Inventing God

In this controversial book, philosopher and psychoanalyst Jon Mills argues that God does not exist; and more provocatively, that God cannot exist as anything but an idea. Put concisely, God is a psychological creation signifying ultimate ideality. Mills argues that the idea or conception of God is the manifestation of humanity's denial and response to natural deprivation; a self-relation to an internalized idealized object, the idealization of imagined value.

After demonstrating the lack of any empirical evidence and the logical impossibility of God, Mills explains the psychological motivations underlying humanity's need to invent a supreme being. In a highly nuanced analysis of unconscious processes informing the psychology of belief and institutionalized social ideology, he concludes that belief in God is the failure to accept our impending death and mourn natural absence for the delusion of divine presence. As an alternative to theistic faith, he offers a secular spirituality that emphasizes the quality of lived experience, the primacy of feeling and value inquiry, ethical self-consciousness, aesthetic and ecological sensibility, and authentic relationality toward self, other, and world as the pursuit of a beautiful soul in search of the numinous.

Inventing God will be of interest to academics, scholars, lay audiences and students of religious studies, the humanities, philosophy, and psychoanalysis, among other disciplines. It will also appeal to psychotherapists, psychoanalysts and mental health professionals focusing on the integration of humanities and psychoanalysis.

Jon Mills, Psy.D., Ph.D., ABPP is a philosopher, psychoanalyst, and clinical psychologist. He is Professor of Psychology & Psychoanalysis at the Adler Graduate Professional School in Toronto and is the author of many books in philosophy, psychoanalysis and psychology. Recipient of many awards for his scholarship, he received the Otto Weininger Memorial Award for lifetime achievement in 2015, given by the Canadian Psychological Association. He runs a mental health corporation in Ontario, Canada.

Philosophy & Psychoanalysis Book Series
Series Editor
Jon Mills

Philosophy & Psychoanalysis is dedicated to current developments and cutting edge research in the philosophical sciences, phenomenology, hermeneutics, existentialism, logic, semiotics, cultural studies, social criticism, and the humanities that engage and enrich psychoanalytic thought through philosophical rigor. With the philosophical turn in psychoanalysis comes a new era of theoretical research that revisits past paradigms while invigorating new approaches to theoretical, historical, contemporary, and applied psychoanalysis. No subject or discipline is immune from psychoanalytic reflection within a philosophical context including psychology, sociology, anthropology, politics, the arts, religion, science, culture, physics, and the nature of morality. Philosophical approaches to psychoanalysis may stimulate new areas of knowledge that have conceptual and applied value beyond the consulting room reflective of greater society at large. In the spirit of pluralism, *Philosophy & Psychoanalysis* is open to any theoretical school in philosophy and psychoanalysis that offers novel, scholarly, and important insights in the way we come to understand our world.

Humanizing Evil
Psychoanalytic, Philosophical and Clinical Perspectives
Edited by Ronald C Naso and Jon Mills

Inventing God
Psychology of Belief and the Rise of Secular Spirituality
By Jon Mills

Every one of the 100 billion people who came before us has died, without a shred of evidence that they live on in some other life. Facing the reality of our death has spawned world religions and spiritual movements, but in this, the Age of Science, we need a new world view that gives individuals meaning and unites us as a species. Jon Mills' *Inventing God* does just this, beautifully and powerfully outlining a humanist perspective that can be embraced by all. This book, however, should not be read just by atheists and humanists, but by anyone desirous of deeper meaning, which is all of us.

Michael Shermer, *publisher of* Skeptic *magazine; monthly columnist for* Scientific American*; author of* The Moral Arc

With this book, Jon Mills brings a considerable clarification to the "atheism" debate by insisting, like the classic sociologist Emile Durkheim before him, on the difference between *God questions* and *religion questions*. Leaving aside the sociological and political questions of religion and investigating, instead, the God questions, Mills enriches the debate with a hitherto rarely considered viewpoint: by not so much focussing upon *what people, when speaking of God, reveal about God*, but rather upon *what they reveal about themselves*—their aspirations, wishes, needs, fears, etc. Written in a clear and elegant style that never shows any contempt for its object, but as well never falls into compromises with it, this book opens up a great chance for civilizing the (sometimes aggressive) discussions between believers and non-believers, not by making them share the same opinions, but by allowing them to get more insight into each other's—thoroughly human—motives.

Professor Robert Pfaller, *author of* On the Pleasure Principle in Culture

Most writers on religion focus on either philosophy—Does God exist? —or social science—Why do persons believe in God? For example, the New Atheists, who are discussed here, limit themselves to the first question and ignore the second. Conversely, social scientists, including psychologists, typically focus on the second question and ignore the first. To his credit, Jon Mills covers both questions and connects them. He does not reduce religion to wish-fulfilment à la *The Future of an Illusion*. He roots religion in a far deeper kind of wish. He does not argue that religion is therefore delusory but rather that the truth claims of religion, for which he prefers the term spirituality, must start with this wish. An amazingly wide-ranging and provocative work.

Professor Robert A. Segal, *Sixth Century Chair in Religious Studies, University of Aberdeen*

Inventing God

Psychology of Belief and the Rise of Secular Spirituality

Jon Mills

Routledge
Taylor & Francis Group

LONDON AND NEW YORK

First published 2017
by Routledge
2 Park Square, Milton Park, Abingdon, Oxon OX14 4RN

and by Routledge
711 Third Avenue, New York, NY 10017

Routledge is an imprint of the Taylor & Francis Group, an informa business

British Library Cataloguing in Publication Data
A catalogue record for this book is available from the British
Library

Library of Congress Cataloging in Publication Data
Names: Mills, Jon, 1964– author.Title: Inventing God : psychology
of belief and the rise of secular spirituality / Jon Mills.
Description: 1 [edition]. | New York : Routledge, 2016. |
Series: Philosophy & psychoanalysis book series | Includes
bibliographical references and index.
Identifiers: LCCN 2015048760| ISBN 9781138195745 (hardback) |
ISBN 9781138195752 (pbk.) | ISBN 9781315620930 (ebook)
Subjects: LCSH: Psychology, Religious. | God. | Religion–
Controversial literature.
Classification: LCC BL53 .M553 2016 | DDC 242/.1–dc23
LC record available at http://lccn.loc.gov/2015048760

ISBN: 978-1-138-19574-5 (hbk)
ISBN: 978-1-138-19575-2 (pbk)
ISBN: 978-1-315-62093-0 (ebk)

Typeset in Times New Roman
Wearset Ltd, Boldon, Tyne and Wear

If God did not exist, it would be necessary for us to invent Him.

—Voltaire

God (gŏd) *n.* 1.a. A supreme being conceived as the creator or originator of the universe. b. The principle object of faith and worship in monotheistic religions. c. The force, effect, manifestation, or aspect of this being. 2.a. A pervasive supernatural entity as divine person. b. Possesses divine properties of perfection, omnipotence, omniscience, omnibenevolence, omnipresence, sovereignty, and aseity. 3.a. The ultimate source, cause, and governance of the cosmos. b. The state or quality of being completely independent, unconditioned, unalterable, and uncaused. c. Self-derived or self-originated. 4.a. Being-from-and-of-itself. b. Being-in-and-for-itself. c. The ultimate ground of all reality. d. Being.

Contents

Proslogion

There is probably nothing graver than the question of God. It consumes waking consciousness and lives in the psychic underworld of humanity. It is always there, invading our thoughts, structuring our social practices, and hence driving interpersonal, political, and economic relations, where the fate of our existence hinges on an answer, beckoning for a response. Billions of people are preoccupied with this question everyday, although it largely affects us unconsciously in ways most people remain unaware of. Although entire cultures are organized around religious custom, the God question is ultimately an intimate enterprise each person must face alone. As a philosopher and psychoanalyst, I remain deeply engaged in this *quest*-ion, one which (admittedly) will likely haunt me until my dying days; yet my somber conclusions offer little consolation in the moment. There is no ultimate destiny (*telos*) other than what we make for ourselves. God is a promise of hope—of peace, happiness, eternal salvation—what we all want, an antidote to hardship, hate, and our undying pain. But we must face the brute reality of life on its own terms, where there are no promises, for we all must find our own way. Each of us must live and die by our own choices and actions, and that is why, in the end, we are all ultimately responsible to answer this question for ourselves.

In this book I argue that God does not exist. More controversially, God *cannot* exist as anything but an idea. The God hypothesis is merely a conjecture *as* supposition based on a fantasy principle conditioned by unconscious illusion sustained through social ideology. Albeit a logical concept born of social convention, God is actually a semiotic invention and symbolization of ideal value. Put concisely, God is only a thought. Rather than an extant ontological subject or agency traditionally attributed to a supernatural, transcendent creator or supreme being responsible for the coming into being of the universe, God is merely a psychological creation signifying ultimate ideality. Here God becomes a self-relation to an internalized idealized object, the idealization of imagined value. This thesis partially rests on the psycho-analytic proposition that mental processes and contents of consciousness are grounded in an unconscious ontology that conditions the production of our conscious thoughts through fantasy formation. Although ideas have both conscious and unconscious origins, their articulation in consciousness is pre-dicated on linguistic constructions governed by the psychodynamics of wish-fulfillment based upon our primordial desires and conflicts stimulated within a social matrix. The idea or notion of God is the manifestation of our denial and response to our being-in-relation-to-lack, and hence the longing to replace natural absence with divine presence. As a result, God remains a deposit of humanity's failure to mourn natural deprivation or lack in favor of the delusional belief in an ultimate hypostatized object of idealized value.

New atheism

Religious scholars, theologians, and philosophers of religion will likely balk and moan at my dismissal of the God hypothesis, which they take as sacrosanct in a long established tradition of religious studies that is (pur-portedly) fundamentally epistemologically agnostic at best, despite having carved out a permissible space of unquestioning devotion to the study of the God construct. I certainly do not claim to resolve the God debate, which is next to impossible due to unrelenting human desire, nor am I interested in a sparring match with the theologians and religious scholars who will predictably criticize me based on my lack of observed convention for not addressing the large literature base on the subject matter. I have no intention of engaging the discourse in the philosophy of religion that is accustomed to preaching to a narrow (albeit erudite) audi-ence with a circumscribed agenda who finds the loquacious atheist an unsophisticated philistine or unwelcome trespass. This book is about dealing with the spiritual question for people who are in search of meaning and greater transcendence when they cannot believe in tradi-tional religious principles and theological presuppositions. The spiritual problem I will address here is about the struggle the human psyche (ψυχή) or soul (*Seele*) has with itself in its own process of becoming.

Although I am respectful of the myriad differences in belief systems and opinion (*doxa*) individuals and cultures maintain with regard to the God posit, it does not mean that I agree with or equally support the relativism of beliefs. We should not confuse proper social etiquette with intellectual inquiry, academic seriousness, or the pursuit of truth. Therefore this project is likely to be deemed by believers as polemical and devaluing of peoples' religious tenets, especially by individuals who view their faith as part of their identity, upbringing, or a way of life, and in cultures where religiosity largely defines the social customs and mores of its peoples and daily communal practices. As a humanist I wish to avow that I have no ill-will or malice toward anyone who believes in God. As a practicing psychoanalyst and psychologist, I think I understand many of the psychological motivations for why people are drawn to believe, and even have empathy for their need for God, as it is reflective of human nature. And as a philosopher, I can appreciate the need to justify our warranted beliefs and devise arguments in support of them, even if they are fallible, as most things are.

Although atheism is nothing new, it has garnered a new interest amongst the intelligentsia and public at large within the past decade. We may largely attribute this shift to the secular movement that has gained increasing visibility and incremental momentum by emphasizing reason over faith and pressing into service political reform.[1] However, the post-9/11 response to religious fundamentalism was instrumental in ushering in a burgeoning level of social self-consciousness that spawned the dawn of new atheism, one that is much more clamorous, intolerant, and virulent toward organized religion of virtually every persuasion, especially Islam. Sam Harris' devastating indictment of religion in *The End of Faith* (2004) broke the mold of political correctness by condemning the social institution of religion, which simultaneously gave America a catharsis and sparked a new public outcry against the oppressive atrocities of culturally entrenched brainwashing under the name of God. Academics soon came out of the woodwork. Philosopher Daniel Dennett published *Breaking the Spell* (2006) at about the same time evolutionary biologist Richard Dawkins took the world by storm with *The God Delusion* (2006), followed by journalist Christopher Hitchens in *God is Not Great* (2007). These gentlemen inherited (or manufactured) the illustrious tag "The Four Horsemen", dubbed after the Four Horsemen of the Apocalypse, a term which has apparently stuck in popular culture. This publicity nicely symbolizes the vehemence and spitefulness against the psychopathology of religion these new missionaries would like to exterminate.

---

1 A good example of this is the motto of the American Humanist Association, where "Good Without God" is its slogan, a political activist and lobbyist group that consistently advocates for religious and governmental reform within the United States.

What is further unique about their work and influence is that they have gained international prominence by breaking into the popular trade market-place, which is unprecedented in history. This speaks volumes about the discerning taste of an educated public whose appetite for God is waning. Other noted academic atheists writing during this time period (who are slightly less radical) are Victor Stenger, Michael Martin, Michael Shermer, and Anthony Grayling, all of whom have made significant contributions from the standpoint of science, skeptical philosophy, and humanism.

In today's globalized dissemination of information technology, new atheism is a visible player on the World Wide Web, where columnists, bloggers, and televised public debates sponsored by major universities (e.g., Notre Dame), religious and scientific organizations, and international forums are readily available on YouTube as theists and atheists stand-off in both moderated (hence formally structured and supervised) and unmediated settings where spontaneous dialogues and vitriolic exchanges make for good entertainment. This worldwide phenomenon shows at the very least how captivating this topic currently is to secular and theistic audiences alike, and how it has come to loggerheads between science, theology, and sectors of society whom themselves identify with a particular religious faith.

I am not into polemics like some vociferous atheists such as Christopher Hitchens,[2] Sam Harris,[3] Richard Dawkins,[4] and others,[5] or in their

2 Before he died, Hitchens was so provocative, militant, and unrelenting in his condemnation of religion that it remains surprising that he was not murdered by Islamic extremists rather than succumbing to esophageal cancer. Unlike Salman Rushdie, we may speculate that he subverted a *fatwah* only on the condition that he was an infidel and not a Muslim.

3 Harris (2004) is so combative in his views against the "monstrosity" of "religious lunacy" (p. 236) and in advocating for conversational intolerance, that he travels with bodyguards because he has received death threats from both Muslims and Christians alike (see Oppenheimer, 2010).

4 Dawkins is probably the most famous (if not infamous) public defender of atheism from esteemed academic pedigree. Yet he is a sarcastic polemicist. In *The God Delusion*, he tells us:

   The God of the Old Testament is arguably the most unpleasant character in all fiction: jealous and proud of it; a petty, unjust, unforgiving control-freak; a vindictive, bloodthirsty ethnic cleanser; a misogynistic, homophobic, racist, infanticidal, genocidal, filicidal, pestilential, megalomaniacal, sadomasochistic, capriciously malevolent bully (p. 51).

   Elsewhere (1989a) he writes: "if you meet someone who claims not to believe in evolution, that person is ignorant, stupid or insane (or wicked, but I'd rather not consider that)." He furthermore announces that "faith is one of the world's greatest evils, comparable to the smallpox virus but harder to eradicate" (Dawkins, 1989b, p. 26).

5 In *Darwin's Dangerous Idea*, Daniel Dennett (1995) bluntly tells us that anyone who does not believe in the scientific idea of evolution "is simply ignorant, inexcusably ignorant" (p. 46) based upon childish belief and irrationality. In *Breaking the Spell* (2006), he also continues in his typical provocative style by making a comparison between "a parasitic worm invading an ant's brain and an idea invading a human brain," which he goes on to say "probably seems both far-fetched and

apologists, reactionaries, or theological defenders such as William Lane Craig, Alvin Plantinga,[6] and David Bentley Hart,[7] but I am bound to offend believers because this cuts to the heart of what truly matters to them, what is in their souls. In polite social circles, this issue would not be addressed so forthrightly because interpersonal nicety and pleasantry in community settings, even among a few acquaintances at a party or social gathering, is appropriate to the context and preferred by most. But this forum is different, which is ultimately about a critique of ideas. In the vicious world of cut-throat academic politics and disciplinary ideology, where truth is embattled, descent is abhorred, and every idea and proposition is up for fair game, I hope to weigh in on this ongoing dispute as an outsider in search of spirituality without God.

---

outrageous" (p. 5); however, despite that the "comparison of the Word of God to a lancet fluke [tiny parasite] is unsettling," he is making the point that an *idea* can affect people's minds no differently than an infectious pest. Equally provocative, in his style of sardonic humor, Colin Howson (2011) refers to the argument of faith based on unseen evidence as "simply oxymoronic sophistry" and further lists the types of evidence reported to have been seen by believers "such as the Turin shroud, angels in clouds, Jesus crucified on a telegraph pole in Louisiana (a climbing shrub when viewed close to), countless sightings of the Virgin Mary (once in a loaf of bread) and so on" (p. 35, fn.4). Also in his critique of Stephen Jay Gould's non-overlapping magisteria (NOMA) thesis, he accuses him of "intellectual treason" and concludes that his theory is "simple nonsense" (p. 37).

6 Plantinga (2011), an analytic theological philosopher, refers to Dawkins as "sophomoric" (p. 17, fn.23), but he is more brutal in his criticisms of Dennett (see pp. 33–49). He concludes:
    Dennett and Dawkins remind one of a certain kind of religious personality with which we are all too familiar: if you disagree with them, you are not only wrong, but wicked, and should be punished, if not in this world then certainly in the next (p. 33).
    Stephen Jay Gould also once referred to Dennett as "Dawkins's lapdog."

7 Hart (2013) is the most acerbic polemicist against "the new atheists" I have read. He is unbridled in his criticisms, using a combination of condescending ad hominems, refutation by laughter from *ex cathedra*, straw men arguments, infantilizing dismissals, and hasty generalizations he applies to all atheists, as is they are all the same. This is transparent when he refers to the "plenteously contended, drowsily complacent, temperamentally incurious atheist" (p. 5), "jaws firmly set and eyes fiercely agleam" (p. 113), who is "buoyantly coarse," "simplistic," and "lacks the conceptual means" (p. 15) to understand the sage ways of theism. In the form of a reversed argumentation from mimesis, Hart accuses the new atheists of a "sheer lack of intellectual curiosity they betray" (p. 21), and who embrace "ultimate absurdity" by denying the transcendent realm of the supernatural for naturalism, which Hart charges is "indistinguishable from pure magical thinking" (p. 17). Hart concludes that: "I do not regard true philosophical atheism as an intellectually valid or even cogent position; in fact, I see it as a fundamentally irrational view of reality" that "is a kind of obliviousness to the obvious," which "must be regarded as a superstition" and "a fervently resolute will to believe the absurd" (p. 16). One cannot refrain from reading Hart's criticisms of atheism as an angry, reactive emotive polemic based on the negation of negation through ridicule and employing a spate of informal fallacies tantamount to freshman philosophy. On the more serious reflections Hart makes with regard to God and metaphysics, I will take up later; however, I see no point in participating in the mud-slinging that keeps atheists and theists from having more respectful dialogues.

One attitude that sets me apart from the "new atheists" is that I am neither intent on denouncing people or ethnic groups via a refutation of their religions, historical customs, or contemporary belief systems, nor am I interested in offering a critique of religion or its systemic abuses. All these issues are (of course) very important and germane to our understanding of contemporary cultural variances, geopolitical frictions, fundamentalism, ethnic warfare, and human suffering as a whole, for these anthropological realities carry noteworthy ideological, political, and economic ramifications. But they will barely concern us here. What is unique about my reflections on this topic are broadly twofold: (1) We should not confuse the God question with religion, which is more of a critique of metaphysical postulates rather than human societal practices; and (2) What is missing from most atheistic analyses is a proper exposition of the underlying psychological dispositions and unconscious conflicts motivating this debate, which more properly accounts for why human beings have the need to invent God.

Without prevarication, most of the new atheist literature is about a repudiation of religion, which is often explicitly and/or implicitly linked to a denial of God as though the two constructs are equivalent, when they are not. The God question is ultimately about the legitimacy of postulating a supreme being, while religion governs human social life and ways of being in relation to others. Often religion reflects a whole host of communal and cultural factors that are historically contextualized and sociologically embedded as part of one's thrownness or facticity, and these structural fabrics within a given society may have nothing to do with the relevance or viability of belief in a supernatural creator simply because cultural creeds and value practices are conditioned. It is important not to conflate the God posit with religion and treat them as if they are identical. I do not think that the question of God is the same as the problematic of religion, although they usually involve interdependent relations that are mutually implicative. Throughout this investigation I wish to remain focused on the God posit as a philosophical object of inquiry that may be theoretically (categorically) separated from religious institutions, policies, and habits, as well as psychologically explained. By demarcating our scope of inquiry, I hope to avoid the myriad shortcomings that occur in current discourses that pit religion or pious convictions against those who negate the existence of God by collapsing them under the same rubric. What is most important to emphasize is that I wish to remain attentive to the question of legitimacy in predicating the ontology of God rather than analyze the historical, contemporary, and ecumenical details of sacred writings and faith practices belonging to the Abra-hamic monotheisms, let alone the ancillary variegated religions and mystical traditions that are scattered throughout the world.

In addition to this stipulation, there has been a profound omission within current atheist literature elucidating the psychological variables informing the need for God. One danger in equating the God construct with religion is that it does not allow for nuances in the psychological dispositions moti-vating individuals and peoples who selectively adopt various aspects of their faith (idiosyncratically and pragmatically) without the literal belief in scripture, nor does it fully capture all the traditional reasons why religion has become a social and political backdrop for moral teachings, law and order, and ethnic cohesiveness governing a particular polity. These are complex and overdetermined processes that require careful sociological analyses, something I am not prepared to do here. Claiming that religion per se subjugates people to ignorance and irrationality, and that it is the source of all human monstrosities and suffering (a) presupposes there can be no rational justification for belief, and (b) displaces the fact that often the abuses of religion are enacted by psychopathic men and fanatical groups who misappropriate sacred texts and annex the so-called word of God (itself a manmade invention) as a purveyor of power to exploit and suppress weaker parts of society and to control the masses (typically women and children), especially in non-democratic nations and developing countries. We must not confound fundamentalist teachings and radicaliza-tion with the normative beliefs and practices integral to a certain religion within a given culture. Although all religions (including their co-extensive, reformed, and modified versions) always stand in relation to their original historical radicality, that is, as tenets represented by fundamentalist dogma, the psychological constructions of personal and cultural identity, along with freedom and individuation in selective praxis, makes any generaliza-tion dubious. This conflation furthermore ignores the reported positive benefits that come from religious faith and practice, which is empirically verified to be the case for many peoples.[8]

---

8 The emphasis on the different social functions of religion have been exemplified by Emile Dur-kheim's (1915) work and elaborated by a number of contemporary scholars (see O'Dea and Aviad, 1983, for an overview). Religion provides (i) support and reconciliation; (ii) offers a tran-scendental relationship that promotes security; (iii) sacralizes values and norms of society; (iv) provides standards for critically evaluating established norms; (v) facilitates identity func-tions; and (vi) aids in the passage through the life cycle.

It may be argued that it is not religion itself (which is much more than observing scripture) that creates human atrocities, but rather the evil that men do based upon the use (and distortion) of holy books (once again created by man) to accomplish certain self-serving ends and gains. In itself, this is not a very good argument for irreligion as it is too reductionistic and adheres to a simple economy of ideological causality. Conversely, there are certain religions that do not require a godhead to explain or govern human activities, such as various sects of Buddhism and, more obscurely, Mimamsa Hinduism.[9] Jainism is also a good example of a religion that preaches non-violence and self-restraint and believes that the universe was not created and will always exist. One can claim, like Grayling does,[10] that these examples are not true religions, but rather philosophies of life, yet this quibble does not answer to the fact that over a billion votaries world-wide identify themselves as religious adherents of these largely oriental traditions. To make religion itself the source of world *pathos* is to commit a category mistake by not partitioning off pathological from benign forms of human desire and perversion. Here any analysis of religion should remain contextualized and contingent upon multifaceted dimensions that spur, domesticate, and derange a given society.

Since Freud, a psychological analysis of humanity's perennial pining for a divine object has been virtually ignored. The central arguments made against God are usually from the standpoint of science, such as from evolutionary biology, physics, cosmology, and more recently neuroscience, not from psychology let alone psychoanalysis. When philosophers chime in on the matter, they usually represent the Anglo-American tradition of logical positivism and naturalized critique, or they adopt materialist methodologies popular in the philosophy of mind that rely heavily on evolutionary viewpoints and contemporary brain science, not on the unconscious complexity of mental processes, personal agency, resistance and defense, transference, fantasy projection, compromise formation, transitional phenomena, attachment and selfobject needs, imaginary and symbolic representations, and the dynamics of wish-fulfillment that explain underlying psychic motivations and conflicts reductionistic paradigms failure to capture. Here I hope to offer something novel to the discussion that compliments new atheistic perspectives.

9 See Biderman (1981) for a discussion, pp. 127–128.
10 A.C. Grayling (2013b), p. 16.

The term "atheist" has historically been deemed a dirty and dangerous word, a label that would not only get you beheaded or burned at the stake in distant times, but it is currently used to justify state execution in many Muslim parts of the world. The term has acquired a certain sense of psychological repugnance and repudiation among many devout factions of society because it signifies an innate badness for the simple reason that it stands in opposition to mass cherished beliefs. But etymologically, the term merely represents the view that one is godless (Gk. *atheos*: *a-*, without + *theos*, god), just as the term "agnostic" means that one does not know (Gk. *agnōstos*, unknown). For all practical purposes, atheists are merely those who do not believe in God by virtue of the fact that they cannot see any evidence for it or buy into the premises that bind theists in their convictions. Here we do not need to import an inherent hostility in this position, for it is merely an impersonal or indifferent attitude of rationalism (although emotionally laden) that stands in dialectical relation to faith. And what is etymologically interesting about the word "faith" is that it is derived from the Latin *fidere*, to trust. By contrast, atheists lack confidence in believing. In other words, they do not trust popular opinion.

The term "antitheist," however, signifies a more aggressive stance of radical negation and militant opposition that is adamantly against theism, which is in vogue by some secular humanists intent on abrogating religion itself with the political (as well as moral) motive of introducing educational and cultural reform. As a subjective reflection, I suspect there is a certain degree of pleasure that is operative in the universal renunciation of the religiously devout (that is, cryptically speaking, the intellectually inferior other) when academic "brights"[11] belabor the issue contemptuously. Perhaps this is a good example of narcissistic differences that titillate intellectual debates, but I do not desire to "rub it in" the faces of the pious to make my point. Secular intellectuals are committed to a cause, just as those who are religious zealots, because they passionately believe in their calling on the voyage of reason. Here I do not begrudge them, as they are dedicated to a noble quest as the pursuit of truth and the eradication of human suffering, only that I do not embrace this form of aggressivity via negating the institution of religion to make

---

11 This is Dennett's (2006) self-adopted (and rather pretentious) term for nonbelievers who are adherents of naturalism: "I am a *bright*" (p. 21).

my case. In fact the term "religion" signifies a principle that connects people together strongly in unity or communal belief (Lat. *religio* < *ligāre*, to bind), the content and context of which are subject to variation. This reflects the natural need for human attachment.

It can be argued that atheism is itself a form of religion based on a union or consensus of belief in a certain worldview premised on negation, although many contemporary humanists would cringe at such a suggestion. They would likely claim (and I agree with them) that religion historically and linguistically represents a fallacious worldview based on unsubstantiated beliefs in a supreme supernatural creator, emotional prejudices, and political oppressions that institute a social code of dogmas designed to regulate the behavior of masses. But the point I wish to emphasize is that moral causes in the name of truth, knowledge, freedom, and justice may be framed from different vantage points and life perspectives, and in order to understand them in the service of education, liberation, and societal betterment we must be willing as humanists (namely, those who embrace an ethical stance toward humanity) to validate people's internal psychological dynamics and subjective felt experiences in order to enter into a meaningful discourse so we may together fashion a space where mutual recognition is possible. Negating religion *in toto* does not accomplish this goal, for it is tantamount to negating otherness in general and only fortifies an animus that is at cross-purposes for fostering open and sincere dialogue.

People ultimately want to feel a sense of acceptance and connection to others, and the psychological craving for safety and emotional security in our relationships and attachments is a reflection of the human need for God. The secularist philosophizing with a hammer is not only a sure way of buttressing resistance and perpetuating misunderstanding, it closes off avenues for productive reform by maintaining rigid oppositions rather than gleaning insight into the psychological ingredients the belief in God symbolically supplies. There is no need to obliterate peoples' proclivity for religion let alone deracinate their need to believe, only that we need to understand *why* humanity is inclined to think this way in order to introduce an intervening reflective level of self-conscious awareness that points toward the truth of being in a world that does not require God to function or give meaning to existence.

I am not invested in nor impressed with the need to convert others into my way of thinking. A free mind will derive its own conclusions. Education will do its own work over time. What is most important is that these judgments are chosen. Here we must invite believers and skeptics alike to set aside their emotional biases and try to be open to receiving another perspective where the moral, aesthetic, and spiritual fibers of the soul still flourish and have purpose despite the fact that God is nowhere to be found.

On the question of predication

Instead of offering a defense of atheism via a critique of theism or organized religion, or by engaging and reiterating all the philosophical arguments that ferret out the minutia of these sundry problematics, which could easily fill entire volumes, I wish to offer a brief treatise on the philosophical and psychological variables motivating this debate. Here I hope to approximate many non-theist, agnostic, and secular humanists' views on the matter, which may be said to reasonably represent what non-theistic belief represents to a secular audience. Rather than presuppose or accept as valid the postulation dating from antiquity to modern day theology that a supreme being or beings exist, only to offer arguments in support of this presumption, I reverse the presupposition and start with the predication that no such being exists and offer arguments for why this is so. Here I use naturalized psychology as our guide.

Every human experience—from instinct to desire, sensation, perception, emotion, imagination, and thought—is psychologically mediated, and this is an uncontested logical and scientific fact.[12] It is beyond dispute. Whether we determine that proper philosophical and/or theological arguments are *categorically distinct* from psychological ones, it does not negate the fact that human beings are psychologically constituted. Therefore, any attempt to couch intellectual and scientific pursuits outside of the parameters that govern psychological motivations and their constraints is a misguided enterprise. No human experience can exist or transpire independent from our embodied facticity as experiential agents who

---

12 I do not wish to evoke the *Psychologismus-Streit* that was popular at the turn of the twentieth century, such as the antipsychologism Husserl (1900) made famous in his *Prolegomena to Pure Logic* (§§ 17–51), which is Vol. 1 of his *Logical Investigations*. It is generally agreed upon by contemporary standards that logic, science, and epistemology are naturalized processes that involve faculties of human subjectivity regardless of their categorical identifications or objectivity, and that it serves no purpose to bifurcate psychology from philosophical naturalism when making determinations about the human mind.

are sentient-desirous-feeling-conscious beings who cognize. Therefore, all propositional attitudes and rational postulations about being and reality are mediated by mind. This naturally extends to the God construct.

When one closely examines contemporary scholarly research in religious studies, there is a preponderance of discourses that predicate God's existence without even taking into account the most elemental questions: What do we mean by God? Following our definitions, Does God exist? Why would we even posit God? Why hypothesize about let alone assume the predication of God? Here I am referring to the pedestrian God of the common man reflected in every monotheistic Abrahamic religion (Judaism, Christianity, Islam) as a supreme agency and transpersonal creator of the universe. Alvin Plantinga nicely summaries this theological position as "the thought that there is such a person as God: a personal agent who has created the world and is all-powerful, all-knowing, and perfectly good."[13] Other contemporaries such as Richard Swinburne also define God as "a person without a body (i.e. a spirit) who necessarily is eternal, perfectly free, omnipotent, omniscient, perfectly good, and the creator of all things."[14] Note that Plantinga and Swinburne use the terms "person" and "personal" when referring to a divine deity, which reflects the consensus held by most theologians and philosophers of religion.[15] This type of God, I argue, is not very believable because it hinges on a transubjective or suprapersonal metaphysical realism that makes God a superordinate Self with a personal identity. Here we should not equate God with logical inference, symbolic abstraction, a unifying principle, category of the ultimate, informational nexus, or an energetic force governing and saturating the cosmos, which are potentially more comprehensible and less anthropomorphic—hence more philosophically defensible because they address other possible definitions, meanings, and functions we can attribute to a godhead. Instead, as the vast majority of believers in monotheism would contend—and I mean those who actually believe in and practice their faith—not irascible academics or theologians

13 Plantinga (2011), p. ix.

14 Swinburne (2004), p. 7.

15 Cf. Anselm's Prologue to the *Monologion* where he refers to the "substance" of God as a "person" (p. 4). By way of contrast, Spinoza's (1992) definitions are less personal: "By God I mean an absolutely infinite being; that is, substance consisting of infinite attributes, each of which expresses eternal and infinite essence," whereby God is "in itself and is conceived through itself" and is "self-caused." See *The Ethics*, Part I: Concerning God: Definitions 6, 3, 1.

in the Ivory Tower, God is necessarily conceived to be a superhuman creator or supernatural supreme agent. From this perspective, does the God question even make sense?

Why do we postulate God, let alone assume there are reasons for God's existence? Although these questions have a long anthropological and theosophic history, they virtually stopped being asked after the publication of St. Thomas Aquinas' *Summa Theologiae* [ca. 1256–1272], which laid out the question of God's existence in three articles: (1) Whether the Existence of God is Self-Evident?; (2) Whether it Can be Demonstrated that God Exists?; and (3) Whether God Exists? This impressive contribution to Western theology is the last in its genre to focus on the ontological question of God (until it was resurrected by Descartes). Philosophy of religion since then has focused on ways to expatiate and defend these basic premises. Today out of the over 300 identified professional journals in religious studies in the academic world, covering multiple languages and countries, there is not one that is devoted to atheistic studies.[16] And a perusal of these leading scholarly journals will reveal not one article in recent times devoted to the negation of God's existence. Perhaps this is due, in part, to the inherent bias and politics of publishing, where editors and reviewers promote their own ideas and agendas at the expense of secular points of view that are in opposition to their own; but it is nonetheless a curious artifact that contemporary scholars are not asking whether God exists. Why is the most fundamental question not being asked; and furthermore, why is God's predication taken at face value?

I suggest that the God question is not permissible in scholarly (religion) journals because academics do not want to undermine the profession in which they practice. If you draw into question or delegitimize the institutionalization of God, let alone jeopardize your livelihood, this has discernible consequences that can impact on peer recognition and acceptance, promotion and tenure, funding resources and endowments, and political bodies that can affect one's career advancement, not to mention

---

16 According to the journal ranking listings on religious studies compiled by the SCImago: Journal & Country Rank indicators, which is powered by Scopus, an internet database that lists the leading academic and scientific journals based on referencing and rank classifications in the world, not one journal is devoted to atheistic studies as of 2013. The only scholarly journal (not magazine) I am aware of that is friendly to atheistic thought is *Essays in the Philosophy of Humanism*, a journal of the American Humanist Association.

you could end up in the unemployment line. But may I also suggest that the topic is unsavory to most, and it violates a certain sense of balance or harmony among social affairs. There is also the mindfulness about not doing violence to a sacred ideal, which speaks to the human sense of conscience and empathy in being respectful of illusions other people live by in a world besieged by uncertainty and strife.

Having said that, this position is ultimately infantilizing to believers: to not question one's beliefs (whether invoked by others or self-generated) and to not ask for rational justification under the guise of political correctness (or to avoid embarrassment, or to assume the other is fundamentally incapable of an intelligent response) is to assume they are developmentally and/or cognitively limited and in need of pity rather than treat them as adults responsible for logically defending their faith. To think otherwise is to succumb to a profane condescension that already objectifies believers as irrational children inept at genuine self-reflection or critical analysis. Here I would say that emotional predilection based on cultural conditioning and human longing is a steadfast resistance reason itself is hardly capable of vanquishing. But the will or right to believe is hardly a logical justification for belief itself. The masses, I suggest, do not critically engage reason, for the inner call of feeling and desire thinks for them.

Following Augustine, Anselm, and Aquinas, theologians start with the presupposition that "God exists," which is "self-evident," when we may ask, How do you know that? According to Aquinas, "the existence of God is self-evident" because, following Aristotle, "the predicate is the same as the subject,"[17] that is, God's existence is self-predicating. But this is a tautology. You cannot define God *into* being no matter how you define your propositions. Should we take for granted that a *sensus divinitatis* is implanted in us by God so that we are epistemologically equipped to know the Almighty, or is this merely a fantasy? I argue this is an illegitimate premise to begin with, for it begs the question of presupposing the very existence of the object under critical inquiry, when we must first set out a justification or ground for predicating it in the first place. Although there are many sophisticated attempts (philosophically, methodologically, exegetically, kataphatically) to provide logical parameters,

---

17 See *Summa Theologiae*, Vol. 1. Part I, Question II: The Existence of God, First Article, *Obj.* 1; *Obj.* 3, *answer*.

emendations, and redirecting shifts in emphasis to justify the God construct, they hardly touch on the original question of *why* we predicate God's existence. It is simply a presumptive given. Although believers will say that God's existence is "self-evident," and that nonbelievers do not understand the scriptures, ecclesiology, eschatology, the scholarly arguments, the phenomenology of religiosity or faith, spiritual or mystical experience, the reality of revelation, and so on, it is incumbent upon believers to address whether the most basic proposition of God's predication is even justified, and if so, under what conditions. Even in the apophatic tradition of negative theology (*via negativa*), which defines God by what "He" is not, this still presumes God's existence, the very thing one has the burden to prove.

For Anselm, God is the greatest of all possible things we can conceive—"that than which it is impossible to think anything greater" (*id quo maius cogitari nequit*); and since actuality is greater than just an object of thought or understanding (*intellectus*), God *must* exist in reality.[18] Following this line of reasoning, this would mean that all objects of cognition must exist in actuality, for what is not thought is not capable of being cognized, so therefore they do not exist. But if this were the case, then nothing thought could be false, for all objects of the intellect would confer their truth as existing. Hence there would be no distinction between a mental object and its actual existence, for both would be identical. All notions or objects of thought would necessarily correspond to an actual entity *in* reality, not merely a fantasized object. What this means is that there would be no distinction between thought, fantasy, and an existing correspondent object that is objectivity real. If this were the case, it would follow that anything you imagine is real as an extant thing or being that actually exists as a concrete entity or substance. But just because you have an imaginative idea does not make it an autonomous entity that subsists in the universe independent of mind. Yet a more basic problem with this argument is the epistemological difficulty of claiming that anything actually exists corresponding to what we think.

Following in Anselm's footsteps, Aquinas certainly provides one of the most sophisticated series of arguments for God's existence, which are versions of the teleological argument by design, the ontological proof,

---

18 See *Proslogion*, Ch. 2: "there is no doubt that something than which a greater cannot be thought exists both in the understanding and in reality" (p. 100).

and the Five Ways, in which he largely uses Aristotle to justify on his behalf. Rather than engage the minutia of these arguments, which has been done *ad nauseam*, I would like to stay focused on the notion of predication; namely, why and how God is predicated to *be* and *is*, and, more specifically, how God is conceived to be a "person."[19] The attribution of God's ontological status to personhood is particularly problematic given that this elevates human provenance to the province of divinity.

The parallax between religion and science

Current debates still loom large in academic circles about the compatibility between religion (usually referring to the monotheistic traditions) and science (specifically empirical naturalism), where they are often portrayed as incommensurate and pitted against one another in firm opposition. Here I will not address those nuanced issues because I wish to remain focused on the question of predication. But I wonder if, sometime in the future, society will replace the pedestrian God as personal creator with Holy Science. We see this possibility emerging especially within the

---

19 In scripture, God is mainly referred to in the masculine gender, until the post-feminist introduction of the neutral term "person" took its politically correct position. Theologian and psychologist John Burke (personal communication, 2012) points out there are at least three direct quotes from the Old and New Testaments (King James Version) where the person of God is referred to: Job 13:8; II Corinthians 2:10 (but also examine Corinthians 5:13); and Hebrews 1:3. The word for person in the Job passage is *panim*, which is usually translated as "face," but in this instance, it is translated as "person." Job 13:8 states: "Will you accept his person? Will you contend for God?" The word *panim* is found 400 times, with about 100 instances referring to Yahweh, the God of Israel, usually "related to another substantive, or as a proper name, whether part of a construct phrase, by means of a possessive suffix, or, in a few instances, through immediate context" (*Theological Dictionary of the Old Testament*, Vol. XI, p. 591, translated from German). The word is sometimes also translated as "face, front, top, appearance" (p. 590). The II Corinthians 2:10 reference is interesting: Paul says, "To whom you forgave anything, I forgive also: for if I forgave anything, to whom I forgave it, for your sakes forgave I it in the person of Christ." The Hebrews 1:3 reference is the most profound:

Who being the brightness of his glory and the express image of his person (Me - God himself), and upholding all things by the word of his power, when he had by himself purged our sins, sat down at the right hand of power.

The word used for person in this case is *hupostasis*. In Hebrews 1:3, *hupostasis* is used more or less philosophically to denote reality or being: Jesus Christ as the Son is the "stamp of God's [immortal or transcendent] being" (*Exegetical Dictionary of the New Testament*, Vol. III, p. 407, translated from German). But we may speculate that based on the Latin *persona*, derived from *personare*, "to sound through" (< Etruscan *phersu*, a face or mask), God is not referred to directly as being a person because God does not sound through a mask, but rather is directly ascertained as The Eternal One (e.g., when asked his name by Moses at the burning bush event, he states "I am that I am," in other words, eternal living reality).

burgeoning fields of physics, evolutionary biology, medical technology, and psychology. With the purported discovery of the Higgs boson particle, will science announce?—We have discovered the underlying fabric of the cosmos! Here, the argument goes, there is no need to evoke God, because science will have explained how this operates in nature. Because we can explain how it appears (although unobserved, such as dark-matter/dark-energy—itself problematic) and operates in the extant world, we don't have to posit another source or cause. With the aid of mathematics, computer programs, experimental methods, sophisticated equation models, and statistical analysis, will science proclaim to have transcended God? Or will they merely purloin the concept to suit their needs? Here contemporary philosophers of religion are to be commended for pointing out how science parades as priest.

Even if this scenario is plausible, perhaps even justifiably sound, it will not be a sufficient universal explanation. As dialectically predicted, we can anticipate the opposite conclusion: God pervades nature and is the source, animation, and cause of the universe. If something like the Higgs boson particle—that unseen and unobservable entity—exists, which according to the Standard Model of fundamental particle physics is responsible for creating mass, and hence belongs to the invisible sea of elementary particles including virtual objects that pop in and out of existence, is it so phantasmal to entertain the notion that a godhead is behind the scenes of the quantum world as an informational process system governing all aspects of reality? The so-called "God particle," as the story goes, may be considered proof of God's existence (as the unifying function governing the interrelatedness of all things on the most fundamental micro-quantum level). In philosophy, we have always called this metaphysics.

It is also predicted that there will be a middle ground of undecidability—a limit, boundary, or check, where there is no discernible synthesis—the Kantian *Ding an sich*, Fichtean *Anstoss*, or Žižekian parallax where no unification is possible—the void, gap, or limbo in which we find ourselves. This is the underworld of paradox, of agnostic uncertainty wed to the foreclosure of knowledge, the ineffability of boundless wonder. It is also the den of unease and angst, of melancholia and dearth, in a word, unhappiness. Uncertainty, vagueness, and indecision breeds existential anxiety and intolerance for ambiguity. Humanity will predictably reveal its ambivalence, insecurity, and *Unbehagen*, for I cannot envision a pristine Hegelian sublation (*Aufhebung*) where all dissimilarity is amalgamated into a holistic totality or cohesive category of completion where all difference is dissolved into unity. Rather I envisage a future where there will always be a Kantian divide between belief and fact, revelation and observation, mystery versus certainty, transcendence versus occlusion; in other words, God *vs.* Nature. And without this seamless synthesis, humanity will simply continue in its process of discord and persistence. This certainly comes with moments of progression, as well as atrophy, with respite, reprieve, and approximations of Aristotelian contentment or simply being "happy" (εὐδαίμων) trickling in from time to time. But the question of "ultimate unity" and "ultimate reality" will likely be left to the philosophers, theologians, mystics, and new age physicists who will predictably redefine what they mean by God. Here God potentially becomes whatever you signify God to be, hardly a satisfactory answer to either science or the humanities. In the end, we remain in the gap of a sublime ignorance, itself sublime.

Perhaps the most perplexing (if not unanswerable) question is the mystery of existence itself. Why is there something rather than nothing? Why is there Being? What explains the being or presence of the universe as a concrete and experiential reality that is simply *here* or *given* as part of our thrownness into the naked thereness we find ourselves immersed in, what we typically call world and life? Traditional theistic accounts believe that because we cannot causally explain the mystery of Being— why it is here, or more precisely, that there is even existence in the first place, this becomes logical grounds for positing God's existence *necessarily*. Following this line of argumentation, some go so far as to say that it is logically impossible to explain why there is existence itself without appealing to God. For the naturalistic philosopher or scientist, Being or reality just *is*. The theist can't buy this casual acceptance of the givenness of the natural world and must insist that such intellectual lassitude is no explanation at all. It does not account for existence, and certainly does not explain *why* let alone *what* causes reality to exist. But we may ask, Does this really matter, let alone justify the leap to speculative theology as an explanation? Regardless of whether we can satisfactorily answer to the ultimate origins of existence, the fact remains that we are here in the physical universe and God is nowhere to be seen.

As an antidote to such ambiguity, classical theism preaches that existence comes from God's infinite Being, which is eternal yet procreative, while the naturalist would say that nature or existence is simply furnished and empirically imparted, that which is assumed as elemental to the physical and experiential world in which we find ourselves situated. The epistemic tension endemic to both positions is that, when it comes to the question of ultimate origin, this is fundamentally unknowable. Whatever metaphysical speculations are advanced (by either theology or science), we are basically left with beckoning the question of evidence.

The natural philosopher or scientist takes existence for granted without trying to answer why it is so, only how it may be expounded from how we find or encounter it; while the theist opines that existence must be explained as coming into being from an ultimate cause that has no cause, because God is self-caused, unconditioned, or the ground of its own being. The agnostic (and indifferent) scientific attitude attempts to bracket the question of why there is existence per se and merely accepts it as that which is present. In other words, it is futile to ask why. The theistic response is discontented (if not infuriated) by the passivity of this stance. The naturalist replies that it is the most logical thing to accept because this is the way we find the universe with or without God, so the appeal to a prime absolute cause is not only epistemologically intractable, it is pointless and based on the desire to know that which we as humanity can never truly know in any definitive way. This does not make the argument from God any more plausible than just accepting the world as we encounter it without appealing to anything else other than what merely *is*. This furthermore assumes that the universe was caused, and moreover, that it had a first cause that is itself uncaused, when this line of argumentation ultimately leads us into an infinite regression of causes and the *aporia* of how something can exist without being caused. It is arguably dissatisfying that we have no ultimate answer to the reason of existence, namely, why the universe exists at all, but we do not need to provide an answer to this *mysterium* to accept what is given. This is the tenet of scientific realism.

Physicists are divided in their metaphysical views on the origins of reality: while some espouse a steady state theory of the universe as having always existed, and hence always will (even accounting for process and change), the preponderant consensus is that the beginning of existence was brought into being by the spontaneous burst of the big bang. Of course one may ascribe infinity to the universe that also entails temporal points of initiation, inflation, succession, fluctuation, and entropy with respect to their parameters and vicissitudes, but one version of the big bang championed by Stephen Hawking and similar minded colleagues is that the physical universe came into existence all by itself. It is no wonder why critics of naturalism find this proposition just as magical as natural scientists find the God posit. Here the binary (and paradox) foisted upon us is that either the cosmos or God is self-generated (regardless of the question of eternity), and we must choose one explanation over the other. Although one may espouse a meta-physics that equates the cosmos with God, classical theology insists that the universe is conditioned on and exudes from God's eternal presence, hence it is the a priori basis for all that is and all that can ever be. But the same problem resurrects itself in both propositions: appealing to a natural universe *or* transcendent creator that has always existed in eternity still begs for a causal explanation of how the cosmos or God came into being in the first place, each of which flounders in offering a viable answer. We may very well want to dispense with the question of *why*, as this presupposes an ultimate purpose or meta-physical intent to the universe, when all we may observe, experience, and analyze is *how* the world of objects manifest without importing an anthropic bias. We may very well end up accepting the hypothesis that all we can defend is a theoretical view of naturalized teleology without inferring an ultimate cause.

Contemporary theological crusader David Bentley Hart urges us to return to a view of God as Being, in fact, the absolute fullness of Being as such,[20] as exemplified by the great mystical traditions of East and West. For Hart, God is not conceived as a supreme (personal) being or agency, but rather as Existence itself. Here we may say he espouses a mystical idealism. Yet he still engenders God by the customary mascu-line salutation, and makes God the unconditioned, eternal, infinite ground of Being that is a *supernatural* force (hence an agent of action by neces-sity) underlying the fabric of the cosmos and sustaining all of reality as we know and experience it. In fact, Hart makes extreme indefensible gen-eralizations such as: "It is the supernatural of which we have direct cer-tainty, and only in consequence of that can the reality of nature be assumed."[21] Those who champion a supernatural first cause to the cosmos

---

20 See *The Experience of God: Being, Consciousness, Bliss*, pp. 30, 109–123.
21 Ibid., p. 96.

have already naturalized God by introducing causal relations into the natural world, which would make God subject to the same laws that govern empirical confirmation, even if we were to concede that God invented such laws. Those who wish to impersonalize God and make it eternal Being in-itself have the same problematic, for Being must appear as natural phenomena.

From the standpoint of subjective experience, we do not perceive or experience Being, only *beings*, that is, particular objects in a process of becoming—things we encounter in relation to our minds and other tangible properties that populate our mental and material encounters with reality. Everything that we encounter in our existence and in our relation to existence is particulars or instantiations of being-as-becoming: the abstract notion of Being or Existence is primarily a mental relation or universal logical category, and hence the complexity of thought as it engages the imperceptibility of the experiential manifold of objects. Of course, this abstract encompassing principle, classification, or genus we attribute to Being is comprised of an infinite sea of processes and particularities belonging to it: we experience particulars despite comprehending the universal in which all particularity participates; yet this universal is a conceptual relation, not an empirical one except insofar as we experientially encounter our own thought. Moreover, any apprehension of universality is mediated by internal psychological processes. Desire, sensation, affect, perception, fantasy, and ideation are naturalized occurrences because they require embodiment to be executed and realized: even if we view the psyche or soul as a sophisticated psychological agency, it is nevertheless dependent upon its corporeal counterpart we customarily call the brain and central nervous system, hence thought is enmattered.

Ancient, medieval, and Arabic philosophies, as well as Eastern mysticisms, have encumbered our historical consciousness by introducing a false dilemma between material and immaterial substance and/or energetic forces that comprise mental life and the actual universe: this is the fallacy of ontological dualism where spirit and matter are conceived as separate essences that may consist and subsist apart from one another independently. Given this view has been emphatically discredited by both philosophy and science alike, and does not stand up to logical scrutiny let alone empirical accounts, we must throw down the proverbial gauntlet and summon the evidential argument—Prove it! Show me one thing that is immaterial. Provide empirical demonstration that incorporeality exists.

One may object to this challenge and retort that the very category of immateriality by logical definition is not capable of empirical demonstration because it is not subject to the same laws as the material world by virtue of its incorporeality. Yet this tautological assertion simply begs the question of what constitutes an immaterial instantiation as well as presumes that extranatural laws exist in the first place. If immateriality is merely an a priori category, analytical truth, or logical relation to its dialectical counterpart as a theoretical abstraction, then anything that is posited to be immaterial or supernatural is destined to lack demonstrable proof.

A logical proof is not the same as a real fact of the actual world. As I will repeatedly argue throughout this book, you cannot define something into existence, namely, God. A concept is not the same thing as an object. Even if we grant the proposition of immateriality or supernaturalism the logical category of existence, it is still nonetheless confined to human thought and semiotic conventions, which are dependent upon energetic-material processes that permit mentation to emerge, and hence are conceived through our embodied facticity as psychophysiological agents. Have you ever truly experienced something supernatural, that is, outside of or in excess of nature? No, because all experience is embodied and subject to natural processes, even if the subjective perception of events *appear to be* beyond or outside the purview of natural occurrences. All experience and thought is contingent upon our naturalized psychobiology *by necessity*, or we would not experience anything at all.

Some proponents of phenomenology would readily object to this naturalized characterization and be quick to evoke the claim that all intentional activity is the work of spirit, which eschews scientific rationalism or naïve objectivism and displaces human consciousness for material reduction. Here the view is that the vitality of soul is based upon its irreducible subjectivity grounded in the lived aspects of perceptual and reflective knowing of the immediate parameters of experience as they are directly encountered through the phenomena of awareness.[22] The notion that consciousness, especially the lived phenomenology of experience, should be equated with or devolve into some kind of physical substance or spatial locality in the brain becomes an obscene insult to the freedom of psychic reality. For the record, I do not espouse material reductionism or non-reductive physicalism, which still categorizes mental functioning

22 See Cecile Tougas' (2013) representation of the Husserlian school, p. 91.

as an epiphenomenon with no causal powers or properties of its own, as I have the upmost respect for the phenomenology of freedom that fuels people's psychological experiences and perspectives of the world. But it would be a mistake to view consciousness as existing independent of our material embodiment. Because consciousness exudes from, persists, and is organically extended in space and time within our transpiring brainstems, the proposition that consciousness is an immaterial unextended substance is simply fallacious by all modern standards, which is especially foreign and antiquated to contemporary neuroscience.

One may be tempted to invoke the argument from language or mathematics as an example of the reality of immateriality, such as the non-materiality of numbers or human ideals that inform our societies despite the fact that they cannot be located in spacetime nor have they ever been realized here on earth (e.g., transfinite numbers or universal peace). One may be tempted to refer to mathematical laws as logical ideal relations or immaterial entities with objective properties, the phenomena of time, the presence of ideas, and incorporeal intelligibles that resist physical reduction, but as long as human mentation is required to conceive and perceive of such phenomena, and cognition necessarily depends upon material embodiment, it seems to beg the question of whether these instances exist independent of mind as some types of realism would proffer. For example, the belief in mathematical realism contends that mathematical entities exist independent of observers; but even if this were true, they would be naturally occurring objects that would be subject to discovery by an *observer*, hence an embodied subject, so the whole argument becomes circular and incoherently unsubstantiated (in principle) as to their immaterial existence independent of human ideation or perceivability.

Even though non-corporeal intelligibles do not exist anywhere in extrinsic space as real objects, they are nonetheless concepts that inhabit our thoughts and structure our interactions with the world. Words, thoughts, and numbers are in fact mental objects. The idea of ideality, of abstraction, of mathematical theory such as the notion of the transfinite whole, are conceived through mind, yet these complex processes are interdependent on the brain, hence an embodied organ. And even if we concede in principle that an idea is not physical matter in a spatial location in time (except conceived in our heads), it does not make it immaterial in-itself independent of our thoughts that construe it to be so. When we signify or speak of energy, it must also be enmattered, as it cannot be actual or realized without instantiating itself in a naturalized medium, such as the Higgs field. Energy has a counterpart to matter yet inheres in it; in fact, according to the field of contemporary physics, it is the ground or condition for matter, therefore it is materially instantiated. And if energy is mere potentiality that has no counterpart to physicality, then energy is merely a theoretical abstraction, hence an idea. But energy without a medium becomes a vacuous concept, for it would be destined to remain not-actual.

The mystery of why there is Being at all, in terms of explaining its origins, must contend with the enigma of our givenness. This is not a solution, nor is it satisfactory, namely, that something merely *is*, but without an explanation as to why or what lies at the fountain of its cause or the reason why things are this way, we are still obliged, nonetheless, to accept the universe as it is disclosed to us. This is perhaps the contention and crux of the matter for theology. In order to answer to why things exist at all, God becomes the functional rationalization behind everything. This also serves a psychological explanation of causality, one we can never prove, but one that appeals to our emotional natures. Perhaps this riddle is unanswerable by definition. We may simply have to contend with accepting presence as such and observe the teleology of nature or Being as a purpose without a cause.

I cannot answer the conundrum of Being, for I am unable to resolve it. But this does not mean that we should or must think that there has to be an original cause or ground for the brute facticity of existence, let alone conjure up a supernatural entity, force, or energy that sustains the cosmos beyond what we can reasonably know and explain through our own natural encounter with life and the manifold of objects that are presented to us in our experience of the world. It is not incumbent upon me to prove why there is existence, only that we do not need to appeal to a divine being as the reason. Is there any point to positing a cause if the universe is eternal? Why assume an original temporal instance of absolute beginning that precedes the succession of all natural events when this is moot and irresolute, subject to language games, scholarly sparing matches, and intellectual masturbation? If either God or the cosmos is eternal, would they not be both equally given? Regardless of what side you sit on the fence, we are all left with the agony of explaining how anything originally got here.

I am convinced that this debate will never be adequately resolved unless God manifests or reveals itself directly, that is, *appears* to humanity as a metaphysical force (whether corporeally or immaterially) with sensuous properties and empirical consequences that stop people(s) dead in their tracks and stimulates a new order of self- and social-consciousness. But this is not probable by any stretch of the imagination, even though one could argue it is not strictly (theoretically speaking, so they say) impossible. Yet theory and proof often collide. Theoretical (logical) proof alone is impotent without an empirical counterpart, unless it is relegated to the stipulated domain of ideas. But when ideation is touted as evidence of extant correspondent facts without empirical correlates, it suffers a mighty blow from the impartial hands of reason. Here intellect (*logos*) and experience (*empeiria*) require a simpatico. In the end, what is real must be made actual.

People have a penchant for dichotomies, exemplified here as pitting religion against science, for the human mind has a need to refrain from synthesizing away opposition as a way of preserving the substance and qualities each affords on their own terms. In a way, each carries its own truths and mythologies, notwithstanding they proclaim to cancel each other out. Such recalcitrance underscores a fundamental resistance to the abolition of difference, despite that the striving for God, I suggest, is based on the need for unitive experiences. This is a psychological argument that is impossible to escape. We all want to integrate experience in order to make sense out of and give meaning to phenomena; and at the same time we gravitate toward particularized experiences that vitiate universals because we imbue them with personal value. The psychomythology of the God construct speaks to both universal and relativized experiences of the need to merge a personalized account of spirituality with a transpersonal ontology.

The nature of belief and faith in either religion or science is instantiated through naturalized psychology, in other words, the doctrine that no human activity is possible without mentation or cognition. No amount of philosophical argumentation, scientific experimentation, or theological maneuvering can change the fact that any proposition is posited by and mediated through our mental faculties. Here the God question is fated to be epistemologically unrectifiable; but what is indisputable is that God is a human idea.

If metaphysical inquiry collapses into epistemology, then we may only revert back to the bifurcation between the empirical and rationalist traditions of knowledge. Here experience and science is embattled by logic and pure reason, when both are operative and co-exist at any given moment in tandem. The project of modern philosophy was to attempt to unify this dichotomy, and yet, despite the rise of idealism that boasted a synthetic holism, we are still in the Kantian gulf that divides the two separate discourses and desires. On one hand, we have the desire to know (*pace* philosophy and science), and on the other, we have the desire to fulfill our desires irrespective of truth, reason, or reality. This tension in human consciousness has divided loyalties; yet all of human activity—from cognition to action—is fundamentally based on psychological foundations. In the end, we may ponder, will evolution and physics become the new God? Will divine truth be illuminated by hallowed science (< Lat. *scientia*, from *scire*, to know)? Or is this another psychomythology born/e of social convention designed (sometimes with great hubris) to appease our anxiety to know? In either supernaturalism or naturalism, we pine for an ultimate explanation.

Imagination and the creativity of logic

That God's predication is taken for granted, as if this is a self-evident fact or truism, suggests that historically humanity has always looked toward transpersonal realms to explain the most basic metaphysical questions. In many ways this seems natural, because the tendency to posit some greater supraordinate causal factor is operative psychologically as a by-product of wonder, for the active intellect desires to know.[23] When paradox, mystery, and *aporiai* are not resolved by the intellect alone, it becomes reflexive to resort to imaginative, speculative thought (even if abductive), for this serves multiple psychic purposes, such as the need to impose meaningful structure or order on cognitive uncertainty as an illusory means of pseudo-control designed to neutralize our anxieties. The faculty of imagination,[24] especially fantasy, is a cognitive organization that medi-

---

23 Recall the opening line of Aristotle's *Metaphysics*: "All men by nature desire to know" (Bk 1 [A], 980a25).

24 Robert Pfaller (2014) nicely articulates the range of imagination as:

> the repetition of a past idea, the expansion of a current one, or the invention, through a new combination of existing elements, of an idea that had not been present before. The ingeniousness at work here fulfils exclusively those functions that serve the knowledge of the world: at most, perhaps, it exaggerates a bit, carries it to excess, feigns a little too heavily, and this makes sure that we . . . imagine all possible things and some others as well. (pp. 213–214)

Cf. Kant (1781/1787), *Critique of Pure Reason*: "pure imagination . . . is one of the fundamental faculties of the human soul" (A 124) responsible for the formal operations of knowledge.

ates between desire and reason, which could potentially explain the impetus behind basic predications of existence, hence giving rise to Hegel's dictum: The real is the rational, and the rational is the real. In other words, there must be a reason to existence. The rational intellect ponders what it experiences and/or comprehends, and this is most assuredly grounded in psychological motives fueling appetition, consciousness, and wonder. When explanation is lacking, reason reaches for a greater overarching purpose or cause to explain that which is unexplainable. God becomes an extrapolation or natural extension of human longing, because in the absence of meaning and understanding, our intellectual faculties gravitate toward intuitive and logical explanations even though they are steeped in imagination, emotional propensities, and wish-fulfillment. When reason cannot answer the most essential cogitations, we revert to what is primal and basic—natural desire (*Lust*) as an antidote to lack (*manque*). Here is where imagination intervenes. And imagination is not possible without reliance on an unconscious ontology.

Beginning with the late modern (epistemological) turn in philosophy through to German idealism, in the great works of Kant, Fichte, Schelling, and Hegel, imagination intervenes and mediates between intuition (sense perception) and thought (rational judgment). Freud canonized this idea with the advent of psychoanalysis. Therefore, there is always an unconscious domain that infects any conscious apperception and conceptual determination with fantasies about the object of conscious thought and perception. What this means is that imagination is necessarily conditioned on unconscious processes. Following the principle of sufficient reason, there must be an original ground for every mental event that stands in relation to every mental object. In other words, all conscious activities of mind come from prior states of unconscious organization. Hence the God posit is mediated by imagination and fantasy, and cannot be approached or apprehended by pure reason alone. Reason necessarily requires an unconscious ontology, for consciousness is conditioned on its archaic primacy.[25] Faith becomes a wish under the guise of the Kierkegaardian "leap" from reason, what psychoanalysis would attribute to unconscious motivation.

If much of the world is prepared to take this leap of faith, probably knowing very little about the scriptures, scholarly disputes, or logical

---

25 Although I have outlined this position in *The Unconscious Abyss* (2002a), see my discussion in *Origins: On the Genesis of Psychic Reality* (2010), pp. 54–55.

arguments involved, than what does this tell us about the human need for divinity? It means we lack. Here we should not stray away too quickly from the qualitative press of desire experienced as a psychic *need*. For billions of people, there appears to be a deep-seated psychological significance in the pining for a reality we know nothing about yet covet. At best, we can unequivocally conclude that the craving for God speaks to a human want that people phenomenologically experience as a felt requirement, as though it is a biological necessity, such as hunger or thirst. Perhaps this is simply spiritual hunger, which, I argue, is not the same as the God posit. Yet spirit is conceived by believers to emanate from the *intellectus divinus*, the presumptive mind of God, rather than the craving human intellect in search of meaning and satiation where none is currently found.

Certain theologians, such as the Christian philosopher and apologist William Lane Craig, would no doubt (predictably) accuse me of committing a genetic fallacy, namely, that just because one can show how a belief originates does not make it *ipso facto* false. This claim assumes that the origin or source of a belief is irrelevant and fails to consider the truth or falsity of a proposition within its current context. A statement or event is either true or not true and must be judged on its own merit. In short, it does not matter how a person acquires belief in God, only that the belief should be adjudicated based on the worth of its argument. Although I certainly agree that the veracity of an argument should be based on its merit, I do not agree that genetic accounts are irrelevant. In fact one should appeal to origins to determine if the conditions under which one acquired certain beliefs are based on sound principles in order to justify the validity of the premises. Most religious beliefs are based on childhood conditioning and reinforced by the obedient consensus of those around them, supported by an appeal to authority and custom, not on critical investigations that logically and scientifically analyze the rationale and empirical parameters of propositions that correspond to verifiable and replicable facts. What happens psychologically is that certain emotional properties are attached to beliefs that favor certain wishful conclusions without undergoing logical scrutiny, and hence form a self-justified basis for the belief in the legitimacy of the belief itself via auto-suggestion. Here the belief that a proposition is legitimate does not mean that the belief itself is legitimate, let alone true. It simply becomes unquestioned dogma. The thought that a belief should be judged without reference to how it is acquired assumes that beliefs are construed by pure reason alone (untainted by passion or affect), when this simply goes against sound psychological science.

Beliefs do not exist in a vacuum. There is no such thing as an intellect that is ontologically separate from other psychical faculties, because the human mind is a dynamic complex totality comprising all biopsychosocial processes, which are interconnected and bound by interrelational events underlying organic order. If we accept the principle of sufficient reason that there is a primordial origin to the mind that unconsciously conditions all mental processes, then all logical and rational arguments are the sublation of intervening and mediating forces that have their source and energy within our primal embodied constitutions under the influence of evolutionary pressures. Although the truth and falsity of propositions and beliefs should be contexualized and arbitrated within the present structural form of an argument, it does not negate the relevance of the past, especially if a poor argument or unreflective belief is unsound or fallacious. In fact, the niggle of "genetic fallacy" is often used as a red herring designed to obfuscate the argument from origins by making it appear illegitimate when it may have everything to do with why a person prefers a certain belief system and not another. Here both the integrity of the belief and the conditions under which they arise may prove to be symbiotic despite whether we can adduce the truth or falsity of the belief itself. Spouting off accusations that questioning the grounds from which a belief is acquired is an informal fallacy of logic or pseudo-reasoning does nothing to negate the fact that beliefs are originally derived from earlier experiential sources that have informed the current epistemology of the subject. In this context, there is no such thing as a genetic fallacy, especially when it comes to the idea of God. Furthermore, when we examine the psychodynamics of belief from a psychological lens, we often discover that the need to believe is governed by emotional rhetoric ultimately justified as an argument from desire.

I have never met anyone who has converted to theism based on the classical philosophical arguments for the existence of God, such as the ontological proof, the Five Ways, or cosmological and teleological accounts.[26] Those who I have met in life and in clinical practice who find

---

26 Because there are so many variations of these arguments, it becomes difficult to categorize them all. If we were to try to summarize them, what stands out are the temporal and modal cosmological arguments, the argument from first cause, possible worlds, necessity, design *vs.* chance, probability and teleology, the anthropic principle, ethics and the problem of evil, deflationism, and the question of immortality. And the list goes on.

theism convincing always speak from a heartfelt place of longing, emotion, and personal experience. The desire for God is all that they need to sustain their faith. Although my psychological arguments are not designed to disprove the ontology of God, which I will leave for a more proper logical and empirical critique, it is impossible to deny without credulity that our psychological dispositions inform our capacities to form a priori and a posteriori judgments in the first place. Therefore, the psychological bases underlying our capacity to form any beliefs condition all arguments for the existence of God.

What keeps us from asking the most basic questions: Why assume God? What grounds do we have for doing so? Why do we predicate God's existence when we could predicate its non-existence, or at least begin from a standpoint of methodological doubt, or alternatively, agnostic inquiry? Was the universe created or has it always existed in some form *ab initio*? Does it make sense to posit a definitive beginning or origin to reality when this question always evokes the further (regressive) question of pre-beginning or pre-being? Does the universe require causation or creation, let alone does it have to have a creator? Does existence itself have to stem from an initial cause? Necessarily so? And if so, why not posit infinity as an unconditioned cause without having an original cause? Recall that the ancients used the term *cause* (αἰτία) to mean the reason or explanation for something happening. We are linguistically and culturally conditioned to think in terms of linear time and sequential (determined) antecedent events that transpire in space, when this argument is fated to succumb to an infinite regress, as we have no way of knowing the answer to an ultimate origin. Perhaps these questions are so far lost in history, tradition, academia, and custom that to posit them is to evoke an antiquated sophomoric naiveté. But I am not embarrassed to ask—Why God?

What is certain is that God is an idea. The question of whether it is a true or false idea is moot, because you can have a sincere justified assertion or warranted belief that is either true or false, yet by definition unprovable. You can claim that an idea does not prove the existence of something other than a set of coherent logical relations that correspond to a proclaimed theorem signifying an independent metaphysical reality, yet there is a distinction between a logical relationship and an ontological actuality. Logical *relata* can be perfectly coherent and justifiable within their own methodological procedures and modes of specialized discourse, but it does not mean that they can define into existence (either through definitional semantics or formalized mathematical-symbolic procedures) the very thing they wish to prove. Logic cannot define an extant God into existence *ex nihilo*. No proposition proves itself. In other words, a statement alone cannot offer proof. A premise must have an independent ground or source of reason that provides evidence for its truth separate from its conclusion(s). To say otherwise is simply begging the question.

Can a logical relationship tell us something about the actual world if analytic judgments based on deductive logic are built on a system of definitions alone? Just because definitions are classified as being logically true or coherent (that is, non-contradictory) and reliant on technical principles based on a consensus of people who invent and adopt the premises and procedures *in toto*, does not mean that we prove or deduce them into existence. Existence is not a proposition. Logical proof for an unconditional existence-statement is not the same as proof for existence itself. Here God simply becomes a linguistic proposition within a semiotic system or lexicon of human meanings—hence a *definition*, not an *actuality*. In other words, we cannot define or think God into existence.

In the end, it does not matter if one's argument for God's existence is successful, for when all is said and done we ultimately want proof—not arguments. We want to *see* it and experience it for ourselves, and this is always an appeal to empirical evidence. You can have the most thoughtful philosophical argument for the existence of God, but if you don't provide tangible evidence, it won't convince anyone other than those who have already made up their minds. The fixation of belief as an unwavering identification to a non-negotiable and unalterable set of ideals is impossible to break in people who are psychologically committed to their passion or will to believe. In the end, we believe in what we want or desire to be true and then formulate arguments to justify our beliefs in the wake of our subjective prejudices and presuppositions of truth simply because they are emotionally dominant. Whatever we subjectively experience, affectively feel, or intuit to be the case, we are more persuaded that they are real. Here reason is eclipsed by the life of feelings and fantasy ubiquitous to psychic reality. We cannot reason God into existence any more than we can attribute the actuality of the physical universe to be the sole product of our minds. The epistemic correspondence of thought to a mental object is the most we can accredit to the predication of God's existence, itself the invention of an idea.

Axioms

Ab Initio

God as Thought Experiment:

I Definition of God

A What Constitutes God?

I God

1 God is conceived to be greater than which nothing greater can be thought.
1a This constitutes supremacy, therefore God is supreme.
1b Supremacy must exist in actuality and in truth, not as mere thought or possibility, therefore God *is*.
1c God is actual and real and exists as Supreme Being, for nothing greater can be conceived.

2 Supreme Being has no bounds or limits, therefore God is boundless and limitless, hence unconstrained and eternal; for anything less would be fallible, finite, and imperfect.
   i   As unalterable.
   ii   As unchanging and unchangeable.
2a Therefore God is Absolute Perfection and Infinity.

3 To be unconstrained, perfect, and eternal, God would have to be unconditioned, uncaused, and entirely self-sufficient.
   i   As self-derived, self-caused, or self-originated.
   ii   Being-from-and-of-itself.
   iii As self-essence.
   iv As absolute independence.
   v   Being-in-and-for-itself.

4   In order to be supreme and perfect, God would have to possess the following properties:
   i   Omnipotence
   ii Omnipresence
   iii Omniscience
   iv Ultimate Goodness

4a   To be omnipotent is to have unlimited universal power, therefore God is the ultimate force, will, and authority in the universe.

4b   In order to be the ultimate force, God would have to be the ultimate originator or creator of all that *is*; for only supreme power would be able to create existence. Therefore God is the source, creator, and cause of all existence.

4c   To be all powerful, to have no limits or constraints, would mean that God is everywhere at once and permeates all things.

4d   Therefore God is Being and is present everywhere at all times and in all possible realities.

4e   To be all powerful and ubiquitous would necessitate possessing ultimate knowledge, for no being would be supreme without knowing all that is and all that is possible.

4f   Therefore God is the omnifarious knower of ultimate knowledge as unsurpassable intelligence.

4g   To be supreme and perfect would also entail ultimate goodness, for anything less is imperfect and fallible; therefore ultimate goodness as a virtue is an essential property.
   i   This would entail any ancillary attributes or instantiations such as benevolence, beneficence, beauty, grace, beatitude, etc.

4h   What is ultimately good is of supreme excellence and righteousness.

4i   That which is supremely good and moral is the epitome of Value, the Ideal and highest of all values.
   i   That which is desirable and to be desired and pursued.

4j   Therefore God is a moral agency, for that which is ultimately good is right, just, pure, and virtuous.

5   To be Supreme Being, cause of all existence, of paramount intelligence, ultimate goodness, and ideal value would make God a divine agent.

5a   Therefore God is personification.

5b   As divine agency, God's personification is the epitome and ideal of its personhood.

5c *Ergo* God is a person.

6   What is actual is real, and what is real is true, therefore the person of God is ultimate Truth.

2 The existence of God

A Can the existence of God be proven?

I Existence

1   *Existence* is defined as that which *is*, that which has being or presence.
   i   Is present in the current moment.
   ii   That which is the case and real.
   iii   Is manifest, hence actual.
1a To exist is to *be*, to have actuality, to be alive.
1b To be is to exist in actuality and have reality or life.
1c To exist is to occur, to take place, and to be present in space and time.
1d To exist is to be and manifest as a thing, entity, mode, process, or manner of being that is evident.
1e To exist is to persist and continue to be.
1f To be is to belong to a specified class or group with certain discernible qualities, attributes, and characteristics.

II Proof

1   *Proof* is understood as the conclusive demonstration of a given assertion based on evidence that is incontestable.
   i   Proof must depend upon evidence that establishes the validity of the proposition(s) in question.

2a *Evidence* is understood as facts or data that indicate and furnish proof for which judgments are based to derive discernible conclusions.
   i   Evidence should be present, plainly visible, clear, and conspicuous.
2b *Facts* are understood as having actual demonstrable existence; in reality and in truth, actually.

i   Facts are something done and presented as objectively real.

ii   They *are*.

iii   They can be occurrences or events.

iv   They must refer to something substantial, instantiated, or performed and be objectively (extraspectively) verified.

2c   *Data* is information as something given or assumed based on determined facts or propositions used in order to derive specified conclusions or decisions.

2d   *Demonstration* is the act of making evident.

i   As an act of proving.

ii   Through conclusive reasoning or presentation of facts.

iii   As an illustration or explanation by experiment or practical application.

iv   To show, reveal, display, operate, exemplify, or manifest by adducing evidence.

2e   *Validity* is a state or quality of being well-grounded, sound, efficacious, and based on well-founded conclusions. Validity may be achieved in several ways:

i   By the correct application of certain specified rules determined by linguistic, mathematical, and logical operations governing conventional systems of discourse derived from human consensus.

ii   By methodological observation, measurement, calculation, and experimentation via tests, trials, replication, and statistical analysis operating within the scientific parameters of reliability and the principles of verifiability and falsifiability.

III Coda

3   Following our operational definition of the criterion of evidence (2a), God's predication would not meet the empirical standards of existence (1, 1d) because God cannot be proven (2) as a fact (2b) or demonstrated to exist as an actual reality (2d), for God has neither appeared nor manifested (1, 1d) as an actual being or entity subject to methodological observation or investigative science (2eii).

3a   Therefore the existence of God cannot be proven.

3b   Following the parameters and conventions of systematic logic, it is possible to offer legitimate arguments and formal (deductive-symbolic) proofs for the existence of God that contain valid premises from which justified conclusions may be derived, or where they are correctly inferred or deduced from the premises (2ei).

3c   However, they would not meet the criteria pertaining to facts (2b).

3d   Although arguments can be logically coherent, God's predication is based on speculative propositions and confined to formal boundaries governed by the human laws and rules of predication and demonstration, hence confined to thought, conception, or abstraction rather than fact.

    i   As warranted or justified belief (which can be true or false).

    ii   As faith.

3e   Hence proof becomes a definitional dynamic, not an objective fact, although it may be valid (2e, 2i).

3f   Definitions are based on linguistic conventions and semantic structures of language or grammar as social constructions instantiated within culture and sustained by consensual rules governing semiotics and meaning systems.

3g   This relegates the concept of God to a cognitive object, intentional stance, mental property, or psychological faculty of mind.

3h   Predicate logic embraces coherency, preciseness of definitions, and the correct application of specified rules to structure arguments and derive reasonable conclusions. The applications and procedures that govern formal logic or analytic judgments devolve into the domain of ideas as mental objects and abstract systems of rational thought following prescribed rules of semantics and deduction.

    i   Following logical rules of demonstration, the most we can say is that proof is based on assent to conventional lexicon and methodological operations governed by consensus, social construction, and linguistic determinism that appeal to human norms and values.

    ii   No proposition can be proof of itself.

3i   Existence itself is not a predicate. You cannot define being into existence. We cannot warrant the leap from logical forms or ideas to a category of actuality *qua* empirical reality; that is, as incontestable and definite existence, or the presencing of being of a real Being as such.

3j   Therefore the formal conditions surrounding the logical applications of proof of God's existence can only be confirmed as a mental object determined by human discourse posited by the psyche.

3k   Hence God exists only as an idea.

3 The non-existence of God

A Is God's non-existence self-evident?

1   We have determined that in order for something to exist, it must have being and presence as a real entity, and manifest itself as something actual.

1a We have determined that evidence must be presented as facts or data that furnish proof and demonstrate existence that is incontestable.

1b God's predication does not conform to the requirements governing empirical reality.

1c God is not present or manifest.

1d God's predication does not meet the criteria constituting a fact.

1e God's predication cannot be objectively verified.

1f God cannot be demonstrated to exist in actuality as factual truth.

1g Therefore, God is not evident as objectively real.

2   God's predication is based on absence.

2a If God's absence is posited to exist, then there is no formal ground to determine the verity or validity of non-existence other than its own non-manifestation.

2b Non-existence is self-evident based on a lack of presence as nothingness.

2c Therefore God's non-existence is self-evident for nothing is present nor is being presented; hence this failure to appear constitutes the actuality of non-existence.

B Can it be demonstrated that God does not exist?

1   Under the criteria necessary to demonstrate evidence, God is not evident.

1a What is evident is God's absence.

1b Absence is evident when nothing is present.

1c Nothingness demonstrates a lack of presence or being.

1d Non-existence is evident when there is nothing.

1e Therefore nothingness and non-existence are co-extensive.

1f When nothing is present, non-existence is self-evident.

1g God's non-existence is self-evident by virtue of *absentia*.

1h Therefore God's non-existence is demonstrated.

C Can God's Non-Existence be Established?

1   We have determined that God is not evident, manifest, or factually demonstrated to be real based on absence or lack of presence.

1a God's non-existence is self-evident based on a failure to emerge or appear in actuality, for that which exists must appear in order to be actual.

1b Therefore lack of appearance constitutes the presence of non-being based on the principle of non-manifestation.

1c That which does not manifest does not exist.

1d Since God does not appear, is not present in reality, nor has ever manifested as actual, God's non-existence is established.

2   If we abandon the empirical criterion of evidence and justification, then predication, proof, and demonstration are relocated to the realm of thought and human mentation.

2a As ideation, God is a mental object of predication.

2b As a mental or cognitive object, God's predication is actual only as experiential ideation.

2c Ideation is the product and projection of mind.

2d Ideation and projection are generative *acts* of mentation conveying psychological dispositions inherent to subjectivity.

2e Psychological dispositions as mental processes underlie all acts of ideation.

2f Conceiving God is both an act and object of thought.

I Coda

3   God does not exist independent of mind.

3a Therefore, God does not exist as an autonomous ontological entity or extant being.

3b God cannot exist without mind.

3c Therefore, God exists only as thought.

3d Without thought, God does not and cannot exist.

3e Therefore, God is the invention of an idea.

Chapter 1

God as a metaphysical question

God does not exist. God is merely an idea—a mental object, the invention of imaginative thought championed by reason yet conditioned on desire. We as humanity have devised this myth and it is likely here to stay because world masses cannot live without it. Although there is a rational tenor to predicating God's existence, reason is ultimately mediated by fantasy.[1] God is the product of a collective ideological fantasy fueled by unconscious illusion ensconced in the basic desire for wish-fulfillment. It is easy to appreciate why the human psyche is compelled to invent the notion of God as an ultimate metaphysical reality, because billions of people have a profound need for God. People want consonance, love, enjoyment, satiation, perpetual peace, joy—no one in their right mind would deny these universal yearnings! Yet for believers, a secular existence fails to meet this felt necessity. It is deeply comforting to believe in an Ideal Being, for one's anxieties, conflicts, and emotional pain are mitigated by believing in a divine beneficence that promises a satisfying afterlife. This hegemonic fallacy—the belief or faith in such an afterlife—makes personal, daily existence more tolerable with the dream,

---

1 This is a major tenet of psychoanalysis, however, it may be said to originate in antiquity. Aristotle anticipates Hegel's psychology when he suggests there is a sort of unconscious intelligence at work that mediates images and stored objects within the abyss of the mind. Originally laid down and retained as sensations, "after-images" can take on a life of their own, as we may observe in dreams and fantasy, and are reproduced by the faculty of imagination as re-presentations that are unconsciously derived. This is why Aristotle states: "Thinking is different from perceiving and is held to be in part imagination, in part judgment" (*De Anima*, 427b28–29). Notice that imagination and thought intermingle. Here we may appreciate why Hegel (1830a) claims, even with stipulations, that "phantasy is reason" (*EG* § 457). In other words, unconscious valences intervene during any act of thinking, especially in fantasy formation. Because reason is a developmental achievement, it is grounded upon our natural embodied constitution that acquires advanced forms of cognition through human maturation. Therefore, reason is the epigenetic evolution of its prior shapes that transform yet derive from our natural corporeality as desire, sentience, affect, and the life of imagination (see Mills, 2010).

that deep down, sometime in the future, when you *perish* you will have everything you desire but are deprived of in your momentary life. Death no longer becomes an ending in-itself, but rather an Eden where all cherished wishes and values are realized—the Perfect World. God is a signifier for flawlessness, salvation, everlasting tranquility, or any qualitative value that signifies perennial happiness or bliss. As the product of fantasy life, God is solely a coveted fiction.

Proof and negation

> Every reflecting mind must allow that there is no proof of the existence of a Deity.
>
> —Percy Bysshe Shelley[2]

Certain philosophers may claim that you cannot prove a negation, namely, God's non-existence. But I would ask, How is it that you cannot prove the non-existence of something when by definition there is nothing there to prove? We do not need to prove a negative, especially when there is nothing present. Negation is self-evident by virtue of absence. It doesn't take a natural scientist to demonstrate objective reality. Negation or absence is obvious and indisputable, a plain truism. There is nothing there to predicate other than negation. The burden is in proving how there is something out of nothing, how there *is* when what appears or manifests is *not*, literally no-thing. We do not even have a proper predication because we are positing (concrete) existence (not ideation) in the face of nothingness, a so-called hidden presence when there is salient absence. If the only thing that presents itself is absence, how can the predication of existence negate this apparent negation? In other words, if God is predicated to be yet is occluded, does this not beg the question of what constitutes the properties of existence? If anything, negation is the one thing that you can prove because nothing appears. Here we may side with Hume: "It is an infinite advantage in every controversy, to defend the negative."[3] Translation: that which is not evident needs no coaxing.

The philosopher is never called upon to prove a negative, for the burden is on the one predicating existential affirmation, here God's existence. The

---

2 This was the final sentence of his 1811 anonymously published pamphlet, "The Necessity of Atheism," for which he was expelled from Oxford for refusing to denounce authorship to the university authorities.
3 David Hume (1755), p. 598.

laws of induction and inference speak of reasonable and common sense ratios of probability to support likely conclusions based upon evidence some believers wish to categorically disqualify as truth or knowledge because it does not yield absolute certainty. However, is that good justification to negate a negative, let alone a good reason to live one's life by, when there is no evidence (which is missing, hence does not exist) to support such a supposition? Just because something cannot be proved with absolute certainty does not make it *ipso facto* false. Moreover, theists or deists would have us believe: "Because it is not certain that God cannot exist, it is at least equally certain that God exists." According to this way of thinking, any concession to the limits of proving a negation provides proportional (if not equal) logical grounds for positing an affirmation (which at most is an inference, and a poor one at that, based on a non sequitur where the conclusions do not follow from the premises). This reasoning is further based on the value of abstract possibility (itself a mental construction) rather than on mere probability, as if the possible supersedes the probable, especially when there is no tangible data to warrant this leap to metaphysical heaven.

Positing divine being to annul non-being (itself the negation of negation) is to privilege a lop-sided logic that assertion *itself* cancels negation when the assertion is a vacuous statement that lacks a present referential object; while the negative is self-evident by virtue of the fact of nothing being present. Rather than set the bar to zero as a mutual inference based on the laws of induction, the predication of the existence of an absent object does nothing to negate this apparent absence. I do not grant that the proposition of God's existence holds the same level of probability as the apparent nothingness of the (mental) object we are positing. And when philosophers are called upon to prove a negation, they wittingly revert to the proof from *modus tollens*:

$$\frac{P \rightarrow Q, \neg Q}{\therefore \neg P}$$

If (p) God exists, then (q) God would not be absent.
(q) God is not present, hence absent.
Therefore, (p) God does not exist.

Although this is a valid proof based on propositional logic, all one has to do is quibble with the premises to manipulate the desired outcome one wants. But here I am appealing to empirical facts: God's lack of presence gives no evidence for God's existence. To quote the new atheists, "the absence of evidence is evidence of absence." Given that most knowledge claims and scientific discoveries are built upon induction and inference, only to be supported or refuted by empirical evidence, does it make logical sense to affirm the existence of a supreme being when no inductive or deductive support can be indubitably established by appeal to all available evidence? Since when does the criterion of absolute certainty garner the respect to warrant the negation of negation in favor of affirmative belief in asserting "God exists!," especially when there is evidence to the contrary, namely, the absence of the very object in question. The burden of proof is on the one proclaiming existence, not on the one questioning whether something exists. Here negation is self-evident because nothing is present; and in order for something to exist, it must *appear* in order for it to *be*.[4]

The Christian philosopher and apologist William Lane Craig states that the theist need not have to appeal to evidence to know God exists, which is brought about through the inner workings of God's "Holy Spirit ... wholly apart from evidence," and by "miracles," one of which he notes is Christ's resurrection from the dead, as well as the canons of natural theology. Instead, rather than offering cogent or plausible proof, he insists that "it is incumbent on the atheist to prove that if God existed, he would provide more evidence of his existence than what we have. This is an enormously heavy burden of proof for the atheist to bear."[5] How so? Apart from this rhetorical challenge, I do not think the presence of nothing requires anymore proof than what is self-evident, namely the absence of an object, which is tantamount to the absence of evidence. Appealing to the subjectivity of belief as epistemological justification for knowing God's existence based on the invisible workings of a divine ghost is not sound (nor even reasonable) evidence to warrant such a conclusion. Neither is the presupposition of miracles that are said to have historically happened, which defy all natural physical laws; nor is scriptural or theological doctrine proffered

---

4 Recall Hegel's equation of appearance as essence, for nothing could exist unless it is made actual. From the *Encyclopaedia Logic*, Hegel (1812) says:

> Essence must *appear*. Its inward shining is the sublating of itself into immediacy, which as inward reflection is *subsistence* (matter) as well as *form*, reflection-into-another, subsistence *sublating itself*. . . . Essence therefore is not *behind* or *beyond* appearance, but since the essence is what exists, existence is appearance. (*EL* § 131)

Also compare with the *Phenomenology* (1807), § 147.

5 Craig (2007), p. 70.

as good evidence, let alone the imagined intentions or psychological motives attributed to a fantasy object that is presumed to exist. Craig's "proof" is merely the self-projection of his mind. Without providing persuasive argumentation commensurate with verifiable evidence, the theist is simply reasoning in a solipsistic circle.

An assertion of predication is affirmative, but one has the burden of proof. What is it? Where is it? Why does it not stand out or manifest? A proposition is not a proof of itself. And I certainly do not give any credence to Nathan Schneider's definition of proof as "that which makes good,"[6] which relegates evidence, truth, and reason to the scrapheap of relativism. Existence is not a predicate: it cannot be *defined* into actuality. Existence as a hypothetical construct cannot be assigned or unconditionally conferred Being as if it is merely a logical statement that needs no actual proof or substantial demonstration. Logic in itself is a decorous system of abstract inferences that lack substantive properties—an empty formalism, the content of which is arbitrarily supplied by our minds subject to convention. Just because you predicate something does not make it so. One cannot dismiss the request for spatial-temporal location and subsistence when predicating something substantive, such as in the substantive verb *to be*. If we appeal to arguments that God is immaterial and incorporeal, or non-temporal—outside of space and time, ethereal, eternal, and infinite, hence eluding all naturalistic indicators of experiential evidence, then we are positing the presupposition of a being that has

6 See *God in Proof* (2013), p. xi. Schneider's redefinition of proof allows him to take poetic liberty with ordinary experiences we would not typically classify as proof. For example, he surprisingly opens his book with a so-called self-acclaimed proof in God:

> One almost-gone afternoon in November, as I stepped out into what sun remained in the day, a proof for the existence of God took hold of me. I was a freshman in college and had just finished a meeting with a teaching assistant. The department house's heavy wooden door thudded shut behind me. Light; truth (p. ix).

Was it the sound of the door slamming, or perhaps the meeting with an attractive teaching assistant that struck this young man's fancy? Since we do not have first-person epistemic access to his thought processes, we will never know. But if this vague, quasi-mystical, and entirely subjective ineffable form of the numinous constitutes proof in God, then practically anything could constitute proof based upon the idiosyncratic nature of relativized experience imagined by anyone. "I ate a donut. Light; truth." Hardly a defensible criterion of proof. But in all fairness to Schneider, you can glean from his writing that he is a genuinely good soul. His book showcases (like no other I have read) a very authentic, humane, and emotionally open struggle with the God question by someone who craves the spiritual, the good life, and the best for collective humanity; yet he is epistemologically uncertain about his faith despite his belief in God (see p. 227). I applaud him on his individuation process, as we all must travel our own path.

never displayed its manifest existence. The premise itself is illegitimate, for there is nothing to predicate other than a missing object, pure nothingness. Here God becomes a hypothetical mental construct that is hypostatized or reified as a concrete subject (a person, no less). If it is only in one's mind, then how can it be real independent of mind? In other words, just because we think it does not make it an extant reality.

At most we can say is that mind as ideation posits a cognitive (mental) object as the subject matter of its predication, but we cannot ontologically justify the leap from internal ideation (even as coherent logical relata) to external actuality. At best God is a hypothesis, an educated guess or speculative conjecture that is empirically unverifiable. Yet thoughts themselves are empirical (experiential) phenomenon, and the parameters of their content and properties can be scientifically studied and objectively recognized. But with the God hypothesis we have no empirical object other than a mental concept, which is not sufficient to justify (let alone establish) the existence of an autonomous object that inhabits a mind independent metaphysical reality.

A negation, on the contrary, has no onus because nothing is predicated. There is no interlocutor engaging a subject, other than one's own mind. Therefore, an affirmative predication is, at best, a psychological object. If you assert that a negation does not provide proof of a possible or potential object to manifest, then by definition it does not currently exist and the whole argument devolves into possible or potential futures that have not occurred, despite the presumption that you cannot rule out their possible future occurrence. But to me this seems to be eluding the present condition of predication and actuality. Possibility is a mental occasion or instance of futurity—pure hypothetical abstraction, while actuality is real presence not limited to a cognitive object of predication.

The main problem in predicating God's existence independent of any tangible evidence is that it relies on a form of argumentation that attempts to deduce existence from the mere concept of existence. These a priori arguments do not rely on sense experience to lend any credibility to the form of argumentation, but rather on an analysis of concepts alone and their logical relations that pretentiously confer the domain of Being to hypothetical objects of thought, which are held to be knowable independent of empirical encounters. Yet these conventions are confined to the domain of ideas: when we deliberate ontology we must separate our conceptual schemes and what they designate from that which is truly extant.

Predication and empirical reality are two different things: one is confined to mental operations, the other to facts.

It is generally known that Kant forcefully challenged the ontological argument by claiming that existence is not a property or a real predicate, namely, that the proposition "exists" is not a properly defining predicate of God.[7] Because existential propositions are synthetic in nature, existence becomes a logical predicate when such judgments are contingently performed.[8] In other words, the notion of existence is only meaningful when objects of experience substantiate the predication. A concept alone does not confer existence: it is impossible for my idea of God to contain any real properties a priori without an experiential correlate to ground my epistemic judgment that God actually exists as a real object or acquires existence outside of my concept alone.[9] In other words, we cannot conclude that the exact object of my concept exists independent of empirical reality.

Existential statements typically either affirm or deny that something exists. Positive existential statements assert existence, while negative existential statements negate existence. The existential statement "God does not exist" is therefore a negative one. But we must keep in mind, as we have just shown, that God is a concept and not an object. There are no good grounds to think of God as anything but an idea, for there is no counterpart in material reality that would substantiate God as an empirical object. Therefore when theists speak of God as existing, they are in actuality referring to the concept of God as a psychic object. From this vantage point, there is a special relation that is said to exist in one's subjective mind independent of the ontological (external) reality of the concept in question. Therefore the God posit or introject can have different functional distributions in a person's psyche dissociated from the ontological status of God as a real object, and may serve myriad psychological purposes. Perhaps, some would argue, this is a sufficient condition to exonerate the notion of God from the question of ontology. But the God function is still merely a mental relation. It is not a necessary condition adjudicating the question of the existence of God. If a mental relation is all that is justified to establish a communion with the divine, then this phenomenon can extend to practically anything, which potentially imports a whole host of other illusions

---

7 See *Critique of Pure Reason* (1781/1787), Ch. 3, Sec. 4, "The impossibility of an Ontological Proof of the Existence of God."

8 Ibid., A 598/B 626.

9 Ibid., A 600/B 628.

and sundry problematics. Despite the fact that the God introject occupies psychical reality for billions of people, it nevertheless remains a mental construct, the unconscious dynamics of which we will consider shortly.

As we have elucidated, at most we can say is that any existential statement about God refers not to an ontological object, but to the *concept* of God. And all properties attributed to God are an *instance* assigned to the concept of God. As a result, following Frege's amplification of Kant, the predication of existence can neither be a first order property nor a defining property of God.[10] In short, to reiterate the point, existence is not a defining property or a predicate of God.

Richard Dawkins tells us that it is "almost certain" that God does not exist based upon improbable statistical odds.[11] But I would argue that the God hypothesis is not really an empirical question, because if it were, we already have proof in God's non-existence *via absentia*, for God neither has manifested nor revealed itself directly.[12] Evidence is the *sine qua non* or gold standard by which we base and derive our modern understanding of the world, a condition without which it could not be. If the God question was truly an empirical one, then science has already *proven* that God does not exist, for there is no evidence. The very notion of existence employs the predicate of identity, namely, that something *is*. The empiricist's criterion of reality is based on the premise of that which is, that which has presence or being (ὄν, *esse*), namely, something actual. The 'is' of existence (*There is:* $\exists x$) is an existential instantiation. A (re)presentation and conceptual scheme of existence is further constructed based upon the mode in

10 Cf. Nicholas Everitt (2004), p. 54.
11 *The God Delusion*, p. 137.
12 Here God's lack of manifestation should be understood as the failure to directly appear as a substantive (although possibly immaterial) being, not merely revealed or made manifest in the mind of a subject, which can be entirely subjective and construed to be whatever an individual interprets manifestation or revelation to be. Admittedly, it is hard for me to fathom how this manifestation would transpire if God were to appear as anything but a substantive entity. Jung and the post-Jungian spiritual movement have attempted to make God unconscious, and hence one could argue (if you accept Jung's theories) that archetypal appearances from a collective unconscious may qualify as a form of manifestation, albeit it would be entirely confined to subjective experience and interpretation, such as the content and hermeneutics of dreams. Yet this would still confine God to an intrapsychic materialization and not an external (objective) one. My fantasy is that God would have to pervade the senses of all peoples on earth as an experiential certainty in order for God's manifestation to be considered actual; however, we would still have the messy epistemological and empirical criteria to deal with. I could also imagine that if something remotely possible as divine manifestation were to materialize, then there would be a mass hysteria or collective psychosis that would paralyze humanity. Because the bounds of imagination have no bounds, I am content with leaving this thought experiment unexplored for the moment.

which an object presents itself, and our mental apparatus uses various existential quantifiers to distinguish among its attributes or qualities. But with
the God assertion, we have the converse: a being is predicated to exist
based on that which is *not present*, that which does not present itself.
Although most sensible people can generally agree that the universe exists
because it presents itself to us as a manifold of sense impressions, objects
with mass and spatiotemporal locations, and natural processes that we are
necessarily obliged to participate in and acknowledge as concretely real,
the masses often show deference to illogic. Perhaps such tendency toward
deference is partly out of conditioning or habit tied to social custom, but
also out of sensitivity (if not perspicacity and respect) for the needs of all
believers to maintain emotional illusions that serve discernible psychological functions.[13] But this should not dissuade us from the pursuit of sober
truth, no matter how unsavory we find it. We accept the universe as part of
our natural circumstances because we experientially sense it to be real and
substantive, what we are thrown into as part of that which is *given.* So why
should we not impose the same criterion on the question of God?

The *is*ness of identity refers to a real object that exists and subsists, not
merely a cognitive representation of that object, while the *is* of predication refers to a concept or an idea about an object and its representation.
Although we may predicate God's existence, such predication signifies a
mental (ideal) object—a thought—rather than an extant (real) object, for
God is nowhere to be found in the real world, let alone standing out or
above other objects. Instead, God's predication would fall into a category

---

13 Living as an outspoken atheist is a tough row to hoe as a minority in societies that condemn free
speech and inquiry. But social discrimination and marginalization abounds in free societies as
well. Those who question others or speak unabashedly about religious disbelief are often lam-
basted for their deviant convictions and lack of observance to social decorum. Moreover, we are
quick to be labeled as radicals, heretics, or antisocial who thrive on creating interpersonal discomfort in others. We should challenge this political hegemony and militate against it. Yet this
may come with certain costs. An inevitable social distance and alienation occurs when a lack of
tolerance for difference in belief systems is experienced by atheist and theist alike. Cryptic dis-
criminatory practices are prevalent on all stratifications of culture, economic class, and political
dynamics operative within social organizations, from tiny cliques to large political bodies that
collectively determine almost anything, from the fate of how one is treated interpersonally by
others to social policy. This is why many atheists are cautious about offending others because
their authentic, uncensored views could have tangible consequences that encumber the concrete
quality of their lives. This is quite conspicuous in smaller communities where anonymity is
limited or non-existent, which influences everything from social gossip, exclusion or expulsion
from group membership, to ostracism in public schools, business, and communal practices. It is
likely that with increased education, awareness, and social dialogue these emotional prejudices
will acquire reform within democratic countries.

of non-being, for the *is* of identity is not demonstrated nor designated to conform to what we customarily experience as that which exists, except only as a psychic projection or hypothesis as ideation the mind generates through the positionality of consciousness toward an ideal state of affairs it wishes to signify or intend.

My assertion that God does not exist is confined to the world of empirical reality. In the realm of psychic reality, this becomes a whole other matter, for, it bears repeating, the God posit is merely an idea. When I refer to God's non-existence as the predication of nothingness or absence, I mean that it does not signify a concrete actuality, for it is merely a formal abstraction with qualities of denial, dispossession, withdrawal, deletion, elimination, erasure, or privation, and so on; hence positing non-existence dialectically stands in relation to being or real presence. Here what is present is the absence of God. Although the presence of absence as lack has a psychological reality, we should not assume that a thing's absence or lack signifies concealed actuality, such as a supreme being justified by an argument for divine hiddenness. We should not presume there is a transcendent deity in hiding, which is concealed and non-manifest, for that which is real should be manifest, revealed, and openly disclosed. To say that God is hidden, undisclosed, or covered-up is to beg the question of God's existence, let alone any attributed motives or presumed intentions to remain hidden rather than transparent, conspicuous, and unconcealed as divine disclosedness. If we adopt the pre-Socratic notion of truth as *aletheia* (ἀλήθεια) or unconcealment, then God should have disclosed or manifested its being by now. To say God remains hidden to the human world is to say nothing, for absence is not an empirical criterion for being. If this were the case, then anything that has no observational properties, motion, or manifest effects, let alone has never presented itself, could be said to be in hiding. Here the Higgs boson particle may be said to be no different than the God posit, with the exception that physical science can point to tangible evidence even though the detection of subatomic particles largely remains invisible.[14]

---

14 Recent new evidence in support of the Higgs boson was revealed at the world's largest and highest energy particle accelerator, the Large Hadron Collider, which is located in a 17-mile tunnel near the Franco-Swiss border near Geneva, and is operated by CERN, the European Organization of Nuclear Research. The ATLAS and Compact Muon Solenoid calculators detected unusual particles that *manifested*, hence popped into existence, after these collision experiments occurred (see Carroll, 2012; Landau, 2013).

In the context of God's non-instantiation as non-materialization, how can we justify the assertion that there is a divine something rather than an apparent nothing? Given the unequivocal fact that the universe exists, shouldn't the God question be asking, Why is there nothing rather than something? If God exists, why does God abstain from revealing itself? Yet this question presupposes that we as mortal humans should assume the existence of a supreme being in the first place that has reasons not to appear or manifest directly, hence imparting a certain intentionality onto God, and projecting a cornucopia of motives which we are not privy to.[15] But this very supposition rests on the presupposition that there is something behind the veil of nothingness (namely the non-manifested), or more precisely, that there is something *in* nothingness—namely, the inverse of what does not appear. The collective fantasy is that there is a hidden reality—the *Ding an sich*;[16] in this case, a divine invisible presence animating the cosmos.[17]

God as failed hypothesis

The very definition of empiricism rests on the notion that something is observable and potentially measurable as revealed to our experiential senses and cognitive faculties. Although one may claim to experience God as the reality of the unseen,[18] in order to escape the charge of a radical or oppressive subjectivism ("It is true because I say so!"), or crass solipsism or idealism ("I think it, therefore it exists!"), experience must be subject to universal (replicable) criterion that gains validity through verification, which by definition transcends subjectivism for objective consensual agreements or calculations, what we typically—and practically—call facts. From an empirical point of view, God does not exist because there is no observable or tangible object/agent that is manifest or present; hence we cannot scientifically study nothing (literally, no-thing) under

---

15 In *Breaking the Spell* (2006), Daniel Dennett views the concept of God as an "intentional object." Here I wish to emphasize that the intentional stance or object is in fact the human subject whom cannot help but project their own internal human attributes (and dynamic conflicts) onto the *idea* of what is construed to be God.

16 Cf. Kant's (1781) discussion of "Things-in-themselves" as unknowable but thinkable, pp. 27, 74, 87, 149.

17 Stephen Maitzen (2006) argues that according to the argument of divine hiddenness, "God's existence is disconfirmed by the fact that not everyone believes in God" (p. 177) based on an uneven distribution of theistic belief due to a dwindling reduction in the demographics of theism.

18 See William James (1902), Lecture III, p. 53.

the rubric or parameters that define the scientific method. Although we may charge science with its own hegemonic agendas,[19] here it may be argued that the God question is not a legitimate scientific topic because it does not meet the basic requisite of falsifiability through testability.[20] In other words, if you cannot falsify a premise through the potential refutation of conjectures, then anything is potentially true. How can you observe, statistically measure, or quantify something that eludes the sensuous world? How can you refute that which does not appear if the presupposition in question does not allow for an empirical assessment? By positing the existence of something that is not observable or manifest, verifiable or falsifiable, one dislocates the object in question away from science to the realm of *thought*. Although thoughts are to some degree introspectively observable and extraspectively recordable, they certainly cannot be dislocated from the thinker or agent entertaining such ideas, even when they become an object of study.

Physicist Victor Stenger claims that the God posit is a failed hypothesis because it does not live up to scientific scrutiny nor pass even simple empirical tests of validity based on all the available data in both the physical and social sciences.[21] If all existing scientific models contain no trace of God, then God would have to appear outside of those models or gaps in systematic observation and measurement. However, this is not a proper scientific argument for it means that the God hypothesis not only defies empirical explanation, it further flouts the possibility of natural description, hence being incapable of providing a plausible account of God as a natural phenomenon. If the God construct fails all attempts to be examined by methodological naturalism through the scientific procedures of hypothesis testing, then science has fertile logical ground to conclude that God does not exist based on lack of evidence. And if the "God of the gaps" or "God in hiding" arguments wish to appeal to supernatural forces as explananda, then the scientific investigation of God is impossible, for such metaphysical postulates are irrefutable by definition because they are not susceptible to empirical falsification.

---

19 One can argue that science fundamentally rests on statistical hypotheses that are in principle unfalsifiable and based on induction; therefore in practice the scientific method almost never employs falsification and is only concerned with reporting statistically significant results that drive and legitimize the political world of scientific publishing.

20 See Karl Popper (1959), Ch. 1, p. 1.

21 Stenger (2007), pp. 11–18, 34, 233, 237.

But abstracting God outside the realm of scientific investigation does nothing to substantiate the existence of God, for abstraction itself conforms to the cognitive and linguistic processes that *define* the laws of predication as human contrivances. Purely logical arguments as language games cannot be equated with the objective (universal) scientific criteria used to arbitrate the circularity of definitions and redefinitions. In the end, science appeals to an objectivist epistemology that follows a replicable method based on empirical facts as the final judge. As stated before, existence is not a predicate, it is an instantiation. The God hypothesis is not only disconfirmed by the available data, it is contradicted by the fact that no empirical evidence for God exists.

The humanities in general, at most a semiotic-hermeneutic science, and the study of religion, theology, and philosophy in particular, are not the same as the natural sciences precisely because they entertain different subject matters and employ different methodologies. Even in contemporary physics, when objects are postulated to exist independent of consciousness, they are still subject to observation selection effects (under the influence of anthropic bias) that must pass the test of a replicable method. Yet non-empirical fields within the humanities are comfortable with making ultimate metaphysical truth claims that support the objective realism of God's existence. This is what is generally meant or implied when God is predicated to *be*, that is, to exist as an external entity independent of people's minds. And if we concede that any object of our sense perception, experiential faculties, and rational contemplation is necessarily predicated on the hermeneutic interpretation of the natural world—in other words, that *all* experience is mediated by mentation and our faculties of cognition—we cannot epistemologically justify the ontological assertion of God's existence independent from mind. In other words, we cannot even conceive of the idea of God's independence and ontological separateness from our own subjective thoughts that, even if shared by others, condition this conception.

Whether we avouch scientific realism, or any of its variants, such as naturalism or critical realism, we are left with the same conclusion: We cannot observe and verify that which does not present itself other than our *ideas* about its lack of presence. This is why the God question, from my point of view, is more properly considered a metaphysical enterprise.[22] More precisely, the God hypothesis conforms to a particular form of speculative metaphysics that has been largely annexed by theology. Because the God construct lacks a verification principle, its proper investigation and meaning(s) is relegated to a speculative philosophy that attempts to lay the theoretical foundations for a grand narrative that allegedly (as *potentia*) lends credibility to a worldview that endeavors to take into account everything as the whole of reality. This Theory of Everything traditionally has centered on the comprehensive understanding, structural interrelatedness, and unification of theology, cosmology, and psychology that systematically attempts to amalgamate the human, natural, and spiritual sciences within a dynamic, coherent complex holism.

Speculative philosophy has its own place in the history of ideas, but we should not compare this with empirical proof. In fact, proponents of logical positivism would say that the God construct is meaningless because it cannot in principle be verified. Yet this assessment displaces the human value attached to the God posit that in itself conveys purpose and meaning to believers. It would be foolish to dismiss its psychological worth as a reified object to humanity, for there is no question that the psychomythology of belief has pragmatic value. God could be said to exist in psychic reality (itself a metaphysical universe), but I would confine these discourses to the realm of human experience, ideation, fantasy, or abstract philosophical ponderings that are purely tentative and hypothetical in nature. They do not conform to the same laws of demonstration or warrant the same determination that we accord the physical universe comprised of the energetic stratification of material substance or informational processing systems that occupy and subsist within space-time in real tangible (hence observable, measurable, and calculable) forms as quantum states or events.

Granted that an idea is substantive, it is not substantial. Although there are many sophisticated and noteworthy metaphysical schemes that

22 In contrast, the linguistic, postmodern turn in Continental philosophy, which developed contemporaneously with Anglo-American analytic philosophy, reduces all propositions to linguistic predications governed by social construction and the conventions of grammatical discourse. In essence, what we *think* is a product of our socialization practices grounded in language. The original content of our thoughts—what we posit, conceive, imagine, or hypothesize about—does not ensure a direct correspondence between the object of thought and an external independent reality. Instead, all ideas are cultural-linguistic mediations. Here the stability of the modern notions of truth, reality, objectivity, and absolutism are overturned by the context and contingencies of society, history, cultural relativism, and linguistic construction. From this perspective, metaphysics is untenable.

address the synergy of mind and matter, including the governing physical laws regulating the universe itself, these endeavors are reserved for the philosophers and onto-theologists who are invested in chasing a logical rationale for a category of the ultimate or absolute, a fundamental unifying or organizing principle to spirit, nature, and cosmic order, and/or the mystical, transcendental, and numinous resonances that pervade human experience. Here such matters should be reserved for discussion on the phenomenology of spirituality, which I will address later, but not attributed to an ontological force emanating from a godhead.

The logical impossibility of God

Speculative metaphysics may posit the ontology of God as an extant entity, but we are only warranted to think of God as a mental object, for no matter how clever one succeeds in providing logical justification, we cannot posit or reason God into actual existence. On the other hand, philosophers have been quite ingenious in their attempts to disprove the existence of God through logic. Disproofs based on deductive arguments have been supported by definitional, doctrinal, and attributional contradictions that nullify the possibility of God. These disproofs include the quagmire of incompatible and contradictory properties, as well as renunciation based on self-contradictory multiple-attributes such as the paradoxes of omnipotence, omniscience, incompleteness, divine freedom and agency, moral perfection, omniconsciousness, and the existence of evil, which are incoherent and lack self-consistency, hence signaling the impossibility of God.[23] Omniproperties (omniperfections) attributed to God are particularly futile arguments that appeal to impossibility in order to ground their alleged possibility, when they are merely self-predicating and circular paroxysms of illogic.

Omniproperty attributions to God rely on a "vicious circle principle" of self-predication, for any property posited either directly or indirectly relates to the divine object in question, hence it is entirely self-referential. Self-predication is not only incongruous and question-begging, it is furthermore *imaginary* because it assumes the *actuality* of the property, capability, or function itself, such as omnipotence, where by definition

---

23 For a nice overview of these detailed arguments see Martin and Monnier (2003), *The Impossibility of God*.

there are *no limits* to one's powers.[24] Superheroes inhabit the cartoon world of comic books and cinema, not reality. These arguments are reflexively circular and appeal to a self-relation to justify their self-predicating existence, such as the predication of God as *causa sui*, the very thing that is in dispute. The premise of omniattributes is illegitimate to begin with because it presupposes the very thing it must set out to prove or demonstrate.

Recently Colin Howson argues that an omniscient God does not and cannot exist based on the application of Tarski's indefinability of truth theorem,[25] which logically proves the impossibility of complete knowledge or truth; not to mention, in surpassing Dawkins' statistical improbability thesis, the probability of God's possible existence, Howson argues, should be set to zero based upon (a) the incoherence and inconsistency of God's so-called a priori omniproperties and (b) the posterior odds relative to all the evidence especially due to the prevalence of evil and innocent suffering in the world.[26]

Here the armory of extremely compelling evidence for the impossibility of God's existence is hard to legitimately rebuke let alone logically dismiss. But just as logic cannot produce an extant God out of nothing, one could argue that it cannot rule out such a possibility *in toto*. Because logical "proofs" and "disproofs" apply only to those who accept certain premises, are willing to grant certain conventions and follow specified rules of argumentation, and adopt their terms, usages, methodologies, and systems of reference, it is not too difficult to evade or reject certain truth premises, or question the validity of ascertained conclusions when the senses of certain terms and their meanings, forms of reference, and rules of demonstration are drawn into question, especially when God is purported to be disproven *a fortiori* based on so-called "fuzzy math." What is interesting to analyze psychologically, however, is why anyone would think that such a possibility of a divine artificer is itself even possible. Here the stronghold of unconscious fantasy overrides the dubious and tenuous nature of our existence and the cognizance of our epistemic uncertainties.

The idea of possibility does not in itself mean to imply that *anything* is possible, only that it signifies a conditional set of indexicals (such as self-instantiated propositions indexed to a person and facts conforming

---

24 Cf. Spinoza (1992), Proposition XV, Part I.
25 Howson (2011), pp. 199, 200, 203, 208.
26 Ibid., p. 133.

to natural laws) that rationally apply to particular contexts and contingencies within the natural world. This means that the forms of possibility must conform to the descriptive laws of nature, which cannot be suspended because they are given or determined. Here the laws of nature do not require a lawgiver. If we accept the premise that the universe participates in and is governed by natural laws, then whatever is possible must transpire within the confines of those laws. If the universe is denied an autonomous existence of its own, hence that it cannot be an open, self-supporting system of contingent facts with statistical variances as essentially incomplete and ultimately impersonal because it depends upon the existence of a supernatural architect that lies beyond or above the natural world as a transcendent being, then God cannot exist because it is logically impossible to stand above and control the whole of nature without also being part of nature itself as a naturalized fact subject to its laws.

If God is said to have willed the universe into existence and it is sustained by this will, then this succumbs to contradiction because God could not remain independent of and permeate the universe at the same time, hence reside outside of nature and not dependent upon its laws, which are the very laws God is purported to have instituted. Furthermore, if God could impose its will on the world it would *necessarily* conform to natural laws because whatever is willed would naturally occur. It may be argued that this is a logically more fundamental fact over any choices God may allegedly will,[27] because any act of will presupposes events that already conform to natural laws, for they would not nor could not occur in the first place. Just as nature cannot be explained by an appeal to something that is not natural, by definition the universe cannot depend on anything that is not a natural fact of the universe.

The abstract (hypothetical) notion of pure possibility only gains popularity as a thought experiment, often designed for amusement by the intellect. The so-called omniattributes and divine properties supposedly bestowed to God such as absolute perfection, omnipotence, omniscience, moral flawlessness, and so forth are the fabrications of human fantasy. They do not and cannot exist in any creature due to their logical incredulity and sheer impossibility. The point I wish to make is that it is not remotely possible to grant the notion of unbounded or unconstrained

---

27 Cf. Gilbert Fulmer (1977), p. 113.

possibility any rational acceptance. It is the power of imagination that generates the fantasy of omniproperties special to God and lends them currency nourished by emotional unconscious factors that inform the cognitive basis for bequeathing them to a supreme being in the first place. This psychological disposition is inherent to man as a wishing animal and nurtures the belief in a rationalized (albeit fictional) account *qua* intellectualized fantasy of potential possible realities that surpass our limitations we are condemned to encounter as fate. The fantasy of a *potentially possible reality* (e.g., God's existence or possible future manifestation) involves a teleological suspension of the laws of nature where no limits, bounds, or restrictions are operative, hence a fantasy of omnipotence. Although we can imagine omnipotence as an abstract idea or object of fantasy, by definition it is impossible because it violates natural laws that govern the world we experience.

One such fantasy is the possibility of futurity that transcends death and the finitude of our natural confines or restrictions, such as our organic embodiment or cultural environs. Futurity is a felt existential anxiety we wish to safeguard against for it is always encroaching upon us like foul weather. The qualia of self-asserted possibility provides the psyche a bit of relief for it endows experience with the felt-intuition or attitude of what things seem to be like or mean to us on a qualitative basis. We often confound our qualitative subjective experiences for quantified objective facts that transcend our personal lives. God's omniperfections and a possible future world of salvation attributed to a Heavenly Father are examples that assuage our nervousness about accepting life and death on their own terms. But the notion of possibility itself is always a bounded concept demarcated by the constraints of reality. There is no absolute condition of unbounded possibility: pure *potentia* is itself a mere fantasy.

The abstract form of potentiality is a theoretical abstraction that does not conform to the demands of objective reality, but it appeals to the subjective finite agent only on the condition that it breaches all conditions. Because it defies logic and conditionality, it is granted an exalted status in the imagining mind. Here the realm of the imaginary confers a certain psychic actuality that defies reality itself, and hence surpasses the limits of reason alone. Although authentic, it is nevertheless a purely subjective act of constructing reality in accord with the wishful fantasies embraced by societies throughout the world. We may refer to this psychological proclivity as the *freedom of fantasy*, but one that remains ensconced in its own illusions. No matter how imaginative (and satisfying) such possible projections of the future may be, we are all obliged by the parameters of our finitude. Here the God posit is the product of dissociation as avoidance of the inevitable we wish were not true, a fundamental denial most of humanity will not and cannot rightfully own because it is too painful to bear.

The God question is really a question of natural wonder. As psychological beings we yearn and speculate that there must be something greater out there, such as an encompassing process, unifying force, and/or an ultimate source to the universe that permeates all reality and binds all phenomena into a synthesizing milieu, which may be proffered via an impersonal metaphysics or natural science. But most of humanity psychologically posits a divine deity as creator and ruler of all. This is a curious artifact of human nature that requires our analysis, for it speaks to a greater collective process that exceeds the lone individual bound to esoteric subjectivity. Here I am intimating the notion of a *subjective universality* that is oriented toward generating meaning structures that point beyond the human mind and given natural world as an explanandum, thereby becoming an inspiration of hope and awe that propels human thought, desire, and action, yet one based nonetheless on a *focus imaginarius*. The ancients referred to this as a cosmic animating principle or vitalism inherent in all things, what we may compare to Plato's *chora*, the womb of all becoming, or Jung's collective unconscious as a transpersonal psyche, the condition and ground of existence, World Soul (*anima mundi*). But what conjoins us in commonality is the substance and sustenance of consciousness, the universality of mind in search of meaning and contentment.

The psychological tendency to project anthropomorphic elements into all objects of thought and experience is an unavoidable onto-structural condition of our psychic constitutions for the simple reason that we are human. We project the intrapsychic dynamics and minutia of our minds into objects of lived experience because the psyche postulates and mediates all metaphysical assertions as propositional dispositions advanced by its own internal nature. The anthropic dimension to the God posit is an extrapolation or natural extension of wonder based upon the human tendency to compare all perceived or imagined things with ourselves, despite the fact that it is a logical error based on a category mistake. Yet from an emotional or unconscious factor, this makes perfect sense. We relate to all objects of thought (whether perceived or imagined) as though they are real and filter external variants through our own inner apparatus and perceptual schemas of reality. Although there are multiple dimensions to reality that structure and color our experience and perceptions of the world, these do not confirm, let alone necessitate, the existence of a supernatural ordering to the universe. All we can reasonably conclude is that the conjecture of any ontological ordering is based on an intractable psychologism that underlies our desire to find meaning and make sense out of natural phenomena, the desire to know.

The problem of infinite regress

Theologians and philosophers of religion often fixate on cosmological arguments for the existence of God to explain the structure of the universe, the complexity of life, and how the cosmos came into being. Cosmologists and astrophysicists equally attempt to answer these conundrums. Both sides must contend with the problem of infinite regress. When the point of origination is said to lie in God's creative act or the big bang, each postulation has the onus of explaining pre-beginning, namely, the prior conditions that would bring about the creation of the universe itself. This appeal to earlier conditions must contend with a further appeal to preconditions *ad infinitum*. In the end, either God exists and has always existed or is self-caused, or the universe has no proper beginning and has always existed or is self-generated. In both instances, either a supreme creator or an impersonal universe has *always existed* in some form as an unswerving constant that is eternal and infinite: something rather than nothing is presupposed as the origin of all that is.

In all versions of the cosmological argument, a necessary existence (hence not contingent or accidental) must be posited in order to escape an infinite regress as the entreaty to an endless or interminable chain of causal events that at some point gives rise to existence itself, which is an incessant trace to earlier antecedent occasions that are said to spark and infiltrate each current moment. Theologians tend to favor some variation of an anthropic argument, which is that the basic facts about the existence of the universe are best explained by appealing to God as the cause of existence, while physicists would attribute causality to processes inherent within the cosmos itself. Here the claim is that the universe was caused and came into being by a cause (hence it *began* to exist), and this cause is

God as the First Cause that is itself uncaused (hence not conditioned on prior causal events that brought about the initial cause of existence per se) because God is unconditioned or self-caused.

Setting aside for the moment that this argument presupposes the very thing it must set out to prove, namely, that a causal agent can be its own cause without being caused or conditioned by prior antecedent events or material-efficient-formal-telic processes that would bring about its self-organizational complexity, even if such circumstances are overdetermined, how do we explain the final cause of causation without reverting to circularity or imposing a self-instituted terminus? Even if the theist concedes to the epistemological limits of knowing the details of God's so-called miraculous powers of self-creation, the unbroken chain of circularity and self-referential premising provides us with no sound justification for positing omnipotent self-causation. Appealing to an omniproperty to explain the omni-act fails to explain how the omni-act is remotely possible, let alone how one acquired the omniproperty to begin with or the mechanisms of how it is self-constituted because it relies on its self-instantiation to justify its presupposed existence, which is the very thing that is in question.

Richard Swinburne summarizes the cosmological viewpoint nicely:

> Arguments for the existence of God have a common characteristic. They all purport to be arguments to a (causal) explanation of the phenomena described in the premises in terms of the action of an agent who intentionally brought about those phenomena. A cosmological argument argues from the existence of the world to a person, God, who intentionally brought it about. An argument from design argues from the design of the world to a person, God, who intentionally made it thus. All the other arguments are arguments from particular features of the world to a God who intentionally made the world with those features.[28]

From this synopsis, we may see that the entire structure of a cosmological argument is circular and self-referential, which ultimately hinges on the teleological notion of divine intentionality. In order to explain the existence of the natural world and its phenomena, God is presupposed as

28 *The Existence of God*, p. 20.

an intentional agent (a "person" nonetheless) who caused it all. Rather than appealing to the phenomena of the world itself, God is predicated to be the designer and architect of all that *is* despite hiding behind an anthropic curtain. Notwithstanding the circularity of the argument, pre-supposing the very thing that is in question as the ultimate cause and explanation of causality itself (one without a cause, mind you) does not explain away the problem of infinite regress. Merely asserting that God is self-caused does not explain how that is possible any more than asserting the universe is caused by the big bang or dark energy or the Higgs field without addressing the question of genesis or the preconditions that brought about the big bang in the first place. Appealing to God may be a satisfying answer for Christian philosophers like Swinburne, Craig, and other apologists, but it does not offer a solution to the question of origins. In a nutshell, the cosmological argument is simply begging the question.

The big question that baffles theologians and physicists alike is the problem of origins. Is there an *absolute* point of origination as creation of the universe, or was something always here? Was there a pre-beginning to beginning? Were there certain a priori conditions that were operative and causally necessary to bring about a beginning? Did the world truly begin, or is science only able to observe and measure its effects or statistical variances through mathematical models to infer a particular point in spacetime when the big bang occurred? Can we infer a prior state of affairs that precedes the big bang or act of creation? Is it a necessary and/ or sufficient condition to posit a point of derivation where energy, mass/ matter, space, and time came into being, or do we need to appeal to a grand designer that brought about such occurrences? If the universe truly had a beginning, did it arise from pure void or nullity? How? What about pre-origins?

Theistic responses to these questions often rest on arguments from fine-tuning, what is said to rely on an anthropic principle, which claims that the laws of physics are finely adjusted to such a degree that the universe could never have come into being nor supported carbon-based life without divine intervention. Put laconically, the arguments from fine-tuning proclaim that because it is so statistically improbable that we are here, that there could even be a life-sustaining universe as the one we inhabit, that there could ever be constants we customarily define as natural causal laws (such as gravity), and that these laws must arise from initial conditions—the conclusion is, "It must be designed." But rather than situate the design argument to the unimpeded and internally derived organizing principles inherent within the universe and organic life itself, where the teleology of nature displays purpose without having to have an *initial* cause, the theist prematurely jumps to the intelligent designer hypothesis where God is said to have created the universe just as we find it, and generously bestows unto God additional omniproperties to boot!

The anthropic argument may be put in the following way:

1   It is a miracle that we are here—that there is a universe that allows and supports life.
2   The fundamental constants and laws of nature that permit and sustain life are so delicately balanced, statistically remote, and existentially improbable that we need to account for how this is possible.
3   Due to such complexity, improbability, and the infinite possibilities or variety of ways we could have turned out, the mystery of existence resists an explanation by chance.
4   It makes no sense that a life-sustaining universe could exist in the absence of an intentional creator.
    Therefore: The universe was designed by God.

Is this conclusion warranted? We would have grounds to expect that a universe that permits human life would surely allow for observers to discover the laws of nature, for what else would we expect to observe? What we expect to observe would necessarily be restricted by the conditions of existence that allow for observers. In the words of philosopher Robin Le Poidevin, "So *of course* the fundamental constants will be such as to permit the development of life."[29] The more controversial claim, however, is that the universe had to be this way in order to permit life and that it was *intended* to be this way by God. Here the cosmological argument is augmented by a teleological explanation that implies that the conditions that allow for the production of life reveal an inherent design or purpose to the universe and that the presence of natural laws is part of the instantiation of that design. The theist is eager to posit the agency of God as designer of the design, however, following Aristotle, a very impersonal account of teleology may be extended to the

---

29 Le Poidevin (1996), p. 55, italics in original. See his comparison between weak and strong anthropic arguments, pp. 54–56, 59–61.

cosmos characterized by evidential purposes behind quantum events as organized processes inherent to non-conscious entities and organisms but without importing conscious intent. And, for sake of argument, even if we cannot successfully defend an impersonal teleological account of the universe, it still does not justify us positing intelligent design by an intentional designer.

For the believer, the values that define the various physical constants that are necessary for life and consciousness to emerge cannot possibly rely on randomness or coincidences, but rather must be chosen and willed by a cosmic intelligence that wanted life to evolve in precise fashions as we know it today. Just because science and the humanities have no absolute answers to why the physical universe is the way it is, does not warrant inventing a supreme entity to explain it all. Not only is a divine Fine Tuner heralded as the solution to why there is something rather than nothing, but that it was deliberately planned to be this way. Even if we were to concede the premise that there is an intelligent design to the universe, it begs the question to assume that there is a grand designer let alone any assumption that a personal being with intentionality is behind the backdrop of creation. How could anyone possibly know that? This view is neither necessary nor sufficient to explain the universe: it is a leap of faith—itself a theological wish with no grounds for proof, even if such "proof" is produced by mathematical formulas or theorems designed to manipulate desired outcomes, which is then passed-off as serious science, such as we may see in some corners of contemporary theoretical physics where incomprehensibly complex equation models dangle a carrot in front of the dumfounded believer, or in probability, propensity, and confirmation theories, which often give the appearance of an exact science but in the end bake no real bread. Once again, a logical proof or mathematical equation cannot produce God's existence out of whole cloth.

Proponents like Swinburne and Craig argue that the universe has an ontological dependence on God, but as we have just shown, this collapses into circularity. This claim not only presupposes God's self-predication, namely, that God constitutes the subject of its own action, but further that the universe could not be occasioned or self-begotten from its own natural configurations and laws. Comparing the origin of the universe to analogies such as Paley's watch or Hume's factory (where an intelligent designer or manufacturer is assumed to set up the complex machinery of the cosmos) is not only a categorical error, because we cannot sufficiently equate a manmade artifact to the structure of the universe, but this position further manufactures a case for the *necessity* of an extrinsic designer by ignoring the naturalized phenomena of self-generation underlying all processes of becoming as a necessary condition of existence. As Keith Parsons puts it, "In nature … order *always* arises from spontaneous self-organization brought about by impersonal causes intrinsic to nature itself."[30] We do not need to go beyond a naturalized account of being and becoming to explain what we can scientifically observe and rationally infer. God is superfluous.

Instead of endorsing the viability of naturalized accounts, theologians prefer the argument from *creatio originans*, namely, that the world was originally created out of nothing by divine action. William Lane Craig explains:

> Now the question is, what could conceivably transform an event that is naturally impossible into a real historical event? Clearly, the answer is the personal God of theism. For if a transcendent, personal God exists, then he could cause events in the universe that could not be produced by causes within the universe. Given a God who created the universe, who conserves the world in being, and who is capable of acting freely, miracles are evidently possible. Only to the extent that one has good grounds for believing atheism to be true could one be rationally justified in denying the possibility of miracles. In this light, arguments for the impossibility of miracles based upon defining them as violations of the laws of nature are vacuous.[31]

There is nothing "clearly" about it. Whether one finds this comical, persuasive, or a garrulous tapestry of sophistry, let us try to unpack this argument for a moment. The "real historical event" Craig's claim applies to is the big bang as the presumed singular point of origin of the universe. In espousing a deterministic model, Craig centers his thesis on the spontaneous generation of a creative act that is issued by a divine personal creator responsible for both originating the material existence of the universe and for conserving Being, all of which challenge our current understanding of natural laws, for how can something simply materialize from pure nothingness and be

---

30 Keith M. Parsons (2013), p. 491.
31 William Lane Craig (2013), p. 386.

sustained by an invisible entity that fractures *and* regulates the physical laws of nature at will? Craig's solution: It could only be a miracle.

Creationists like Craig base their arguments on an appeal to miracles to explain the so-called miraculous while they deny the atheist the right to insist that all events must be explicable from a natural science framework that by definition excludes the miraculous *unless* such said events can be objectively verified or confirmed to violate natural laws. If I interpret Craig correctly here, the theist leaps to the extraordinary explanation when naturalized accounts fail or are truncated in providing an explanation, while the atheist refuses to concede (in principle) to the possibility of extraordinary metaphysical causation that defies naturalism. Here his point that there *could* exist a metaphysical process that currently eludes physical science should be acknowledged.

Theologian David Bentley Hart wishes to extricate himself from the typical view of God as a supreme "agency," yet he upholds the traditional view that God is the supreme "creator" *and* "the infinite ocean of being that gives existence to all reality ex nihilo."[32] Notice here that Hart equates creation with "being itself," whereby being is assigned the properties of *action* out of nothing. This is a logical contradiction, for any creator that acts must have agency to enact events we would properly attribute to the products of creation. If God is merely Being, which is said to be the ground of all existence, then God could be viewed as being no different than Nature itself, a nature that gives rise to itself and all objects in an eternal universe. If we define God as the infinite source of all things and is eternal, uncaused (namely, that it does not depend on anything else for its existence), and is Being itself (in which all subsequent forms of being are necessarily conditioned by its infinite force), then this view of God is no different (in principle) than attributing divinity to the universe itself. What differentiates the theistic position, however, from the impersonal being of nature is that nature is created out of nothing by a presumptive creator.

Hart wants us to believe that existence cannot be explained without an appeal to a timeless a priori supernatural cause he equates with Being that is responsible for "the very possibility of existence as such," which "logically and necessarily" precedes the material universe and produces all physical laws and events in nature, "for neither those laws nor those

---

32 *The Experience of God: Being, Consciousness, Bliss*, p. 36.

states could exist of themselves."[33] But we may naïvely ask, Why not? Do we need to appeal to a supernatural realm to explain what lies before us? Obviously science has come a long way to offer reasonable explanations of natural phenomena through the discovery of fundamental physical constants, such as the processes of gravitational energy, nucleic and electromagnetic force, the speed of light, and so forth. Yet Hart goes so far as to challenge (with great hubris, I might add) that "there simply cannot be a natural explanation of existence as such: it is an absolute logical impossibility."[34] No it is not. The most obvious rebuttal is that existence is simply *given*, part of our natural thrownness, and that existence per se is not caused, rather it is causal. Although this may not be a very satisfactory explanation, it is by no means logically impossible, for if that were true we could offer no explanation at all. Here Hart is merely begging the question of origin.

What does science have to say about the matter? Does it fare any better? Most theists think that we must summon a grand agent that creates the big bang out of nothing, but God is presumed to exist as something. In order to avoid an infinite regress, the scientist focuses on what we can reasonably say about beginning. But no matter what theory is advanced, we still have the same muddle of explicating how something comes into being, and more mysteriously, how something comes from nothing. Recently theoretical physicist Lawrence Krauss has put forth the thesis that the universe comes from nothing, when in fact he posits that energy comes from "empty space," which is essentially *latent* energy that creates all matter mediated by physical laws. Krauss unconvincingly attempts to persuade us into thinking that "nothing" is merely a semantic definition subject to linguistic construction, which is interpreted differently by a scientist, when he in fact displaces all of Western metaphysics by denuding the meaning of "nothing" as being merely a relative term. For example, he rhetorically opines that "'nothing' is every bit as physical as 'something'" for both have physical "quantities."[35] Because Krauss redefines nothing as physicality with quantifying properties, he has invented his own frame of discourse. "Nothing" in the metaphysical sense has always referred to an ontological principle of non-being that signifies *complete absence*, hence, no space, no time, no energetic stratification of

33 Ibid., pp. 40–41.
34 Ibid., p. 44.
35 Krauss (2013), p. xxiv.

matter, no mass, no corporeality or substance, no discernible or inferred empirical properties, and no force or quantum mechanisms whatsoever, which cannot be equated with physicality no matter how clever (or sensationally deceptive in garnering publication in a trade press that was a national bestseller) one is at redefining meanings traditionally held in the history of philosophy to suit self-purposes under the rubric of science. For Krauss, "space exists, with nothing at all in it,"[36] which is the precondition for the spontaneous generation of our inflationary universe. Yet space has energetic processes with physical properties and gravitational forces and pressures, therefore it is not an absolute zero-point of pure nothingness. Here I must concur with the consensus opinion held by philosophers and theologians that even empty space devoid of content still qualifies as something, even if it exists in a quantum vacuum.

We must not confound the field of physical science, which relies on empirical (experimental-observational) and theoretical (mathematical-statistical/simulation) paragons, with the subfield of metaphysics that employ wholly separate methodologies, usually grounded in speculation, logic, abduction, and hermeneutics. Despite the inevitable overlap in physics and philosophy, we must respect categorical distinctions in meaning and methodology that differentiate these two broad disciplines rather than collapsing philosophy entirely into natural science by "operationally" redefining what we mean by our terms in order for them to (nicely and conveniently) fit into a contrived empirical or computational framework where the researcher or subject is dislocated from the research or subject matter under investigation. One could claim that the field of physics is simply trying to substitute the God function for a similar cosmological corollary when positing the Higgs field as an invisible background permeating all of spacetime, which is responsible for dark matter/energy in their spontaneous acts of creation scientists observe in the lab when particles materialize or are inferred based on statistical equations that crunch enormous amounts of data into meaningful units of information. If the Higgs is always there yet hidden in empty space, and is responsible for the generation of all that exists today, including the inflationary big bang, then is this any different from the theological functionality of the God posit? Perhaps this is a good example of wonder at work

---

36 Ibid., p. 149.

in both science and philosophy, for in the lab, on the computer, or just pondering intractable questions, the human mind wants to know.

If empty space is said to *pre-exist* prior to the materialization of the universe, then Krauss inherits a set of conundrums facing the question of infinite regress. Here he is saddled with the same problem as the theologian in his attempt to expound how something comes from nothing. A point of energy before it explodes in rapid exponential inflation in a tiny fraction of its first second of life,[37] which is the premise behind the modern inflationary big bang theory, still needs an explanation of how that energy was derived in the first place out of a sea of nothingness. Victor Stenger argues that the inflationary big bang thesis has passed all stringent empirical tests to date that could prove it false,[38] but this still does not mean that we have solved the riddle of pre-beginning. This energetic organization is propounded to exist prior to the big bang and before it undergoes inflationary eruption, which is averred to bring it about, but it does not answer to how such energy came into being prior to its expansion. Moreover, it does not address the specifics of the preconditions for energy to emerge. In other words, how is the void, nothingness, or empty space organized in such a way as to bring about energetic expressions, not to mention that the *appearance* of energy, namely, what is physically observed, measured, or calculated, may be distinct from its original nucleus or structural process that eludes current empirical classification?

Stenger offers his own view that we have reason to believe that the universe did not in fact begin with the big bang, but rather prior conditions existed that brought it about, including the possibility of a prior universe.[39] Using theoretical equation models of cosmology based on the notion of "quantum tunneling" or fluctuations,[40] he posits that it is conceivable that our current universe materialized from a pre-existing one, which draws into question the notion of an absolute beginning or point of birth of the cosmos. Here Stenger favors the "no boundary model" of James Hartle and Stephen Hawking who claim that the universe has no beginning or end in space and time.[41] This view is in opposition to

---

37 See Alan Guth (1997).
38 *God: The Failed Hypothesis*, p. 117.
39 Ibid., pp. 125–127.
40 See Atkatz and Pagels (1982) and Vilenkin (1983).
41 See Hartle and Hawking (1983). Cf. Stephen Hawking (1988), *A Brief History of Time*, where he says: "if the universe is really self-contained, having no boundary or edge, it would have neither beginning nor end; it would simply be" (pp. 140–141).

William Lane Craig's who challenges such a declaration,[42] instead insisting that the universe began from an initial singularity and has a finite past, hence had an absolute beginning, which he works out in obsessional detail in his kalâm cosmological argument,[43] what Stenger dismisses as an erroneous appeal to a predetermined model of causality, when physical science makes no claims in its controlled observations of atomic and subatomic activity, which are often spontaneous productions without any evident cause.[44] In Stenger's model, using mathematical calculations, he speculates how our world could have tunneled through a previous universe that has "existed for all previous time."[45] Yet here we have the same concerns about infinite regress. Even if we posit a prior universe or universes that conditioned the coming into being of our current one, we will still need to address the notion of what brought the pre-existing universe(s) into being. Positing a metaverse or multiverse only extends the regress farther back in time and down the fox hole.

If the cosmos is considered to come from nothing, either from a God that is said to be the initial cause but is and has always been *absent*, or as energy derived from empty space, we are still not likely to find this a sufficient proof for a theory of *creatio ex nihilio* as it fails to explain how the physical universe can just appear from *no prior state of being*, and moreover, how this transpires *naturally*, namely as an objective certainty explaining the process of empirical phenomenon—not as metaphysical speculation, logical induction, or statistical (mathematical) manipulation that dislocates the phenomenon in question from its natural occurrence. In other words, how can the whole universe just pop into existence as though it is a rabbit pulled from a magician's hat, especially when the magician or the hat is nowhere in sight? If we could irrefutably offer this explanans, then this could be arguably called a miracle.

The problem with temporal and modal cosmological arguments is that they always beg the question of causation and specifically the notion of a *first cause*.[46] And because causation is a temporal concept, that is, it relies on predicating antecedent conditions, events, and outcomes that happen

42 See Craig (2013), p. 381.
43 Craig (1979).
44 *God: The Failed Hypothesis*, p. 124.
45 See Stenger (2006) and (2007), p. 126.
46 Robin Le Poidevin (1996) provides a nice critique of the temporal and modal arguments that ultimately rely on a notion of causality incompatible with our contemporary knowledge of determinism (see pp. 5–15).

at particular instances and places, we cannot posit an original causation that precedes itself in time. Furthermore, if we insist on the notion of a beginning to the universe from a first cause, then time itself would have a beginning. But if this were the case, then the universe cannot have a cause, at least not in any ordinary sense of the word, because this would imply a time that existed *before* the universe began to exist. Nothing could have occurred before this time, that is, before the universe started to exist. This would mean that time itself has a beginning, and hence a cause. But time cannot be the cause of itself nor precede itself, for nothing is said to exist nor occur before time itself. Here time cannot have a cause of its own existence for the circularity of these propositions hinge on the premise that everything that *begins* to exist has a cause. In other words, because nothing can occur before time exists, time cannot have a cause.

While the exact nature of the origin of the universe remains an open indeterminate question and is foreclosed from current scientific knowledge, we neither have to posit nor prove the parameters of the conditions that make the existence of the universe possible to make my case that there is no evidence of an agentic God who teleologically created matter and the laws of physics, nor do we have to appeal to a supraordinate causal creator when there is no cosmological footprint of God's existence. Most physicists agree that the natural constellation of events on macro and micro levels is something rather than nothing. As Stenger puts it, "an empty universe requires supernatural intervention—not a full one. Only by the constant action of an agent outside the universe, such as God, could a state of nothingness be maintained. The fact that we have something is just what we would expect if there is no God."[47] It is more plausible to assume that the universe has always existed in some form, even if it had arisen from previous rudimentary cosmic fluctuations within its sea of eternity, as well as underwent violent change, transmogrification, and expansion, for it is the nature of process reality that allows for transmutational variations and evolutions to instantiate over time. Although I do not claim to resolve this paradox, we need not conjure a supernatural entity to explain the magisterium of natural existence.

47 *God: The Failed Hypothesis*, p. 133.

Chapter 2

Religion as naturalized psychology

When we hear the word God, or its equivalent in other cultures, it imme-diately evokes the notion of religion, its semiotic correspondent. Religion has many names for what God ultimately signifies, such as a divine deity as supernatural intelligence, a supreme Creator[1] or First Cause, Lord of the Universe,[2] the Maker,[3] the Doer,[4] Holy Father, the Unmanifested,[5] the Revealer, the Nameless,[6] the Unconditioned, and the Wholly Other[7] as the condition and ground of existence, where phenomenological experi-ence of the sacred and mystical union with Ultimate Reality may be captured by the term *numen*.[8] Theosophic approaches broadly encompass a religious philosophy where a mystical component to the so-called truth of God as the absolute Ultimate Being and Source of everything is

---

1 "I raise my hand to the Lord God Most High, creator of heaven and earth." (Genesis, 14: 22); Cf. John Calvin's (1845–1846) "God the Creator" (I, iii, i).
2 Maimonides, *Mishneb Torah: The Book of Knowledge*. See section, *Laws on the Basic Principles of the Torah* IV: 7, p. 39a.
3 Saint Augustine (2008), p. 224.
4 Maimonides refers to the preference of *Mutakallimum* Islamic theologians to refer to God as the Doer or Maker rather than a Cause, which according to their argument, implies that the world is caused rather than created, a distinction Maimonides rejects in his discussion of Aristotle's notion of potentiality and actuality. See *Guide of the Perplexed*, Bk I, Ch. LXIX, pp. 83, 87.
5 In the *Yoga Aphorisms* of Patanjali, advanced yogic meditation purportedly leads to mystical union with all-being (see "Subtlety Pertaining To Objects Culminates in A-Linga Or The Unmani-fested;" Sutra I, 45; p. 102). Although the Unmanifested does not become manifest, there is a logical need to posit a Latent or Unmanifest to an underlying, transcendent constant. See Swami Hariharananda Aranya (1981).
6 In Lao Tzu's, *Tao Te Ching*, he discusses the cosmic origin of the transcendent: "The Nameless is the origin of heaven and earth." See Paul J. Lin (1977), p. 3.
7 This term was introduced by Rudolf Otto in *The Idea of the Holy.*
8 Dan Merkur (1996), while interpreting Rudolf Otto (1932), describes the *sensus numinous* as a category of values that inspires majestic awe and splendor, which at the same time is clouded in mystery imbued with an emotional sense of urgency. This phenomenological amalgamation of psychic experience also nicely captures Jung's (1947) numinous notion of an archetype (for a review of Jung, see Mills, 2013 and 2014b).

emphasized,[9] yet there is always a personal element to it.[10] The *mysterium tremendum* inspires awe and mystery,[11] whereby value is attained by believing in Something More that is Other-Worldly, a World to Come.[12]

Religion is ultimately about ontology—about what is "really real," the World of all Worlds. Although some sects of religions are devoid of a God construct, such as in some forms of Buddhism and Shinto, religion has historically attempted to answer to the greater metaphysical questions of Being, especially when it posits a transcendent ideal. For example, we are once again preoccupied with the evolution *vs.* creationism or intelligent design debate, which is a modern day repackaging of the cosmological-teleological argument that challenges the biological sciences. Here *theos* is pitted against *bios* as the reckoning of life. More metaphysical approaches are concerned with the Absolute, Transcendent,

---

9 The seventeenth century philosopher, mystic, and theosophist, Jacob Boehme (1620), provides an account of the origins of the soul and refers to the mystical being of the deity as the "unground" (*Ungrund*). Cf. Andrew Weeks (1991), pp. 146–149. Inspired by the study of Plotinus (see Eric von der Luft, 1994, p. 39), Boehme radically reconceptualized God as the *ens manifestativum sui*, "the being whose essence is to reveal itself" (Refer to David Walsh, 1994, p. 16).

10 This may also be said of Gnosticism. There are many different systems of Gnosticism that offer varying accounts on the nature of first principles and the coming into being of God and the universe. However, a cardinal element of Gnostic thought is a radical dualism that governs the relation between God and the world. Gnostics conceive of God as the "Alien" or the "first" "Life." This appears in a standard introduction of Mandaean compositions: "In the name of the great first alien Life from the worlds of light, the sublime that stands above all," and is reflected throughout gnostic literature such as Marcion's concept of the "alien God," "the Other," "the Nameless," "the Hidden," "the Unknown," and the "unknown Father." Belonging to another (nether) world, the divine alien is "strange" and "unfamiliar," hence "incomprehensible." Estranged from the comprehensible world, the "great first Life" is conceived of as possessing both positive and negative attributes of superiority and suffering, perfection and tragedy, transcendence and alienation from its original being. Further competing dialectical forces are attributed to the godhead, which are understood differently by various gnostic myths and theories on cosmology, cosmogony, and anthropology. The second century gnostic, Basilides, is said to have postulated a primal "non-existent god," which was later taken up by Valentinus who claimed that "there is in invisible and ineffable heights a pre-existent perfect aeon (i.e. a supernatural being), whom they also call Pre-beginning, Forefather and Primal Ground (Bythos), that he is inconceivable and invisible, eternal and uncreated (or: begotten) and that he existed in great peace and stillness in unending spaces (aeons)" (Irenaeus, *Adversus Haereses*, 11). Due to the indescribable nature of the "divine Absolute," the Valentinians were content with using a few alchemical symbols as "Abyss" or "Silence" to represent the ineffable. See Jonas (1958), pp. 42, 49–50, 199; Rudolph (1977), p. 62; Irenaeus of Lyons (1857); and Mills (2002a), p. 206, n5.

11 Otto (1917/1950) also identifies the tremendous and terrifying mystery that is another component of the numinous, where the sense of the holy is apprehensively experienced as overwhelmingly awesome and majestic.

12 See Maimonides (2000): "the final end is *life in the World to Come*" (*Treatise on the Resurrection*, p. 157, italics in original).

or Principle of the Ultimate, or with more abstract equivalents to the universe or energic cosmos as a substitute for a supernatural creator, such as relegating God to Logic or pure thought (divine Logos), an informational principle, or even Nature itself. In all these traditions, God becomes a living system, which is the *matrix of everything*, some sort of Cosmic Mind or suprapersonal agency that exists "out there" in aseity.

Defining God

Because the linguistic term "God" signifies so many different things to different people, ignostics, igtheists, and theological noncognitivists often claim that without consensual agreement on the exact definition of the concept and nature of God, as well as its falsifiability, the question of its truth and validity becomes cognitively meaningless. Here a coherent definition must be presented before the legitimacy of the *term's* existence is even meaningfully discussed. These positions often contend that religious language is inherently meaningless because it is uniformly circular, incoherent, and lacks verifiability. Yet the semiotic term God does signify a meaningful discourse most people can relate to (and they do indeed take a personal position on the matter), whether they believe in God or not, and hence represents an important ideal to humanity. While a definition of God may only be satisfactory to its definer, it becomes important to clarify what the term God is said to reasonably mean to most people in its simplest form, namely, a supreme being as divine agent and creator of the universe.

Although we may characterize God in many fashions, from different cultural anthropologies to variances in religious studies, what I mean by God is this: Any proposition, belief, or faith that there is an independent supraordinate creator, agent, or entity operating in the extant world outside of the living subject or human mind, which *a fortiori* animates or sustains the cosmos, and is viewed as a supreme being that is the primary cause and source underlying all facets of the universe. Theists may wish to qualify additional definitional stipulations, such as the divine agency manifests attributes of personhood, omnibenevolence, omniscience, omnipotence, omnipresence, and other omniproperties; but regardless of these cavils, this form of God, I argue, is merely a fantasy. No such being or entity exists nor could it possibly exist. This is the pedestrian God of monotheism as supreme cause and creator, where the Great Divine resides in the transcendent heavens of metaphysical realism. This view is in scripture: "For from him and through him and unto him are all things" (Romans 11: 36), which is echoed in Augustine who refers to God as "being in a supreme degree" and who is "the creator of everything," "very being itself."[13] And for Maimonides, "everything that exists ... was brought into existence by God."[14] We find this view celebrated in many great theological works, such as in Anselm's *Monologion*[15] and in Aquinas' *Summa Theologiae* where God is deemed "the Maker of man;"[16] only to be further memorialized in Descartes' *Meditations*,[17] all of which is historically conditioned by Plotinus in the *Enneads*,[18] Aristotle in the *Physics*,[19] and Plato in his *Dialogues*.[20]

The Eastern Orthodox religious scholar David Bentley Hart reiterates the classical definitions of God "who is the infinite fullness of being, omnipotent, omnipresent, and omniscient, from whom all things come and upon whom all things depend for every moment of their existence, without whom nothing at all could exist."[21] But he further obfuscates his definition by importing metaphysical language attributed to Greek and Roman antiquity as well as medieval, Arabic, and Indian philosophies, such as those belonging to Sufism and the mystical traditions represented in the *Upanishads*, which introduces inconsistency and contradiction in the way he comes to characterize God. On one hand, Hart wants to champion a defense of God as possessing omniperfections,[22] yet on the other hand he denies

13 *Confessions*, pp. 8, 225, 249.

14 *Guide of the Perplexed*, Bk II, Ch. XIII, p. 94.

15 Especially see Ch. 1: "That there is something that is best and greatest and supreme among all existing things;" Ch. 3: "That there is a certain nature through whom all existing things exist, and who exists through himself and is supreme among all existing things;" and Ch. 5: "That, just as he exists through himself and other things exist through him, so he exists from himself and other things exist from him."

16 See Fourth Article: Whether Sacred Doctrine is a Practical Science? Compare to the chapter on The Merciful in the *Koran* where "In the Name of Allah . . . He created man."

17 *Meditations on First Philosophy*, specifically Meditation 3: Concerning God, That He Exists and Meditation 5: Concerning the Essence of Material Things, and Again Concerning God, That He Exists.

18 Cf. The Good or The One (VI, 9 [9]), 1. "It is by The One that all beings are beings."

19 See *Physics*, Book VIII, particularly his discussion on the Prime Mover, Sec. 5: "everything that is in motion is moved by something, and the first mover is moved but not by anything else, it must be moved by itself" (256a20).

20 In the *Republic*, Book X, Plato refers to God as the "maker" of all things (597d); and in various passages he refers to God as a "divine craftsman" and "cause" (*Sophist*, 265c), the "creator," and the source of "good" and "time" (*Timaeus*, 29e–30; 38c; 53b).

21 *The Experience of God: Being, Consciousness, Bliss*, p. 7.

22 Ibid., see pp. 7, 30.

God "agency."[23] He also views God as the primordial source and creator of existence, not as a designer, artificer, or craftsman of the universe, but rather as an "eternal, not temporal" "act ... bringing into existence the whole of creation, from its beginning to its end."[24] In fact, Hart is adamant when he says that "God's act of creation is understood as the whole event of nature and existence, not as a distinct causal agency."[25] Here God is professed *not* to be an agent, yet a maker "whom" *acts*, but not through "cosmic interventions."[26] Apart from these conspicuous conundrums, how can creation and action be divorced from agency? Moreover, for Hart, there is no beginning or ending—no time—to God's creative act within eternity since it is "timeless;" and hence, by definition, there is no process. Yet acts and events are temporal instantiations, and "nature" and "existence" are spatially embodied within the materiality of the universe, which ensures that reality is a process of becoming. There is no need to impose delimitations on space and time when positing a metaphysics of being, even when espousing a view of the eternal or infinite, for this would eliminate the possibility of flux, change, and transmutation in the empirical universe. The cosmos is not a timeless motionless mass—the stasis of being, but rather a dynamic, experiential self-articulated process of complexity always immersed in a state of turbulent emergence as being-in-becoming.

Hart further assigns God to an ontological category that is "beyond being," which is outside the parameters of the natural universe, yet conditions all of being, in fact "being itself," including the physical cosmos, which it is "always utterly dependent" upon;[27] only then to separate God's essence from the ontology of the world in which it is said to belong and depends upon to exist. This becomes further problematic when God is viewed as the "unity" and "totality" of everything that *is* despite having a separate ontology and essence, not to mention a "simplicity" in which all "diversity" flows from God's "infinite being."[28] Suffice it to say that these confusional propositions introduce grave logical inconsistencies. For example, how can God be "infinite being" but is "beyond being" within "being itself?" If these murky theoretical details could be worked out, it would still likely commit Hart to

---

23 Ibid., pp. 28, 32.
24 Ibid., p. 26.
25 Ibid., p. 28.
26 Ibid., p. 25.
27 Ibid., pp. 30, 32.
28 Ibid., p. 30.

some type of philosophical *panentheism* where God's ontological composition would be transcendent from the universe in which it inhabits and sustains. More problematically, however, is that if everything that exists is dependent upon God's essence, yet is separate from God's essence and divine Being, then this position devolves into conceptual and logical incoherence: if all of existence is conditioned by God, then all objects and beings participate of God's essence, hence God's Being, or they could not exist, for they are extensions or manifestations of God that, although modified and differentiated in form, must remain reliant on God's essence.

These contradictions are further compounded by the scholarly disputes within the subfields of theology that debate over the minutia of competing cosmogonies and theogonies, not to mention the metaphysical consequences of such disparate interpretations that introduce myriad incongruities in the way we come to characterize God. Notwithstanding the plausible validity of metaphysical discourse, mixing metaphysics with supernaturalism can easily lead to a confusion of tongues, especially when speculative metaphysics is arbitrarily culled from competing systems in the history of theology and philosophy with relaxed respect for theoretical boundaries. For these reasons, I prefer to retain the traditional theistic definitions of God that emphasize supernaturalism, creationism, and supreme agency.

There is no evidentiary or verifiable proof for believing that God is *anything but* an idea; and even philosophical rationalism is severely challenged, because, to reiterate the point, you cannot simply reason something into tangible existence. Furthermore, if we import a transcendent realm independent of the energetic-material universe, where space and time are suspended for a non-embodied, atemporal, cosmic paranormal order, then are we not embracing an equally improbable antiquated vitalism, animism, panpsychism, anthroposophy,[29] or some form of unsophisticated shamanistic folk lore?

---

29 I have in mind the founder of anthroposophy, Rudolf Steiner, who developed a method of perceptual, intellectual, and intuitive attunement to a purported "objective" spiritual world, which has developed into an international movement applied to many different disciplines. It has also been harshly critiqued and largely viewed as a cult, although academics would favor the value-neutral phrase "new religious movement." Dan Merkur (personal communication, 2011) tells us that anthroposophy, as well as other theosophical systems:

> teach visualization practices, so that people can travel out of the body on the astral plane, [and] perform actions there that ostensibly cause results on the material plane (i.e. accomplishing magic), etc. These practices have practical results, that is, they produce visions that blend autosuggestion with unconscious manifestations, and [are] routinely interpreted in fantastic ways that are self-deluding.

There is an inescapable psychologism and anthropomorphism inherent in assigning human characteristics to a cosmic creator entity, especially when there are purported to be subjective dispositions and predilections assigned to a supreme Will or divine Personality. For example, the (Christian) scientist Francis Collins, who spearheaded the Human Genome Project, unpretentiously declares that God "takes a personal interest in each one of us."[30] Psychological properties attributed to God furthermore take on hypostatized qualities, to the point that they may be viewed as belonging to a supernatural *macroanthropos* as opposed to our own psychic projections. If one's definition of God does not include or imply a personal (individualistic or subjective) element as divine agent or agency, then what is the point of calling it God? Here God merely becomes an abstraction, impersonality, or category of values one aspires to attain or fulfill. If the deist proclaims that God is Creator but is not a person or agent, such as an ultimate force or source behind the cosmos, the same arguments against creationism as Supreme Cause equally apply; and if the pantheist insists that God is the universe itself, then physical science has come a long way in understanding and explaining God. But this is not how most people conceive the meaning of God. These qualitative quiddities in definition are what theologians and philosophers perennially debate about; yet they are not the concerns of common masses who believe in monotheistic conceptions of God as a supremely divine being.

The moment you dislocate the God question from theistic religion (with its presuppositions of creationism and holiness), God no longer becomes God by normative standards. God signifies much more to believers than a mere impersonal force in the universe or the cosmos itself. This latter view more properly conforms to naturalism, *Naturphilosophie*, a philosophy of living, or a transcendental perspective on life and the universe. The primordiality of Being—the sheer presence and expanse of existence itself—should not be equated with divinity. If the deification of Being becomes what we typically refer to as God, then that's not God to me. That's naturalized psychology, or what philosophers typi-

---

30 See Collins (2006), p. 6. Notwithstanding the fact that Collins has no way of justifying this spurious epistemological claim, this statement is particularly vulgar given the millions of innocent children who die each year due to thirst, starvation, malnutrition, infectious diseases, lack of medical prevention, intervention, and care, and the inhumane casualties of neglect, abuse, crime, and warfare that saturate our planet. If God takes a personal interest in these children, then it is only to see them suffer and die a cruel fate.

cally call phenomenology. For the vast majority of theists worldwide, belief in the God posit remains a belief in the existence of a supreme creator conforming to the philosophical tenets of metaphysical realism, namely, as a celestial entity that ontologically exists independent of our minds.

The sociobiology of religion

Sociobiological accounts of religion have focused on the notion of evolutionary forces operative within culture. Since Richard Dawkins' introduction of the theory of memes in evolutionary biology,[31] which he puts forth as the cultural equivalent of genes, it becomes all too seductive to boil everything down to biology. Here we must be careful to avoid material reductionism, as the overdetermined processes and instantiation of culture is a highly complex system irreducible to organic substrates that govern the physical dynamics of genes. Although the concept of memetics has been criticized for its simplistic correspondence to natural selection,[32] we are justified, I believe, in questioning to what degree culture, and specifically the social institution of religion, is reflective of evolutionary forces in the psychological development of the human race.

For our purposes, it is sufficient to mention (without going into all the details) the two main principles of Darwinian evolutionary theory: selection and adaptation. Biological determinants are clearly at play when we speak of natural selection, which proponents like Edward O. Wilson and Dawkins emphasize when making extensions to religious phenomena, however, the degree to which they are driven by biology, are by-products of selection, or are based on cultural evolution is disputed.[33] Wilson believes there is a certain "biological advantage" to religious practice as it secures identity within group membership,[34] while Daniel Dennett sees religion as parasitic with no real adaptive value, much like a virus that

---

31 See Dawkins (1976).
32 See Michael Ruse (2013), pp. 513, 518.
33 Kate Distin (2011) has extended the theory of cultural evolution to include the inheritance of discrete units of information broadly defined in terms of natural language and artefactual language invented by human activity (such as economic and technological exchange, as well as music), which is synthesized and transmitted via metarepresentations that convey such information on larger organizational stratums reflective of social systems. The degree to which these environmental informational processes actually transmute genetic structures is a vogue topic within the burgeoning field of epigenetics.
34 Edward O. Wilson (1978), p. 188.

destroys its host.[35] Here I will not be so concerned with the biological mechanisms of natural selection; rather I wish to focus on the question of adaptation.

We cannot separate the person from culture any more than we can dislocate the subject from the object: self and otherness, individual and group, singular and multiple, particular and universal are dialectically conjoined. Our being in the world presupposes our biological embodiment as an organic fact of nature that stands in relation to the environmental contingencies that impact our psychological mediations on those imposed state of affairs. It makes no logical sense to believe that an individual can stand separate from the cultural ontology in which one is born any more than a society can exist separately without the ontic[36] participation of agents who compose its membership. Whether adaptation is biologically selected or not, the question of individual versus social adaptation based upon religious belief and practice is coextensive and contextually dependent upon specific contingencies, whether that reflects the intrapsychic dynamics of an individual or the cultural fabric in which people live and interpersonally interact with others. Adaptation is biologically and socially informed: one cannot devolve into the other, only that certain ontological conditions must be operative when we speak of biological and cultural organisms.

Whether our discourse is about the individual or the collective, when it comes to adaptation we are talking about how certain psychological compromises designed to protect the psyche from threat (what we customarily call "defense mechanisms" or unconsciously derived methods of coping with anxiety) transpire on multiple parallel levels of personal and social (i.e., political, economic, and religious) organization. These unconscious enactments are attempts at adaptation, that is, they are designed to protect the mind (and by extension a social system) against real or perceived dangers that threaten the integrity of the organism so it can continue to function and adjust resiliently to exigencies that are forced on it from external *and* internal constraints. In other words, there are certain pressures and prohibitions that are intrinsically derived, not only from the internalization of culture, but also from our natural embodied constitutions, instinctual drives (*Triebe*), and impulses that need to be defended

35 *Breaking the Spell*, pp. 3–6. Also see his section on "Toxic Memes," pp. 328–333.
36 Here I employ the Heideggerian (1927) distinction between the ontic, which applies to human relations, versus the ontological, which applies to the question, meaning, and truth of Being.

against or combated with defensive counterattacks that attempt to neutralize the anxiety that is generated internally. Religion is one such example of psychic adaptation. The question is, How effective is it?

The evolutionist notions of replicators, of encoding, of copying, of memesis or emulation (such as imitating behavior or mimicking what people see and experience every day), of inheriting information that is culturally disseminated on metarepresentational levels as part of our neurocognitive processing systems—presupposes its orientation toward social adaptation that is unconsciously enacted, just as biological activity is automatic, teleonomic, and regulatory for an organic system. From the standpoint of psychology, that is, what animates the soul or makes a person think, feel, and behave, adaptation is ultimately about the nature of defenses and their functionality in the human psyche. The sociobiologist's task is slightly different from the psychologist's, which is more directly concerned with understanding how natural selection operates as causal biological mechanisms of adaptation in the form and direction it produces in particular species. Selection presupposes a modified type of teleology (what we may call teleonomy) insofar as it functions in ways that are oriented toward desired ends, much like a heart that is designed to pump blood, but not all variations in species are adaptive based on empirical calculations that over 95 percent of species that lived in the past have long perished. Chance and causality are co-determinants in this equation, just as by-products of evolution with no adaptive advantage are logically probable. So the questions become, To what degree is something adaptive and likely produced by natural selection versus what is not; and if so, what would be the probable mechanism behind its appearance, hence its cause?

Given that religion is a primal force in human civilization that continues to motivate and drive individual and collective behavior, one would be hard pressed to ignore its connection to evolutionary biology. In fact, Edward O. Wilson makes religion an epiphenomenon of biology, yet one based on group selection that carries survival value for our species. For Wilson, all creation myths and their accoutrements are driven by emotion and are an essential bond designed to maintain tribal unity, strengthen group identifications, institute social order, insure personal security, and provide meaning to life and death—all of which have adaptive worth. As a "Darwinian device for survival," organized religion is the biologic expression of tribalism.

Such an intensely tribal instinct could, in the real world, arise in evolution only by group selection, tribe competing against tribe. The peculiar qualities of religious faith are the logical consequence of the dynamism at this higher level of biological organization.[37]

Wilson can be criticized for his simplicity, instead insisting that human consciousness and culture are irreducible to biology and are highly overdetermined, complex organic systems that belie the reductive causality Wilson is content in adopting. But for our purposes it is enough to say that the human brain is hardwired in some mode to fashion these communal bonds that lead to circumscribed forms of religious custom regardless of their content, which have undoubtedly evolved just as consciousness, language, and civilization has in human history. Here the mechanisms of evolutionary biology that are adaptive to group survival are non-consciously (hence automatically, prereflectively) sustained and interact with cultural variances as well as the idiosyncratic organizations peculiar to one's personality development within a given (contextual) social ontology.[38] The point is that it is neither necessary nor sufficient to make religion the sole product of evolution in order to explain the sociobiological principles that are at play in our psychological analysis of the unconscious motivations informing the need for God. Just as individuals and societies who harbor belief in God and organize their lives around religious affiliations—even extending to group identifications and disidentifications that may mirror early tribalism and clan rivalry (namely "My religion is better than yours!")—these individual thoughts and cultural conventions are not *experienced* as biological productions, but rather as psychological ones, hence qualitative states of consciousness. In other words, for masses it is natural to think and feel this way toward the God posit as a complex expression of our intrapsychic and intersubjective natures, not because our bodies make it so.

37 E.O. Wilson (2012), p. 259.
38 In the relatively new field of epigenetics, scientists are advancing the notion of how culture mutates genetic structures (more specifically, gene expression or their cellular phenotype, that is, functional modifications in the genome that do not alter the underlying nucleotide sequence of DNA, some of which are purported to be inheritable) and biological adaptive systems based on environmentally encoded infiltrations (both good and bad) that further affect neuroplasticity within brain development. What this means is that environmental factors can causally alter genetic traits and their structural expressions (some in a relatively brief period of time and in successive generations), not merely that biological determinism is our ultimate destiny.

The sociobiological organization of religion is the sublation of our evolutionary rudiments that inform our psychic experience of the social world. Our tendency to attribute agency to God is one such outcome of evolutionary psychology based upon our unconscious perceptibility of agency-detection schemata we employ in our manner of relating to the animate and inanimate world. Michael Ruse nicely points out how these automatic biological processes can lead to premature beliefs about supernatural forces in our most basic environmental encounters:

> Natural selection designs the agency-detection system to deal rapidly and economically with stimulus situations involving people and animals as predators, protectors, and prey. This results in the system's being trip-wired to respond to fragmentary information under conditions of uncertainty, inciting perception of figures in the clouds, voices in the wind, lurking movements in the leaves, and emotions among interacting dots on a computer screen. This hair-triggering of the agency-detection mechanism readily lends itself to supernatural interpretation of uncertain or anxiety-provoking events.[39]

From this depiction, we can readily appreciate how paranoiac factors have evolutionary currency for they safeguard against danger and increase the likelihood of survival, but they can also lead to extreme distortions in imagination and thought processes that may be maladaptive to a given individual or group. Here we may see how folk psychology engenders various illusions (as well as delusional beliefs) that may have some adaptive value for a given culture, but it can readily be critically negated (even pathologized) if a competing culture or oppositional portions within a given social system challenge such instinctual beliefs and attitudes, as we may observe in the antitheistic secular movement today.

The concept of agency-detection is the biological equivalent of unconscious defense systems designed to ensure the organism's survival. Freud referred to the self-preservative drives that were enlisted by the ego in our everyday functioning, as they were designed to secure satisfaction and avoid pain in accordance with the parameters of reality, a reality that could be easily distorted under the rubric of immediate pleasure seeking motives governing unconscious impulses. Although we may be hardwired

---

39 Ruse (2013), p. 517.

to be paranoid based on the fear of predation, we may be equally inclined (hence dialectically oriented) toward seeking peaceful and/or comforting ministrations (in physical reality and thought) as a means of containing and/or quelling our primal anxieties. If our attributions to God are not paranoiac in nature, then we can appreciate how our projection onto God as divine agent is a particular form of idealized transference enlisted to mollify our primordial fantasies.

For evolutionists, the main question becomes whether or not religion is adaptive to the human race. If not, why is it still around, let alone pre-occupy the consciousness of most of the world's inhabitants? Many athe-ists see it as a parasite sucking the life out of culture, where the psychopoesis of God is viewed as an inevitable tragedy of human folly that does more harm than good by instilling ignorance and irrationality. Yet given its sheer magnitude and variation in human culture, it is hard to dismiss the fact that it is psychologically adaptive to world masses, or it would have been long abandoned and extinguished. This does not necessarily make it ultimately beneficial to human society, nor does it guarantee it will survive in the future, but it is unlikely to disappear based on what we know about unconscious defense.

We may further say that the variances in world religions that precipi-tate interculture/interethnic/interfaith tension and conflict, as well as the microdivisions and narcissism of minor differences that exist and prolif-erate in same religious enclaves within a given society, is reflective of a clash of values that are fighting for adaptation. From Exodus to the Inqui-sition, the Crusades, and contemporary warfare and mass diasporas in the Middle East, we do not need to look far to see how tribalism is still very much alive today. It is obvious that the biggest threat facing humanity is other disgruntled human beings based on hegemonic ideologies, differing value practices, and a fundamental clash of ideas. Here the God posit is central to our perpetual world discord in its bid for adaptation and con-tinued existence.

The fallacy of divine sense

In the tradition of Aquinas and Calvin, who claim that God endows us with a *sensus divinitatis*, or natural faculty to believe in "Him," the Chris-tian analytic philosopher Alvin Plantinga argues that faith is a special type of epistemic experience that justifies belief in God, which transcends the faculties of reason alone.[40] Here a special sort of cognitive ability to sense and know the divine is said to be created by God and implanted in us a priori, which is experienced as a natural tendency to form a belief in "Him."[41] This proposition assumes (a) the existence of God to begin with, which is presumptuous; (b) that we are equipped with a "special" epistemic faculty apart from reason, which was (c) created by God, hence relying on premise (a); and furthermore (d) placed in the human mind by intentional design or God's teleological action. If we do not concede to premise (a), then premises (c) and (d) are gratuitous. The crux of the argument is therefore centered on how we come to form a belief in God, what Plantinga claims is based on a reformed or modified species of epistemology.

Plantinga argues that one does not need evidence to justify the properly basic belief that God exists,[42] which he avows is primary and natural, for it is self-evident and self-referentially confirmed by the believer's internal experience. He tells us that "it is entirely right, rational, reasonable, and proper to believe in God without any evidence or argument at all."[43] This appears to be a dominant trend held by contemporary theologians. William Lane Craig explains: "the primary way in which we come to know God is not through evidence but through the work of his Holy Spirit, which is effectual in bringing persons into relation with God wholly apart from evidence."[44] Without trying to be unsympathetically flippant about these assertions, the main thesis seems to be, "If I believe it is the case, then it's true." Here "belief" seems to be a rather fluid category not contingent upon any evidence or proof whatsoever: the criterion of subjective experience is all that is needed to warrant its justification. In other words, as the claim goes, people's tendency to naturally form a belief in God under normal cognitive circumstances shows

---

40 *Where the Conflict Really Lies*, pp. 60, 181, 263–264.
41 See Aquinas: *"the knowledge of God is naturally implanted in all,"* and "To know that God exists in a general and confused way is implanted in us by nature." (*Summa Theologiae*, Vol. 1. Part I, Question II: The Existence of God, First Article, *Obj.* 1 and *Reply Obj.* 1.) Cf. Calvin's claim that God bestowed us with a faculty "by natural instinct," which purportedly existed "from the womb" to be able to sense His divine presence (see *Institutes*, I, iii, 1; I, iii, 3). This may also be called an *intellectual intuition*, insofar as there is a reason to believe in what we intuit to be true.
42 Nicholas Everitt (2004) provides a nice overview and critique of Plantinga's reformed epistemology where he shows that theistic belief is at most derived belief, hence not properly basic belief, and even if it were, it would still be begging the question of God's existence (pp. 17–29).
43 Plantinga (1983), p. 17.
44 Craig (2007), p. 70.

that we are naturally constituted to do so by God. Providing our beliefs are formed by uncompromised mental faculties within appropriate environments untainted by "the noetic effects of sin,"[45] then our beliefs are warranted. According to Plantinga, the awareness or perception of God produced by this *sensus divinitatis* is often experienced as immediate and palpable to warrant basic belief.[46] The believer feels this so sonorously and profoundly that one is justified in knowing that God exists.

In attempting to be fair to the theist, we need to empathically place our consciousness into the experiential world of the believer who intuits and/or feels the presence of God, which phenomenally resonates as a primordial irrefutable knowledge that is reinforced by the experience itself. Here something is said to be experientially felt, perceived, or intuited in us that unquestionably tells us it is substantive and true, which is believed indubitably, or at least that it has a real presence to the point that it is neither skeptically entertained nor disputed, hence it is believed. In response to requests to offer a reason to believe in such a proposition, the theist would likely say "I experience it, that's why I believe it." But is experience enough to warrant the leap to a metaphysical factor? And could this not be explained as a psychological disposition to perceive the phenomenon in question conforming to a preconceived belief system superimposed on this mystical encounter or distorted by unconscious transference fantasies? Craig's invocation of the Holy Spirit, on the other hand, to support such epistemic beliefs clearly imports a fantasy object that we are asked to accept prima facie when no evidential support for this proposition exists. It would follow that such a claim is merely grounded in personal belief independent of verity or verification principles supported by correspondent facts. But knowledge of one's inner experience is different than the independent truth or verity of a proposition. It is incumbent upon the theist to show how an inner experience of God corresponds to the concrete ontological reality of God's existence independent of personal internal experience conditioning the grounds for belief itself. At most we may only conclude that God is a psychological object irrespective of metaphysical realism. Here what the believer claims to know

45 Ibid., p. 84, fn.4.
46 Plantinga (2000), p. 181.

is merely an internal experience (whether that be a somatic or affective feeling or intuition grounding a belief) corresponding to an *idea* of God.

Plantinga argues that belief in God is basic and requires no evidence or reasoning apart from one's current conscious state of mind. It does not matter if one's beliefs are certain, infallible, or even true, only that it is permissible to have them without any supportive evidence other than it should be treated like an informational datum any criteria of proper basic beliefs must accommodate. In other words, all the theist needs to have to justify belief in God is the experience itself, for as Plantinga notes, "experience is what justifies me in holding it."[47] Here the experience of God is sufficient to ground the justification for the belief that God exists. But we may ask, What if your belief is false, or distorted, or based on a delusion although it may be an authentic one? If experience as sincere first-person warranted belief is all that is needed to justify a proposition, then we are entitled to believe in anything no matter how feeble the premise or shoddy the conclusion may be. If one is said to be justified in belief without any supportive arguments, then whatever I wish to believe is radically definitive (even if egoistic or solipsistic) without requiring external supports or constraints informing such inner experience. In other words, if inner experience is all that is needed to substantiate genuine belief, then truth is reducibly subjective and relative.

But this position must contend with the criteria of evidence or objective facts corresponding to external reality, for any thought could be deemed real, that is, independent of one's subjective experience, such as the psychotic productions of a schizophrenic mind. This is not the type of rational belief a reformed epistemologist wants to champion, yet it is an inescapable consequence of such a position.

Defending the permissibility to believe in what one wants to believe based on psychological experience of an intrapsychic nature is not the same as a supportive rationale grounding a justified belief based on a sound reason to do so. The argument from experience is intimately associated with the argument from desire. Here we cannot escape the psychological attributions assigned to the need to believe in a certain set of premises (such as the theistic proclamation to know God exists) when this so-called knowledge is confined to the way one prefers to think. In the end, lacking any appeal to supportive evidence or rational justification, one may simply

47 Plantinga (in Sennett, 1998), p. 152.

devolve into an epistemic position based on cognitive distortion or psychological naïveté grounded in fantasy, superstition, and/or wish-fulfillment. This is tantamount to saying: "I believe what I want because it feels true or right to me." Here it would be more proper to say that one imposes their subjective right to fashion their internal world of beliefs according to how they want things to be rather than how things truly are. This defensive function is a good example of what Dennett would call a "belief in belief"[48] based upon psychological dynamics motivating the need for God. Although one may offer an argument for why one has the right or will in believing what one believes, contra William James it does not necessarily make it valid or correct. "I experience God, therefore God exists" is at most a psychological proposition based on internal experience and has no generalizability apart from subjective posit with no objective grounds or reasons to justify what one believes is actually true.

And what do we make of the role of "sin"—itself a theological invention? For Plantinga, the person who is incapable of perceiving or knowing God is clouded by sin, which produces a malfunction or blockade in the *sensus divinitatis* occluding one from knowing God.[49] Of course this would apply to the atheist who denies any knowledge of God and claims to dispossess the faculty itself. Is this denial the result of sin, or is it a warrant basic belief? Here Keith Parsons rightfully notes that, according to Plantinga, since warranted belief in God is rational based on reformed epistemology, and unbelief is due to cognitive malfunction in the divine sense, this would make atheism irrational.[50] The upshot is that if one cannot locate a *sensus divinitatis* in oneself through sincere first-person introspection or lack of directly experiencing the presence of God, then one is morally corrupt and asinine. This is equivalent to saying that if one cannot perceive and know God, then one is flawed in some fundamental way. Here we may feel Plantinga's harsh superego as he passes judgment (not unlike Moses) on those who do not experience the world the way he does or thinks they should. If one's warrant basic belief is based on intrapsychic bona fide experience one claims is immediate and tangible, assuming one has a normatively operational cognitive apparatus, than would not Plantinga's argument equally apply to those who do not intuit or have direct knowledge of God? Blaming those who have no

48 *Breaking the Spell*, pp. 6, 200–210.
49 Plantinga (2000), pp. 184–185.
50 Parsons (2007), p. 110.

knowledge of God due to turpitude or cognitive malfunction is simply a projection due to negation and splitting based upon an unconscious threat to the integrity of their ego (and the insecurity of one's intellectual argument) overidentified with a particular fantasy constellation they very much wish were true. Just as the theist may claim that the atheist is blind to God due to sin and depravity, the atheist may equally declare that the belief in a so-called divine sense is illusory, if not delusional.

David Bentley Hart evokes another variant of reformed epistemology when he attempts to resurrect a defunct Platonism by professing an argument from experience that is based on a so-called "forgetting" of our knowledge of God upon birth. In his words, "the most important things we know are things we know before we can speak them," what is of the "greatest immediacy" yet something we attempt to block out from our minds when we grow older through defensive posturing. Notice his use of psychological vocabulary: we "put them out of mind ... and make ourselves oblivious to them, and try to silence the voice of knowledge that speaks within," knowledge of God.[51] For Hart, "wisdom is the recovery of innocence," "the ability to see again" that which has been "forgotten."[52] Despite the long tradition in late modern philosophy and British empiricism that points out the inconceivability of innate ideas—from Locke to Kant and Hume, which is further endorsed by neuroscience today, Hart's epistemological predilections informed by "Platonic" ideals suffer a romantic fate unsubstantiated by contemporary cognitive science, which empirically shows how neural networks are developmental achievements forged through personal experience, and hence are structurally and functionally incapable of inheriting knowledge of God at birth. Any so-called knowledge of God is the sole product of culture.

The *sensus divinitatis*—the faculty to sense and believe in God,[53] may be explained by psychological motivations due to social conditioning any child encounters at birth in our globalized multicultural world where diverse religious practices are historically embedded. Given the ubiquity of faith practices and teachings operative within the social matrix of any culture, not to mention the globalization of information technologies that

---

51 *The Experience of God*, p. 9.
52 Ibid., p. 10.
53 Contra Aquinas and Calvin, John Locke (1690), in *An Essay Concerning Human Understanding*, Bk 1, Ch. III, Par. 8, elaborates this discussion in his section on: Idea of God not innate. Also see David Hume's (1739–40), *A Treatise of Human Nature*, Bk 1, Sec. V, Of the immateriality of the soul, where he concludes that any argument in support of the soul as substance "is absolutely unintelligible" (p. 298), as is the case for the immortality of the soul (p. 299).

allows practically anyone to access knowledge at the touch of a computer mouse, why would we need to appeal to a divine principle to account for the prevalence of belief in a divine presence when we can more readily account for it through naturalized anthropological practices?

Belief in God is psychogenic. Leaving aside for the moment the impact and reinforcement of parochial education, this is partially derived from ideational deposits of childhood that leave emotional residues informing entrenched belief systems promulgated in any society simply because they are too powerful to resist. Children do not have the cognitive equipment to think about or analyze such matters properly due to their paucity of rational development, self-conscious awareness, and capacities for abstract thought, which are maturational (and neuropsychological) achievements. It is perfectly natural to believe what other powerful authority figures proclaim to be true when we are children, because we do not have the means to think otherwise. As children we do not possess the advanced neurobiological-cognitive facilities required to question the verity or logical justifications of what our parents or elders teach us: this comes with brain development, education, self-reflection, and critical thinking. These archaic emotional prejudices (based in ignorance, fear, and awe) form the psychological edifice of meaning structures we later call "faith" to justify the belief in something unseen, unexplainable, and empirically unverifiable. This fantasy system, I argue, is what unconsciously organizes and sustains the belief in God, which has become institutionalized in the social environments we find ourselves situated and immersed.

Plantinga's so-called reformed epistemology of having an implanted sense to know God is closely related to certain proponents of the "innateness" argument for religious belief that is thought to be biologically determined.[54] In today's climate of neuroscience, where all human psychological experience is boiled down to brain structures and synaptic mechanisms, it has become vogue to reduce the capacity for knowing God to a crass material determinism that is responsible for it all. Notwithstanding the contributions of naturalized explanations of group selection on adaptation and the evolving brain, it has become all too superficial, banal, and one-dimensional to situate the locus of belief in

---

54 See Newberg and D'Aquili (2001) who claim that belief in God is rooted in "the wiring of the human brain" (p. 129).

God to neuronal patterns rather than see how the sophistication of consciousness as a self-organized systemic achievement can produce neurochemical-biologic effects of its own. Just because the brain may be scientifically observed and measured by technological methods and neuroimaging techniques such as functional magnetic resonance imaging (fMRI) and positron emission tomography (PET) scans does not mean that mind is equivalent to its physical locality. In other words, we should not simply assume a one-way causal relation among brain processes that determine the productions of consciousness as an epiphenomenon, but rather human consciousness should be conceived as an evolved organic matrix that equiprimordially and reciprocally determines physical effects that transpire in the brain as a dialectical two-way, causal systemic informational and relational exchange of events. We cannot justify the belief in absolute (hard) determinism when it comes to biological organisms without shouldering a presumptive causal bias, especially when the complexifications of consciousness may exert a causal influence on how the manifestations of brain activity are understood. Here the God posit that is professed to be innately implanted in the human mind a priori is more readily explained as the product of a posteriori experience that stimulates cognitive functions and leaves its effects on neuronal activity.

Proponents of mental determinism that rely on reductive epistemologies based on brain discourse grounded in neuro-ontology commit a mereological error by demoting psychic complexity to its material constituents alone, not to mention being guilty of the fallacy of simple location or misplaced concreteness where human consciousness is said to be found in a reducible particle.[55] Here the intricacy of an organic whole or gestalt is reduced to its parts as neuroscience mistakenly conceives of mind *as* brain. Yet this naïve determinism supporting the conclusion that mind equals brain still continues to be in fashion. Here Phil Zuckerman cogently points out that based on the sheer numbers of atheists worldwide, which is estimated to be at least 500 million in total, "any suggestion that belief in God is natural, inborn, or a result of how our brains are wired becomes difficult to sustain."

Innate/neural theories of belief in God cannot explain the dramatically different rates of belief among similar countries. Consider

---

55 See my discussion and critique of reductive material ontologies in *Origins: On the Genesis of Psychic Reality*, pp. 10–12, 251, 263n9.

Britain (31%–44% atheist) compared with Ireland (4%–5% atheist), the Czech Republic (54%–61% atheist) compared with Poland (3%–6% atheist), and South Korea (30%–52% atheist) compared with the Philippines (less than 1% atheist). It is simply unsustainable to argue that these glaring differences in rates of atheism among these nations is due to different biological, neurological, or other such brain-related properties. Rather the differences are better explained by taking into account historical, cultural, economic, political, and sociological factors.[56]

The notion that theism or belief in God is implanted in us naturally at birth or is neurologically innate or genetic is manifestly untenable.

It may be further argued that positing a *sensus divinitatis* bestowed by God is begging the question because it can neither be empirically confirmed nor disproven if an individual who claims to possess it is relying on subjective experience or felt intuition alone to justify the belief in such a faculty. This proposition ultimately collapses into relativism peculiar to a particular subject's reported self-experience because it is based on first-person assertions that cannot be properly empirically tested or objectively investigated. At best we can only report on our own inner phenomenal experiences, but it does not (magically) make them real as independent, persisting external (eternal) objects, only as objects of thought qua ideas. As Freud tells us, "If one man has gained an unshakable conviction of the true reality of religious doctrines from a state of ecstasy which has deeply moved him, of what significance is that to others?"[57] As human beings, we try to convey our inner experiential lives to others who do not possess the same thoughts nor have first-person epistemic access to them, even though we may share a consensus on any topic of inquiry within a particular mode of discourse. At best we can say is that the self-possession of such ability is based on psychological dispositions that favor this particular explanation of one's inner lived experience. This means that the most we can say is that the subject's belief in this so-called faculty is based on a self-relation to one's internal experiences, which are not subject to objectivist (empirical-epistemic) criteria; hence the claim in itself proves nothing.

---

56 See Zuckerman (2007), p. 61.
57 *The Future of an Illusion*, p. 28.

> Religion is based, I think, primarily and mainly upon fear. It is partly the terror of the unknown and partly, as I have said, the wish to feel that you have a kind of elder brother who will stand by you in all your troubles and disputes. Fear is the basis of the whole thing—fear of the mysterious, fear of defeat, fear of death.[63]

None of us want to face the thought of a final ending, especially on our death beds as the lights go out for good. Russell professed that belief in God has nothing to do with intellectual argumentation at all and everything to do with emotion and a wish for safety.

Colin McGinn refers to the "cosmic loneliness"[64] that besieges us in our realization that we are alone in the universe, yet we yearn to connect with others because we are cut off in our essence. God supplies a wonderful antidote to our persistent solipsism and existential isolation by offering a communion we can attach to as something outside of ourselves (and in Mass consume as a wafer). The human proclivity to envision a personified higher power with whom we may have a personal relationship helps assuage the uneasiness of life alone in an impersonal universe. Our intrinsic sense of aloneness is reflected in the fact that each of us are confined to the theater of our own thoughts and inner dialogues that no other person can experience directly even if such epistemic experiences are conveyed or communicated to others. Here we form a relationship to our own minds and sense of self as the metaprocessing of information and the cacophony of competing desires, wants, compulsions, revulsions, and so on that create an ocean of inner ambiguity and restlessness we deeply want conciliated and resolved. This cosmic loneliness is an extension of the inevitable solitude we inhabit even when we have copious people in our lives and an interactive world we are constantly engaging. Our private sense of inner aloneness requires a certain degree of psychic resilience, as it takes mental fortitude to contain, channel, and ameliorate various internal pressures, urges, and defensive processes that beleaguer our psychological equilibrium and internal accord. Fantasy formation helps alleviate these inherent tensions of uncertainty, ambivalence, and need for object relations.

Based upon the nature of internalization, as we acquire internal objects through our experiences of the world, our unconscious ego fashions a

---

63 *Why I Am Not a Christian*, p. 22.
64 See Jonathan Miller (2004), Episode 1.

variety of mental representations and nexuses to fantasy constellations our minds manufacture. Our internalized object representations provide the contents for fantasy systems to manipulate and relate to. This naturally extends to the God introject as a particularized fantasy relation we construct in the wake of our cosmic aloneness. This is further overdetermined by the social forces we are thrown into that condition the contents of this fantasy object each individual (within their cultural matrix) must assimilate for themselves subject to further manipulation in content and form by unconscious agency. Beginning with any type of internal communication with the fantasy object, especially in prayer, we forge modes of relatedness to a God object, even if ever so slight or ambiguous, as this fantasy relation ensures that we are not alone.

In my private and professional discussions with those who are religious, agnostic, and secular, there is often a concession people genuinely confess to, which is a felt need for God in order to make life meaningful; and they particularly need something outside of themselves to bestow purpose and value on this world, which would be utterly empty and worthless without it. As David Bentley Hart puts it, "If there is no God, then of course the universe is ultimately absurd … in the end it is also quite, quite meaningless."[65] This sentiment seems to echo an existential futility in having to make meaning for oneself as a traumatic revelation to life. This revelation mirrors the developmental traumas each child encounters in having to confront the incursions of reality, especially when we realize that the social world does not revolve around our infantile geocentric identities. The narcissistic injury to our inchoate egos left over as a deposit from early childhood is unconsciously memorialized and resonates as a sense of entitlement the self refuses to abandon. This festers as a grandiose prerogative and expectation we secretly harbor in not having all our wishes and caprices fulfilled, the disillusionment of which an infant immediately encounters when the maternal object or social environment fails to meet its needs upon demand. Religion may be said to attempt to neutralize this traumatic revelation, despite the fact that religion is borne of a traumatic reaction to life.

It may be argued that the social institution of religion is the result of human developmental trauma instantiated in the early throes of the childhood of the human race. Informed by the evolutionary tendency to impute agency to natural events, engage in sense-making, and form shared

65 *The Experience of God*, p. 19.

beliefs that promote group survival, the earliest religious traditions may be said to be humanity's proto-scientific attempt at explaining our place in the world and coping with the trauma of living. It burgeoned in myriad forms through myth and folk psychology in response to the hardship, emotional pain, and *pathos* of early mankind, and was erected as a means to make sense out of natural phenomena, institute social cohesiveness, curb base aggressions and carnality, control human behavior, and to emplace meaning and purpose in the face of austerity instated by the impassive staidness of an indifferent cosmos. The recognition that being able to summon a source of explanation to understand natural phenomena unknown to societies in the past (such as physical and mental diseases, laws of chemistry and physics, etc.) was also a powerful psychological method of social control that was politically and pragmatically exploited by privileged classes who had authority, wealth, and power. Since the social advent of religion is human civilization, it has survived and flourished mainly because of its institutionalization. Now that it is solidified in all societies throughout the globe and is an inextricable part of cultural verve and character, religion is no more likely to disappear than the reality of the external world, for it is the product of human nature. The only reasonable question is that of futurity, namely, how religions will transform or mutate in substance and form in light of cultural evolution.

God as the inversion of our *pathos*

Belief in God is pathological, as it is an expression of our suffering. For the Greeks, to be human is to suffer. Our *pathos* (πάθος) is to create God through thought, the invention of mind, and we are compelled to do this precisely because we lack. The human condition is suffused with psychic pain, what modern society is quick to label as pathology. Riddled with anxiety, deprivation, uncertainty, and daily adversity, the believer postulates the opposite of what we experience—the negation of our suffering and finitude through the fantasy of permanence, fulfillment, and immortality, where we achieve abundance, plenitude, and deep satisfaction—*eudaimonia*.[66] In modern psychiatric parlance, we have come to call this a form of dissociation, if not pollyannaish denial.

---

66 This is Aristotle's term for happiness, the end goal of all action for the good of man. See *Nicomachean Ethics*, Book X.

The notion of God is unconsciously conditioned by a fantasy principle. On one level, the mind interjects a degree of splitting or fracturing into the rational faculty, which compartmentalizes certain elements of information the psyche finds objectionable or intolerable to the degree that it must be negated and banished from awareness. It is in these psychic moments of segmenting-off data presented to consciousness as a refusal of cognitive integration that the mind is unable to register and formulate discrepancies that are in discord with empirical reality. Instead, a certain fictive reality is generated in the mind via reactionary fantasy that maintains these unformulated and unarticulated experiences within its own compartmentalized organizations largely because the mind is overwhelmed in its ability to amalgamate, assimilate, and synthesize a rational unity out of the competing conflicts it is presented with due to the unconscious emotional variants that refuse to accept sober logic. As a result, the unconscious mind presses into service a felt-reality manufactured by imagination via wish-fulfillment as the spawn of desire, which is superimposed on conscious belief systems. The emotional currents that shape fantasy schemes can readily override reason, science, and logic to the degree that certain indisputable facts about the world are suspended in favor of stubborn belief for the simple reason that people want to believe it, itself a self-induced state of voluntary ignorance. This dissociative process also mirrors the psychoanalytic notion of disavowal as a form of negation of accepting certain incontestable aspects of reality on their own terms in preference for a fantasizing principle that displaces critical doubt, skepticism, or rational disbelief.

God does not exist as anything more than a thought conceived by our unconscious fantasies and overlaid on our consciousness as an imagined reality we deeply long to believe in. The idea itself has governed world history and the lives of most of its inhabitants since the inception of our human ancestry—even conceivably other primates who would have had some crude, elemental notion of a powerful Other or agencies operative within the natural world. This concept, namely, this imagined construct, surely would have had its gestation in the minds of primitive man, which was transmitted over the ages as the human race and civilization evolved into its present condition. The idea and belief in God is entrenched in human consciousness and the concept qua idea *as if* God is "really real." Here it is important to emphasize that fictive truths become real truths as a means to neutralize the anxiety generated in the moment of confronting an unsavory reality, which is converted by the processes of denial, repression, disavowal, and/or dissociation. God fictions are thoughts and propositional attitudes, as well as unconscious ideas or mental structures, that have no legitimate counterpart in reality, but they serve an adaptive purpose and are lived out in a pragmatic way in order to enable people to function more effectively in the world. Fictive activity, therefore, becomes interlaced within personality development and serves deep motivational and affective aims tied to fantasy formation. Here fictions serve defensive functions integral to the subject's worldview.[67] But the projective fantasy is that the idea itself (as fiction) is identical with an extant God rather than what the idea signifies. This is an *isomorphic fallacy*, which is the belief that a mental process is equivalent to an actual correspondent object. So the world masses reify the thought to the status of a concrete ontology rather than view the idea itself as a product of our psychologies.

Rather than view God as a semiotic, hence giving birth to a whole host of meaning systems with symbolic functions, there is an isomorphism between the signifier (as thought) and signified (as external object). When people typically refer to God (as the linguistic signifier) they mean that God exists as an absolute correspondent reality, not merely as a metaphor, or more precisely, as a metaphorical function, when this signification is itself the projection of an idea. The idea is mistaken or misrecognized for a substantive (albeit incorporeal) thing rather than a mental event producing such thoughts mediated by imaginative creation. What is imagined, hence created via fantasy and reinforced through the puissance of intelligence, is mistaken for a correspondent reality that is imbued with the predicate of existence and all sorts of idealized psychological properties and dispositions (namely supremacy, omnipotence, and so forth), when these idealizations are the productions of human consciousness.

When reason encounters invariable antinomies, contradictions, or limits to knowledge, the so-called reality or presence of God is said to be understood by a stupefying *sensus divinitatis*, the intuition of a supreme personal being animating the cosmos, when this so-called divine sense is the manifestation of desire, a desire for God. The psychological proclivity to yearn and believe in God is, I suggest, partially based on ideational

67 See Hans Vaihinger (1925).

deposits of our earliest developmental thinking acquired in childhood fueled by cultural conditioning, fear, and fantasy. But unlike typical fairy tales, the God illusion is elevated to the status of divine reality. Like superstition and mythology, fiction becomes hypostatized rather than reflective of metaphorical meaning, and ideas are imagined to be real independent of ideation.

Most of humanity is socially conditioned to believe in God at birth by virtue of the fact of being born into a cultural ontology where God discourse is ubiquitous. No child can escape their thrownness nor is sheltered from this social phenomenon, for no parent or community can inoculate their children against the greater social fabric in which they are raised. Ideas are disseminated outside of our control and approval, for they merely *happen*. Information is simply circulated. Competing stimuli and cultural differences force themselves on human consciousness as surely as television alerts the viewer to a bite of news or a new product for consumption. We are bombarded with a plurality of differences we must confront and assimilate into our personal and familial beliefs and practices within the cultural environs that produce them. Here God is as much a cultural phenomenon as pizza, blue jeans, and dollar stores.

Another reason why the God posit is so reified is that our transference onto God is so powerful. This is the psychoanalytic discovery that human beings universally cannot help but experience reality through the historical lens of their own personal wishes and conflicts. We project our psychic lives onto objects we encounter in daily life, including our hopes, ideals, fears, prejudices, and privations. The transference unto God is an emotional disposition motivated by unconscious discord and desire. The God construct is itself a transference object because it is allotted the greatest existence and qualities of which nothing else could surpass. The attribution of supremacy is fodder for unconscious fantasy life, for the finite and derisory mortal could be squished like an ant in the eye of a supreme beholder. These anxieties (introduced in early childhood when cognitive faculties are undeveloped and immature) spawn a whole underworld of trepidation and fright that are instantiated unconsciously and consciously reinforced by culture and social custom.

These persecutory factors, I argue, which are in no doubt evolutionarily informed by the nature and presence of predation inherent to our animal world, extort mental life to such a degree that civilization had to invent a sublimated way to neutralize such primal anxieties. Here mental life must resort to a form of reaction formation where God the persecutor (as unknown Alien or Other) is turned into God the savior, where only ostensive benevolent and loving qualities are attached to this *imago dei* in its reified supernatural status. Through this inverse psychological maneuver, God is worshiped rather than dreaded—itself a defense designed to annul the persecutory threat, where fear of death and suffering is converted into a *reason* why this would occur, where the individual (soul) is designated to shoulder the onus of responsibility by bringing on divine wrath and punishment based on personal disposition or deed. This message is clear in scripture from Moses to Jesus, Maimonides, and Mohammed—God is to be feared if one's actions are not good and if one's heart is not pure, a legacy dating back to Egyptian polytheistic culture.[68] Here the persecutory objectives of God's unconditioned being are subverted based upon the conditional predilections and actions of mortal fallible men: the persecutory object itself is inverted and displaced onto human agency as the result of personal sin. "God is great, God is good," but He can and does inflict pain and suffering if you are "bad," which humanity brings on itself for violating divine law. Here the God construct doubly serves as a policing agent over the behaviors and conscience of believers, a constant reminder that negative consequences will prevail if one is not decent or worthy of divine recognition.

Humanity's overwhelming need to invent the idea of God is also reflective of the fact that we can't give up on it. This tells us something profound about human nature: we want, crave, seek, pine—hence *require* an object of wish-fulfillment. Billions of people cannot forsake the hope in the possibility that their fantasy is "really real," that is, independent of their fantasy lives and wishes, and that hope and faith become the

---

68 In Egyptian cosmology, Osiris is the Lord of Eternity, King of the Underworld. Emerging from a state of nonexistence, he presided over death and became the supernatural superego that judged the purity of a soul by weighing a man's heart in relation to a feather. Only after passing through a series of gates, caverns, and mounds in the netherworld, and facing a gauntlet of serpents, demons, hybrid monsters, and deadly challenges, such as fires of damnation, was a journeyman to face Osiris on the Day of Judgment. An interesting note is that there is an inherent democracy to the underworld, for the judgment of the heart was initiated by Ma'at, the goddess of truth and justice, where it weighed in the balance of a feather (the symbol of truth) and recorded by Thoth, the god of wisdom, before offering the verdict to Osiris. The fate of an individual's soul was ultimately based on the determination of one's moral character. If the heart was pure (i.e., free of sin and evil), the *ba*-spirit was allowed to pass into eternity and experience a favorable immortality in the blessed Field of Reeds. If not, the guilty party's heart was devoured by a beast (part-lion/crocodile/hippopotamus) and condemned to the cauldron of dead souls that populated the netherworld (see Mills, 2014a).

panacea for their existential malaise. And the cryptic nature of their sub-jective private fantasies is validated and fortified when communal con-sensus elevates this culturally sanctioned, ideological irrealism to the dominion of the "really real." In other words, when everyone around you says "It's true!" you believe them. The need to be accepted by others in a community is more appealing than truth, especially during childhood when acceptance, validation, recognition, and love by parents, family, teachers, and adult authority figures are coveted. Here truth is replaced with fiction and reinforced by society to the degree that belief becomes a delusional property of cultural consensus, a collective *folie à deux*.

God as compromise formation

Psychoanalysis has taught us that since the beginning of the embryonic mind there are a multitude of competing desires, fantasies, and defenses that populate mental life. They all vie for release but they cannot possibly be fulfilled. These instinctual drives, protective defenses, and fantasy con-stellations become more robust and organized as the developing brain matures, but they nevertheless exist from an early age onward due to the emotional and motivational pressures informed by our evolutionary past. Because these mental processes largely occupy unconscious life, and hence are cut-off from conscious awareness, there are innumerable conflicting desires and wishes that are at odds with one another, yet each press for expression and gratification in their own way. In this sense, the mind is a dynamic process system in perpetual conflict. Because it is not possible for every desire or caprice to be fulfilled without resulting in psychic calamity, the mind must produce some kind of negotiated compromise in its execu-tions of form, content, affect, thought, behavior, and qualitative intensity. The result is modified forms of psychical instantiation that are uncon-sciously mediated and expressed as substitutions and transmogrifications of original desire. In psychoanalysis we call this a "compromise formation."[69]

The multicausal fabric of mental life ensures that conflict is normative in the human psyche, which leads to various distributed forms from adaptation to pathology. Following the principle of sufficient reason, every thought, every feeling, every action is precipitated by a corresponding

---

69 Freud (1896) first introduces this notion in his early trauma-affect model of unconscious conflict (see pp. 170–172), which is the basis of modern conflict theory in psychoanalysis.

unconscious derivative or mental act that conditions the production of further acts in accordance with the various compromises they bring about as a result of the interactions with various features of the mind. The competing forces and thresholds at play have no qualitative boundaries, therefore various anxieties and dangers are generated as the mind simultaneously seeks to resolve conflict and restore internal harmony or equilibrium. In the unconscious, there are virtually an unlimited mine of wishes that flow from the cacophony of desire, which generates counter-wishes, resistances, and obstacles to their fulfillment. There are various economic principles in force that seek to regulate these discordances, just as there are various dynamics that generate complexity in organization, form, content, and discharge of energies. This inevitably leads to complex overdetermined systems in the mind that are at odds with one another, yet they must attempt to find some harmonization within their shared co-existence despite the notion that conflict fuels the constant teleonomic, relational, informational, and semiotic exchange of events.

Because the mind seeks synthesis, resolution, and a channeling of natural desire through embodied and ideational units of mental life, there will always be a systemic interplay of tensions between instinct or appetition, the experience and construction of inner reality, and the external world. Compromises occur when various wishes, resistances, and counter-defenses interact and engage with one another in fantasy, affect, and cognition, hence producing a variety of competing psychic agendas all clamoring at once for release and appeasement. It is logically impossible for every urge or whim to be sated without producing more chaos, therefore, something must be altered or sacrificed in order to reach some resolve. Yet this process and its contents are often filtered or barred from consciousness. Instead, what enters into conscious awareness are the *derivatives* of those original compromised impulses and fantasies, such as the need for an ideal object to gratify a primordial wish, but also its counter-reactionary resistance against its gratification because it generates anxiety, negation, ego restrictions, prohibitions, superego punishment fantasies, and so forth. Compromise formations may also embody hybrid or subsidiary dynamic organizations that meet and/or frustrate multiple desires and defenses all at once; hence they are fused into designated fantasy objects, dreams, thoughts, slips, faulty achievements (*Fehlleistungen*), or symptoms. This unconscious activity can be both normative and pathological depending upon the subjective manifestation

in people and their contextual circumstances within the cultural parameters that either permit or forbid the expression of such compromises.

Due to the overdetermined nature of opposing forces in the psyche,
various compromises must be made between the competing organic pressures derived from the body, mental organizations or structures, and defensive systems that govern the agentic mind. The idea of God may be said to
be the product of conflict in the form of a compromise as symptomatic substitution for original wishes as well as competing defensive functions that
are designed to attain pleasure, gratify wishes, neutralize anxiety, avoid
psychic pain, and undo disturbing mental ideation and their consequences
in the multifarious dialectical chemistries that transpire between mutually
implicative/operative forces that oppose each other in the mind. For Freud,
the paradigmatic example of which are manifest in the hysterical and
obsessional neuroses. The God posit is the outcome of unconscious derivatives—at once a fused representational object of idealization and worship,
a restrictive and preventative internalized presence, and an external puni-
tive agent—itself a fantasized solution aimed to end intrapsychic conflict.
This complicated series of psychic operations involves some form of
reorganization in the mental apparatus that redistributes the internal forces
embattling the life of the soul (*Seelenleben*) so that an acceptable or adaptive range of expression can be achieved while satisfying to some degree
the competing interests that press for satisfaction. Here the belief in God
becomes a symptom of our pathology.

God as internal object personifies the dialectical nature of competing
unconscious interests insofar as both wish and defense, emotion and
thought, symbol and symptom may participate in the same fantasy relation whereby each achieves a modicum of gratification. Governed by
oppositional forces within the soul, God as savior also becomes God as
wrath, salvation and damnation, safety and fear, peace and persecution.
The God posit may be generated in response to resistance (e.g., against
suffering, death, personal mortality, and so forth) or instated as resistance
itself (i.e., against cold reality, contingency, etc.). Moreover, it embodies
or symbolizes ideal values and idealized qualities as well as moral
demands and prohibitions: every urge or desire is accompanied by its
inverse relation to its opposing nature. The projection of God's omniattributes in the Abrahamic monotheisms is a case in point. God is the host
of incompatible ideas that are at once libidinal and pleasurable, whereas
God is desired as an unfailing love object, yet is also full of dread, shame,

and guilt, for God becomes a hostile, aggressive, and persecutory introject that evokes moral and predatory anxiety, feelings of worthlessness and inferiority, depressive affect, and punishment fantasies. Each component of a compromise exists within psychic structure and is operative at various levels of unconscious organization. Some may be more dominant while others are repressed or dissociated, yet each subsists as their own micro-agency with assorted degrees of form, valence, and intensity.

Because the God construct is primarily a defensive function, psychic economy is regulated by the way fantasy relations negotiate drive satis-faction, pain affect, and superego injunctions. The God representation inheres in and occupies an element of all these psychic forces in the mind, for defense becomes its emissary. Because all compromise for-mations are relative to a particular individual within their social context by maximizing as much pleasure as possible while avoiding or mini-mizing associated unpleasure, the God object may become more of a source of fulfillment for some yet pain for others. Generally we may say that the God invention is the symbolic fusion of the vicissitudes of instincts or drives (*Triebe*) conditioned by our animal natures after they have undergone inner transformation. The fate of unconscious desire as libido (*Lust*) and primordial aggression undergo energetic, affective, and ideational transmogrifications, which lead to more sublimated rep-resentational and behavioral expressions. Here sublimation acquires a unity containing all elements of a compromise whereby God becomes a transcendent ideal as well as an object of horror, hence representing and satisfying various wishes and conflicts simultaneously. It is not surprising that the monotheistic notion of God historically signifies a deity that is both loving and hateful, invincible yet fallible, perfect yet flawed, whereby a mixture of gratification, defensive renunciation, negation, ideality, and punishment are welded into a single semiotic function. Here God becomes the suprasignifier that quenches a pleasure-seeking wish through the enjoyment of an illusion and simul-taneously penalizes one for enjoying that wish at the same time. Mind covets and rebukes sin at once. Pleasure is always abutted to displeas-ure, hence conflict is unavoidable and ubiquitous to mental life. This ontological fulcrum ensures that God will always remain an ambivalent object to humanity.

The idealized fixation of imagined value

As relational beings, the believing masses cannot accept the fact that we are ultimately alone and there is nothing else after we die. There is no family we return to. There is no bosom. There are no prospects for anything else other than what we experience now or create in our own process of becoming. Many mistakenly, yet quite willfully at times, create the illusion of a wishful afterlife when there is nothing beyond our natural embodiment. Of course we can debate the question of life after death, the transmogrification of matter, mind/body dualism, reincarnation, the transmigration of souls, and so forth, which I would argue is not the same as the God question; however, it is incontestable that the death of organic life is a biological state of finality. Scientific naturalism and contemporary materialism generally argue that mind and body are, with stipulations, virtually identical and dependent upon physiological corporeality, and that the cessation of the physical body is a terminal ending point, as any anatomist or mortician will tell you.

Take for example the narrative myth of Christianity, which I will attempt to summarize in adumbrated pithy form. A child is born from a virgin who was impregnated by a ghost and then proclaimed to be the son of God; whom is then sentenced to state execution and comes back from the dead. You cannot be a faithful Christian and not believe in at least two fantastic cardinal stories: the first being (a) the possibility of a virgin birth—literally a woman who has not had sex with a man, and second (b), that a corpse can come back to life. Nearly all Christians (Catholic, Protestant, Orthodox) believe in three basic tenets: (1) the canon of New Testament scripture, (2) the apostolic creed, and (3) specific forms of church institutional structure.[70] But the teleological suspension of the rational is the most astounding, namely, the possibility of virgin birth and resurrection. Although it is a well-documented fact that religion is a politically driven officialdom that promotes illusory truth in the service of attaining power by fostering intellectual prejudice and servitude, it is unfathomable to think that anyone who is not retarded could possibly believe that a man rose from the grave. The notion of a dead man coming back to life (the myth of resurrection after crucifixion) is the modern day motif of a horror movie—"Divine Zombie Returns from the

70 See Elaine Pagels (1979), p. xxiii.

Dead." Here we hear the echo of Tertullian: *Certum est, quia impossibile*— It is certain, because it is impossible. In other words, "This is crazy, so it must be true." This credulity is hardly a logic remotely worthy of validity.

We pine for futurity (heaven) as an emotional measure to overcome death. We don't want to stop experiencing: the will to live (*conatus essendi*) is instinctual, as the notion of continuation ensures a psychic sense of permanence, for we simply do not want life to end. What we call God—what we think of as an object-relation—is really a *self-relation* to a wishful idea we imagine is an other-worldly divine and beatific supernatural (yet personal) being that exists, and who we are in communion with, when we are in fact only relating to our own minds.[71] This self-relation is indeed an internalized unconscious relation to an idealized object turned into a reified (and deified) Subject, when this fantasized object is in essence a fixation to an *idealization of imagined value*. In psychoanalytic terms, we could refer to the God posit as a product of the ego ideal, which interjects a confusion between wish and reality and attenuates appropriate boundaries belonging to critical judgment in favor of an exemplar view of an ideal self that is impossible to attain yet displaced onto a superior moral agency. Jesus of Nazareth is a good example of the ego ideal, what Jungians refer to as an archetypal image of a perfect self. Yet this fixation to an idealized value-object is tantamount to a delusion, for there is no substantive evidence to prove the facticity of the belief that the Ideal *as* idea is a metaphysical entity apart from the psychological motives that underlie the invention of the idea itself. If what we understand by *delusion* is the fixed belief in something contrary to all evidence against it, then this imaginary idealized object may only belong to the ideational fixations fashioned by psychic reality.

An element of our superego—the seat of conscience and moral judgment,[72] that which stands over and above us in developmental

---

71 It should be assumed that mental contents (i.e., specific ideas or representations of God) are largely, originally derived from interiorized collective, cultural processes introduced in familial, communal, educational, and institutional social life.

72 *Über-Ich* is Freud's term for moral sense, which is a critical-moral agency that stands over against itself and holds itself up to a higher authority. What is familiarly known as the "super-ego" is the modification of the ego or split-off portion of the I that stands in relation to a particular form of identification, namely, a set of values and prohibitions it internalized from attachment figures, familial relations, and cultural experience, ideals and principles the self strives to attain.

importance and idealized value—is itself a valuing microagent or part of our personality that is invested in construing a fantasy system of perfection in all its myriad forms, particularly an Ultimate Object of idealized value. The believer, I suggest, as opposed to a person of faith,[73] harbors a delusional nucleus in the sense that a valued object is extraordinarily idealized and worshiped as a substitute for one's fallible (earthly) objects (i.e., this could be one's parents, society, the Fatherland, Big Other, etc.).[74] What is essential—that is, indispensable, is that an idealized object is worshiped for its imagined ideal value. In other words, the fantasized object of worship is the delusional idealization of imagined value that is attached to the fixated object *within* the fantasy constellation itself.

For the large majority of humanity throughout the world, God, and its semiotic derivatives, symbolize ideality—the conception of absolute perfection. This is none-other than what we prize or cherish above all else— the Good, the True, the Beautiful—Pure Excellence. As our self-relation to ideality, God becomes a signifier for the highest form of valuation imaginable. And the hallowed relationship we form with our values— what we find most worthy—may be the most consecrated covenant that

73 Here I wish to make the distinction between the believer, who takes an affirmative epistemological stance of asserting God's ontological existence, versus the person of faith who may be epistemologically agnostic or uncertain; albeit in phenomenology and practice, there may be said to be a structural tension or ambivalence that underlies both belief and faith. People may rationally reject the God concept while holding in faith an emotional reserve (as hope) that violates reason yet inoculates the self against free-floating anxiety. And the somber hands of reason may deracinate hope and faith to the degree that emotionality is neutered, hence producing an affective backlash of negation and hubris.

74 Although this is in bad taste, I wish to juxtapose an absurd point of comparison to demonstrate the universality of form. It may be argued that, in essence, this delusional hegemony is, with qualifications, analogous to—but not reducible or equivalent to—the pathological organization of the inner world of a paedophile. In De Masi's (2007) discussion of his treatment of a paedophile, the idealized object "promises all manner of pleasure and happiness" (p. 147). Here I wish to emphasize the essential (hence necessary, unconditional, and non-accidental) structure of the similar psychological dispositions inherent to the *fantasy life* of each process, not the specific content or actions of either party. In other words, what is structurally similar is the *form* of the fantasy, not the content or the context. Just as the paedophilic object unconsciously represents the ideal child-self, God signifies the Ideal Other that loves the Ideal Self unconditionally. God, like the sexualized child, becomes a fetish object to love, venerate, and adore: "If I can possess that object, then I will be complete!" It is further interesting to note that the preponderance of paedophiles within the clergy or religious institutions are purportedly, they say, carrying out God's work. Of course, anyone working clinically with sexual offenders has to therapeutically address the almost universal fact that they themselves were victims of childhood sexual abuse and developmental traumas that condition their pathologies and compulsions to prey on children they unconsciously identify as their ideal (untainted or pure) self.

governs the law of the heart, namely, the moral principles that define self-hood and what we conceivably live and die for. If this were not the case, then the history of religious conflict throughout the world in the name of God would be a vacuous testament to human stupidity.

Chapter 3

The need to invent God

Metaphysics is paranoia. The notion of a transpersonal, supernatural creator entity is in reality a very frightful thought. For those in prayer or in the madhouse, I can think of no greater paranoia. For the believer constantly worried about God's judgment or watchful eye, or the psychotic tormented by religious delusions, the common denominator is anxiety. This is why God may be rightfully called The Holy See. Here the very notion of God is laced with an inherent ambivalent factor in felt-relation to our unease and trepidations, for God is both an ideal and a feared, unknown omnipotent object. God therefore serves a dialectical function within the abyss of our psyches that lies at the heart of our anxieties, as well as a promissory medicine to alleviate them. This ambivalent fulcrum, however, is experienced differently for people, depending upon what side of the dialectic (ideality *vs.* a fear factor) is most operative at any given moment. This ambiguous tension between God as good versus ominous is not only historically situated, it is dialectically organized within the concept itself, for ideality always stands in relation to its opposition: both are mutually implicative in any discourse on God.

The transference unto God

A very interesting psychological question is, Why do we as humanity feel the need to talk about God? What does this tell us about human nature? What does God symbolize for the human race? Why does it continue unabashedly—without apology or defense—in our age of reason and science? What psychic functions does it serve? One reason why God is so instinctive and pined after is that the idea itself serves a primordial need for wish-fulfillment via maintaining transcendental illusions based on unconscious angst that torments the psyche. Psychoanalysis has long ago revealed this insight into the matrix of the human mind, for we are besieged by anxiety, despair, trauma, suffering, and human tragedy. Our being is *pathos*, and that is why we need to invent God. We need something to alleviate our fear and trembling, and the antiseptic voice of reason offers little consolation. That is why irrationality and emotion reign supreme in the minds of world masses, for God is the world's greatest defense mechanism.

For Freud, religion is a cultural neurosis, and particularly an obsessive-compulsive type, fashioned "through a delusional remoulding of reality." This is why Freud concluded that "the religions of mankind must be classed among the mass-delusions" of humanity.[1] We may readily witness how cultural observance to ritual, such as prayer, may be construed as a method of displacing obsessionality onto a projected object, and hence compulsively motivated as a way of binding or temporarily alleviating anxiety and paranoiac fear. For example, the Catholic in confessional and the Islamic injunction of multiple daily prayer are each following a certain set of prescribed rituals designed to psychologically assuage anxiety. Like superstitions, these practices as well as other similar religious observances may be said to symbolize this cultural neurosis.

For Freud, the belief in God and future salvation is an illusion and is the source of much human suffering and perpetuated ignorance. Much of his analysis is outlined in his controversial 1927 publication, *The Future of an Illusion*. The Oedipalization of God as the projected father in the sky is undoubtedly his unique insight to the familiar tenets of Judeo-Christian doctrine that reify God as a masculine figure denoted by the personal pronoun "He." This is beyond the mere anthropomorphic hypostatization of God who possesses human attributes with a specific male gender, but to a view of God as a personal authority figure that is in the image of the father who assumes all the characteristics of an Absolute Superego that is both comforting and menacing. Hence, moral conscience, ideal perfection, empathy and compassion, as well as critical judgment, shame, punishment, and guilt are projected attributes believed to belong to God.[2]

Freud's contempt for religious ideologies is well known and exemplified in the following passage:

1 Freud (1930), p. 81.
2 See *The Ego and the Id* (1923). What is not often known among Freud's works is that not only is God seen as the Oedipal father, but also the Devil. Refer to Freud (1923 [1922]), Sec. III, "The Devil as a Father Substitute," pp. 83–92.

> What the common man understands by his religion—with the system of doctrines and promises which on the one hand explains to him the riddles of this world with enviable completeness, and, on the other, assures him that a careful Providence will watch over his life and will compensate him in a future existence for any frustrations that he suffers here. The common man cannot imagine this Providence otherwise than in the figure of an enormously exalted father ... The whole thing is so patently infantile, so foreign to reality, that to anyone with a friendly attitude to humanity it is painful to think that the great majority of mortals will never be able to rise above this view of life.[3]

Recall that the significance of the father is central to the psychoanalytic theory of Oedipalization, when the father is imbued with supremacy and omnipotence in childhood, as well as a rival and moral threat over the child's possession of the mother. This is purportedly resolved through identification with His values and ideals and in obeying His laws.[4]

Paranoia, terror, and dread of annihilation are the consequences if one dares to question the Law or divine command. It is to be avoided at all costs, and is an ingrained psychological defense organized around the horror of non-being, usually evoking fantasies of punishment and death due to anxiety about provoking a revengeful wrath from an omnipotent source. This paranoiac knowledge reinforces the fantasy system that one dare not question the existence of God because it is sacrosanct. The uncanny whispers: "It *could be* real." Such prohibitions become holy dogma, hence the social fantasies underlying ideology, which are unconsciously transformed into persecutory introjects that take on an affective contagion unquestionably fraught with fear of pain, death, and eternal persecution.[5]

---

3 *Civilization and Its Discontents*, p. 74.
4 A Lacanian (1957–1958) application of the Name-of-the-Father may also be applied to the God construct as a paternal signifier, an "Other of the Other" (p. 192), where an ultimate point of signification lies within the Symbolic order. Here the name of the Father—God—is a suprasignifier that institutes the Law into the Symbolic.
5 Recall the book of Revelation 21:8: "the fearful, and unbelieving, and the abominable, and murderers, and whoremongers, and sorcerers, and idolaters, and all liars, shall have their part in the lake which burneth with fire and brimstone: which is the second death." In the West, we likely owe these images to Dante and the medievalists, whom were partly concerned with maintaining political power and influence over the common people through thought control over their spiritual afterlives. It is one thing to remain in servitude to a feudal lord during one's earthly existence, but it is quite another to be eternally condemned to suffering that is other-worldly. And the Koran has capitalized on this notion, for it is riddled with references to eternal persecution from its opening lines, such as "whoever has done an atom's weight of evil shall see it" (The Earthquake), and "the wicked shall burn in Hell-fire upon the Judgement-day: they shall not escape" (The Cataclysm).

For Freud, the principle task of civilization is to defend us against our instinctual nature, that is, to demand a renunciation (or at least a prohibition and curtailment) of our innate tendencies to exploit others and pursue base pleasure at the detriment of social domestication. Civilization by necessity imposes a restriction on the individual, which leads to resistances and hostilities, and as a result causes adversity and anguish. Upon this constraint is added the impersonal hands of feral nature in all its power and dominion, which imposes a certain fate on humanity it cannot control nor prevent, whether this pertains to natural occurrences such as earthly disasters, weather phenomena, or organic death. Humanity is helpless in the face of raw nature, as is a small child in relation to its parents or environmental forces where it feels encircled. But just as children are afraid of storms and wild animals, they equally rely on the protection of their parents—especially the father—against the dangers of the world. And modern attachment theory would concur that parental figures are first and foremost seen as a salve for safety. This is the "infantile prototype" humanity carries forward in its attempt to make sense out of and tame the brute forces of nature, where in ancient times the purported purposes, passions, and wills of nature were attributed to the gods. This psychogenic projection by past civilizations surely had a phylogenetic prehistory, but with the advent of science and discovery of the laws and regularity of natural phenomena, polytheism lost its currency. Yet this did not eradicate the longing for the father's love and protection and the need to alleviate the helplessness and anxiety humanity must endure. In the place of impersonal nature, taciturn and implacable as it is, which the gods of antiquity were imagined to govern in order to "exorcize the terrors" it poses, they too had to "reconcile men to the cruelty of Fate, particularly as it is shown in death," and "compensate them for the sufferings and privations which a civilized life in common has imposed on them."[6] Yet when the gods proved impotent against the destinies of nature in all its austerities, civilization needed to account for these existential absurdities by attributing a divine origin to the universe with a greater purpose and destination that transcended human society and its thrownness.

In order to make human helplessness more tolerable, which at once shelters civilization from insuperable nature, fate, and the hazards and

6 *The Future of an Illusion*, p. 18.

mistreatment that menace people from society itself, a collective store of ideas were slowly developed over the millennia built on the deposits of infantile development spawn from primordial anxieties belonging to the childhood of the human race. Attempting to defy the permanency of death, the ancient preoccupation with the soul's journey in its afterlife speaks to a spiritual faculty where life after death was believed to be an ontological reality. "Death itself is not extinction, is not a return to inorganic lifelessness, but the beginning of a new kind of existence which lies on the path of development to something higher."[7] Overtime, as cultures progressed, the gods and creatures of the underworld of antiquity were *condensed* into the idea of a singular superior intelligence with divine wisdom who created nature and the universe as a whole, remaining a benevolent watchful Providence as moral agent who promises heavenly rewards for goodness and punishment for evil in a supreme court of justice, either in this life or the next. Here the cunning of reason, which belongs to the imaginative faculty, deserves our heartfelt admiration and applause. Mind invents the reality it ultimately wants to inhabit. "In this way all the terrors, the sufferings and the hardships of life are destined to be obliterated."[8] Now that God is conceived to be a person, we may recapture all the intimacies and relations all children unconsciously long for with their father, especially his love, recognition, and forgiveness.

And here we have the gist of the historical beginnings of our transference unto God, which is more prized, precious, and sought after than any other possession in our collective anthropologies based on the sheer magnitude of world believers alone. Whether Freud's narrative of the origins of the mythic idea of God is correct or not, which is moot and inconsequential, he succeeds in showing a nexus between the psychological dispositions and experiences of childhood object relations and their transference onto idealized objects of identification. Although he focuses his arguments on the ubiquity of human helplessness, the need for protection, and the father-complex, he does not ignore the fact that the seed of these affections is rooted in the anaclitic attachment to the mother as the first source of fulfillment and protection against anxiety. This is later transferred to the father (or paternal surrogate) who is viewed as being stronger (whether in the family or as a cultural symbolic). Just as children

7 Ibid., p. 19.
8 Ibid.

sense and absorb the anxieties, powerlessness, feebleness, and felt vulnerability from adults, which are reinforced every day in domestic affairs as their parents and greater societies at large are beset by daily pressures, criminality, war, natural disasters, unpredictable crises, and human tragedies, this basic unrest and nervousness common to human occurrence is temporarily quelled when futurity is turned over to a higher father who holds the touchstone and grace to grant serenity and repose. Here we can say that the God construct is imbued with emotional properties historically derived from humanity's relations to both parents that carry the multiple identifications, ambivalence, fear, reverence, and yearnings for nurturance and veneration that are transferred onto an idealized fantasy principle.

Transitional phenomena and selfobject experience

Psychoanalysis since Freud has tended to focus on the God representation as embodying transitional phenomena, what D.W. Winnicott refers to as an attempt to differentiate self from (m)other inherent in the separation-individuation developmental process, self-experience versus "not-me" possession, and transitioning into personal identity and autonomy through fantasy objects (both illusory and symbolic) as a way of relating to the world separate from one's parents while at the same time developing a real relationship to primary attachment figures.[9] When we refer to transitional objects or processes, popular analogues are a child's pacifier, soft objects (like a blanket), toys, or stuffed animals that are used to provide emotional comfort during times of separation or to substitute for the mother during her absence, but they can be any object or concept that serves as psychic organizers, which allows the subject to transition into developing a psychic space of individuation, independence, and personal control mediated through fantasy. These are cultivated psychic capacities, hence developmental achievements that allow a child to create an internal life and recognize objects that are not identical with the self. Objects come to represent a state of transition from the symbiotic (fantasized) merger with the mother to a differentiated matrix of being separate and existing outside of the child's own existence and relation to the mother. These phenomena may be said to transpire within all

9 See D.W. Winnicott (1971), Ch. 1.

individuals beginning in infancy and forms the basis of imagination, thought, and creativity. In Winnicott's words,

> Transitional objects and transitional phenomena belong to the realm of illusion which is at the basis of initiation of experience. This early stage in development is made possible by the mother's special capacity for making adaptation to the needs of her infant, thus allowing the infant the illusion that what the infant creates *really exists*.
>
> This intermediate area of experience, unchallenged in respect of its belonging to inner or external (shared) reality, constitutes the greater part of the infant's experience, and throughout life is retained in the intense experiencing that belongs to the arts and to *religion*.[10]

Here illusion becomes the *basis* for the initiation of experience, hence it provides a mediatory psychic function within an intermediary space. This "intermediate area of experience" is a border concept and provides the transitionary rubric necessary for fantasy construction. In other words, illusion intervenes in its apprehension and encounter with the real. Furthermore, the relation between reality and fantasy is blurred at this stage of infantile development, where each is collapsed into an isomorphism of the other. Here we may extend this developmental capacity for fantasy formation inherent in object relations to the cultural phenomena of illusory belief in God's existence. This illusion is fostered so early in life that psychic reality is transposed on the belief that the God representation really exists as an objective corresponding fact to one's personal experience, which serves a transitional function. When this is reinforced by the religious institutions of any given society, the God posit is metamorphosed from a transitional object to a transcendent object.

Transitional objects and phenomena are psychically constructed (hence imagined) as a means to secure attachment, sustain maternal comfort and affectional bonds during absences, self-soothe, and ward off depressive anxiety and negative emotional events that besiege the psyche, as well as channel destructive fantasies. But here it is important to distinguish psychic reality and internal experience from objective

10 Ibid., p. 14, italics added.

objects that exist in-themselves separate from the subjective mind. Here we may say that the God concept as object representation is a form of inner reality superimposed on externality that is conflated to be an actual, factual extrinsic entity, the experience of which is believed to be objectively real.

We may never escape illusion, for this is the formative basis of psychic reality. It may be said that everything presented to consciousness is both perceived as the given or found world as intentional meant objects yet immediately imbued with fantasy. And whether real or not, our entire experiential world is interpreted through fantasy constellations. It is the most powerful psychic process we know of, as it is always operating outside of our consciousness and self-conscious reflection, yet it emanates from an ensuing continuum of archaic primacy steeped in unconscious desire. The ways in which we all perceive and build our own internal realities are grafted onto the found given, even if creative fantasy processes dominate only a certain sector of our subjective experiential domains. But the fantasy principle defines our lived experience at every moment—in our sleep and in our waking lives. Maintaining a micro-awareness between fantasized objects and their internal relations in this intermediary space as transitional border phenomena is what distinguishes fantasy from psychosis.

Not only does the God representation function as a compensatory defense *pace* Freud, where an idealized self-image is projected into a grandiose object transformed into a supernatural being, reflecting on the purpose or functionality of such representations as expressions of a person's internal transitional experience will likely lead to the discovery of the psychological parameters or dynamic origins such representations mean to a given individual. At most we can say is that God as an internal object is merely a construal of the psychic aggregates of imago, emotion, qualitative value, and idea rather than an objective reality. No matter what type of introspective knowledge a person claims to have about the experience of God, it does not prove nor make the God representation a real object because God does not present itself to the world as a natural phenomenon that can be known extraspectively, hence independent of any given person's claim to subjective experience. Here we may only attempt to understand how this transitional phenomenon serves a psychological purpose and refrain from making any ontological leap to divinity central to creedal systems, dogma, and doctrinal conditioning fueling particular faith practices. Here we should be reminded that belief in God is neurotic, hence a pathology, both an illusory panacea and an unnecessary continuation of our suffering.[11]

Extending the notion of transitional phenomena as transmutational internal objects that perform a particular self-regulatory function, Heinz Kohut introduced the notion of a "selfobject,"[12] which is an aspect of an object incorporated into the self, usually another person or a part or property of another person, but it can also be an inanimate object or abstract idea that carries a particular quality and performs a certain internal function of maintaining psychic continuity and cohesion of the self. To be more precise, it is the *function* that constitutes the selfobject and not the person, for it is the *experiences* evoked by such objects that allow us to analyze their internal presence and effects. For Kohut, selfobject experiences become the building blocks of psychic reality and serve to mirror the intrinsic worth and integrity of the subject as well as validate and strengthen self-structure. For the believer, the God representation becomes an evoking-sustaining-responding selfobject matrix that maintains self-organization, facilitates healing in the disruption-restoration process, and contributes to the undoing of self-injury incurred by the experiential subject when it undergoes depletion, fragmentation, or emptiness; yet it may be argued that the God posit can contribute to such pathological states as well.

11 In her classic text on psychoanalysis and religion, Ana-Maria Rizzuto (1979) details how the psychogenic belief in God is conditioned on a special object relation to a God representation that serves as a transitional object throughout the lifespan. Although she acknowledges that "God, psychologically speaking, is an illusory transitional object" (p. 177), she maintains that it is not pathological, and in fact argues for why modifications in the God representation throughout one's life can serve as a sign of health and emotional maturity (see p. 49) that is necessary for "the continuous process of psychic integration" (p. 180). But this view does not take into account how earlier transitional phenomena are sublated through psychic differentiation and self-individuation that comes with maturity of the ego that replaces illusion with an appreciation for empirical facts and logical epistemology. The failure of her argument, in my opinion, is why illusion should be promoted, developed, and strengthened rather than decathected and abandoned for truth and reality corresponding to the way we encounter the natural world (cf. Stein, 1981). Here she perpetuates a psychomythology of the potential health of illusion that serves a synthetic, symbolic, or integrative function when we may equally conclude that such an illusorily constructed representation defies objective reality and socially sustains unnecessary suffering due to cultural delusion.

12 Kohut (1971) first makes reference to "self-objects" as "objects which are themselves experienced as part of the self" (p. xiv).

In psychological terms, the selfobject the God representation serves is derivative of unconscious motivations, conflicts, and grandiose longings. It does not correspond to an objective datum, but rather to the transposed properties, qualities, and values the internalized selfobject contributes to psychic economy, which serve to maintain and restore the self from internal rupture. We may say that the God construct preserves specific selfobject transferences as intrapsychic relations to internalized imagoes that evoke and facilitate an enduring state of self-cohesion, even though self-structure is always in flux and undergoes permutations. Such transferences onto God may take on *mirroring* functions, where the sense of acceptance, recognition, and appreciation is conceived as a confirming and validating aspect of the self; or as previously discussed, *idealizing* functions, where the internal resonance states evoke perfection and ideality and conserve a sense of goodness through identification with the infallible idealized selfobject, qualities that are lacking in the subject yet vicariously fulfilled through such idealization, twinship, or merger fantasies with the divine representation.

Although theoretical language differs across the various schools of psychoanalytic thought, whether we are speaking of an exalted protective Father, compromise formations, defensive adaptations, transitional phenomena, or selfobject experiences that regulate self-cohesion and provide internal safety, feelings of worth, self-esteem, or lovability belonging to healthy narcissism, the God construct serves an internal dynamic function modeled after our earliest object representations, emotional relationships, and dissolutions with others within the greater cultural symbolic order that conditions human relations.

The imaginary, symbolic, and real

The psychosocial roles of imago and identification, language and culture, the vicissitudes of desire, and unconscious essence are the sum and substance of human phenomena. We experience the world through our senses, perceive images, encounter appearances, form relationships with others, and construct internal linkages through intentionality and fantasy, all along transpiring within our given material embodiment full of instinct and brimming emotion engrossed in and alongside a specific social environment that informs our being in the world. We attempt to craft a personal identity that is individuated yet interdependent upon family and community, absorb the larger pressures, meaning networks, and knowledge imparted by social institutions, and live out our own private desires and fantasies through imagination, creative thought, and concrete action. All these factors are operative at once within a dynamic system of ontological tensions, what Lacan refers to as psychical registers or realms of being as necessary, interconnected domains of mental functioning metaphorically envisioned as Borromean rings ⊗.

For Lacan, the human being is composed of three orders or registers of mental life, namely, the Imaginary, Symbolic, and Real.[13] The Imaginary (*imaginaire*) is the domain of images, appearances, and illusory projections of our sense of self onto our relation to others and the world, which are largely constituted through fantasy. Imaginary relations are not the way things truly are, but rather the way we experience them to be. The Symbolic (*symbolique*) is the dominion of language and culture that suffuse the wider world, what Lacan refers to as the big Other, where signifiers and semiotic meaning are superimposed through formal linguistic processes that condition the internal fabric of the subject. For Lacan, the human being is largely constituted by language as the discourse of the Other (*discours de l'Autre*), which is broadly subsumed within a social ontology that comprises the symbolic. This ontological order is causally determinative, for we cannot alter being thrown into a social matrix of speech acts and linguistic signifiers that govern the practices and rules of any society. Here the discourse of the Other always saturates human subjectivity and colors our perceptions and desires. The Real (*réel*), on the other hand, is that which is absolute, naturally given, or purely authentic, such as the notion of Being itself, yet it is foreclosed from epistemic knowledge because it is a primordial force that belongs to unconscious nature and is beyond all formal articulation and representability. This is why Lacan refers to the real as the "impossible," as it resists signification in the symbolic order and transpires outside of language. The real is the domain of lack, absence, and negation. As appearance and fantasy, the imaginary dominates our experiential subjective lives,

---

13 Lacan (1953) points out these "elementary registers whose grounding I later put forward in these terms: the symbolic, the imaginary, and the real—a distinction never previously made in psychoanalysis" (p. 95). For an overview of Lacan's epistemology, see my critique in *Underworlds: Philosophies of the Unconscious from Psychoanalysis to Metaphysics*, Ch. 4.

while the symbolic is the causal force that structures a given society by imposing itself through the laws of signification and cultural demands. In contrast, the real is merely given as pure negativity and the materiality of nature, yet all three registers interface with unconscious activity.

Where would God fall into this conceptual scheme? An imaginary mode of relating to the world is based on fictions and illusions we fashion through fantasy, and they operate as a lived sense of reality despite the fact that they are not what they appear to be nor really are in actual existence. They are purely subjective renderings of one's encounter with the world that may have some semblance of correspondence with objective aspects of reality, yet they are filtered through unconscious desire. As imaginary constellations, they serve wishful and defensive functions that present the appearance of reality when they are actually under the influence of illusion or irrealism; or in more pronounced and distorted ways, derealization, that is, when reality testing is compromised or entirely occluded. We are in constant flux through experiential states of transitioning in and out of the objective (factual) world. God representations and symbolic imagery personify the imaginary position as a fabrication of true reality. Because God is not an empirical fact, and provides no real presence of images corresponding to perceptual objects in consciousness, the God posit is the instantiation of the projective human imago—the Image of Man—mistaken to resemble an independent entity with immaterial (albeit ontological) properties condensed and displaced in the form of such images. The imaginary features of God are solely the invention of a fantasy principle grafted onto the visions of how we reckon God to be.

Any collective meaning we have of God does not come from a preordained objective fulcrum of knowledge, but rather is rooted in the symbolic order of language and signification, which is overlaid onto representations of the *imago dei* as construed in the imaginary. Because the real is the mark of delimitation, of undecidability and foreclosure— the *Ding an sich*, that is, a place of impasse, the realm of concealment—a mysterious domain that seems more magical than real as it can never be accessed, it becomes tempting to situate this so-called hidden reality of God in these intercessions of imagination. We may conclude that the Lacanian real is the proper locus of the unconscious as it can never be known nor revealed in-itself. And here the unconscious becomes its own sort of Godhead[14]—at once timeless, transcending spatial location, is asymmetrical and amorphous, and exceeds the law of non-contradiction where all things are possible regardless of contraries, opposition, or illogic. These are the very fantasies that fuel the proposition of the insistence of the real, when it may be argued that the category of the real is also an imaginary construct.

The notion of God permeates all three registers as imago, meaning, and divine hiddenness, where our desire is always the Other's desire, *objet petit a* as lack, namely, the unattainable object as our desire for God itself. Here God is the ultimate suprasignifier, the "Other of the Other," and that which lies ultimately signified somewhere in the symbolic chain, yet is in-itself unsignified, hence shrouded in metaphysical abstraction within the indiscernibility of the real. While God as the master-signifier functions as the Other of the Other, the supreme totality binding and linking the infinite battery of signifiers into a complete unity or neo-Platonic One, this is simultaneously trumped by *objet a* that lies outside the whole, a recalcitrant remainder that dwells outside the realm of the symbolic. Therefore, when Lacan says that "God is unconscious," he is highlighting the formal incompleteness of signification that resists totalization, for the informality of desire rejects integration into the whole. Yet the unconscious is ultimately the Other of the Other, and hence it becomes its own deity, divine inner truth. By attempting to appeal to

14 Cf. In *The Four Fundamental Concepts of Psycho-Analysis,* Lacan (1973) declares "the true formula of atheism is *God is unconscious*" (p. 59, italics in original). C.G. Jung (1952) also posited that God is unconscious when he refers to "the indistinguishableness of God and the unconscious" (p. 469). In *Memories, Dreams, Reflections,* he further makes God synonymous with the unconscious:

> I prefer the term 'the unconscious,' knowing that I might equally well speak of 'God' or 'daimon' if I wished to express myself in mythic language. When I do use such mythic language, I am aware that 'mana,' 'daimon,' and 'God' are synonyms for the unconscious (Jung, 1961, pp. 336–337).

But if God were unconscious, this would simply make God an impersonal force or psychic presence divorced of all omniproperties properly attributed to God by monotheistic religions. Here we are no longer referring to the same historical conception of God that dominates our world discourses. In Jung's analytical psychology, he makes the collective unconscious its own metaphysical Godhead (Mills, 2013), which I argue is a form of transpersonal supervenience or cosmic emanationism (Mills, 2014b) that conditions humanity's subjective unconscious productions. In the end, Jung (1952) concludes: "God is Reality itself and therefore—last but not least—man" (*CW* 11, par. 31). If this is the case, then the Unconscious God loses all divine value. In the words of philosopher Bryan Frances (2013), "such a God does nothing whatsoever to deserve worship, love, adoration, respect, etc. The whole idea of salvation or anything similar goes out the window. And if that's right, then religion is a complete joke" (p. 169).

something wholly other, invisible, archaic, secret, and concealed rather than revealed is to both beg the question of reality and succumb to an infinite regress. At most we can say is that the *concept* of God is experienced in the imaginary as an object representation (imago), populates the symbolic as a formal order (systems of thought/meaning), and is inaccessible in reality (lack), for the interpretation of the real devolves into a social construction determined by language and consensual definitions.

In the Lacanian scheme, it may be said that because the symbolic contains an infinite deferral of signifiers, God becomes the *infinite* yet remains unformulated, unsymbolized, and abandoned to the unknowable real, the very status of which makes God a fetish object of unrepresentability, that is, the unrepresentability of representation as such. Following this line of reasoning, God is merely a linguistic construct. Although God is presumed to exist somewhere in this semiotic mesh of signifiers, it nevertheless remains within a gnostic abyss of ineffability, much like the *via negativa* or unknown God of negative theology. This type of theoretical move institutes its own mythology as the product of its fantasy relation, for here God functions in terms of its absence rather than its presence, and therefore is offered as an antidote to lack obscured within an enigmatic unconscious vapor as divine Thing that never materializes or reveals itself, when what is palpably real is its *lack*.

The sublime object of ideology

Historically, yet systematically articulated since Marx, religion has generally been considered the most exploitive system of ideology repeatedly reinscribed throughout the concrete suprastructures, social organizations, bureaucratic machinery, and institutional authorities that control the masses through economic, cultural, and political hegemonies imposed by the ruling classes. This is why to this day and in most parts of the world, including developing democratic countries, religion (either explicitly or implicitly) dictates the way we think and largely determines the social roles people play in human interactions and communal life. God is the most sublime object of ideology because it is socio-symbolically presented historically as the ultimate (holy) object, a desired ideal truth worthy of devotional worship and sustained through false consciousness that prevents people from seeing how things truly are. As a result, people psychologically construct their own realities through elaborate fantasy systems that are superimposed on imaginary constructions of divine otherness, which are unconsciously fortified and socially maintained. This is why it is impossible to escape ideology, for no one can stand outside of the sociopolitical matrix that constitutes a given social order whether in a religious national state or not.

Philosopher and cultural critic Slavoj Žižek has spent most of his career unmasking the various ideological mechanisms, hegemonies, and fantasy scenarios at play in greater society and inflected through the divided subject that wants social stability and civic responsibility on one hand, yet at the same time to unconsciously indulge their *jouissance* through the excessive enjoyment of breaking prohibitions while simultaneously maintaining a sense of belongingness to the collective. Geoff Boucher nicely summarizes Žižek's position:

> Ideology consists of a relatively fluid set of representations that constitute social subjectivity, together with a core of communal practices that condition the unconscious libidinal investments of subjects in their political community. These libidinal investments are structured by unconscious *social fantasy* and ballast the subject's political allegiances with a kernel of *enjoyment*, which determines a relatively fixed loyalty to the institutional rituals of the political community.[15]

In other words, ideologies are necessary illusions based on collective identifications that allow for social cohesion only on the condition that certain unconscious fantasies may be entertained and enjoyed. In applying a Lacanian framework, Žižek focuses on various aspects of ideology that interpellate the subject through the imaginary, symbolic, and real registers that condition social fantasies through reinforced modes of institutionalization. We may easily see how this applies to organized religion where cultural indoctrination and free-floating signifiers issued from the symbolic and begotten in the imaginary threaten to extract or steal the subject's enjoyment to such a degree that one is compelled to drop to their knees in submission and worship the wholly big Other in order to alleviate the lack and secure a modicum of pleasure.[16] Here we may view

---

15 Boucher (2014), p. 128.
16 See *The Sublime Object of Ideology*, pp. 125–130.

religion (with its various imagery and nodal meaning structures) as homologous to a dialectical oscillation between good and bad, ideal and base, that eclipses the individual for the social fantasy whereby the human agent becomes enveloped in an ontic web of tensions assaulted by master-signifiers that have no final meaning, issued by the desire of the Other as demand and lack (God as ultra-signifier, the Absolute Master, Name-of-the Father, castrating semiotic, etc.), only to simmer in the purgatory remainder or void where *objet petit a*—that unattainable fantasy object peculiar to each person—resides.

The reflective intellect that dares to critique the ideology of the God posit that has indelibly invaded the mass psyche will inevitably encounter the paranoiac epistemological position that militates against the unconscious infighting of negation that threatens to eradicate the Ideal. Negating God is never an easy psychological maneuver for those whom have identified with and internalized this cultural signifier as an idealized psychic introject, because it means negating one's interiority as an osmotic naturalized truth, hence one's felt-visceral identity with the object of identification. As Žižek puts it, the God semiotic speaks to the subject as "I am what is lacking in you; with my devotion to you, with my sacrifice for you, I will fill you out, I will complete you."[17] Here the double reflection of the dialectic says "I am what you want, yet I am unattainable." On a psychological plane, I have witnessed patients agonize over their inner spiritual ambivalence, and even admit this of myself, as well as observed how certain destructive processes are released, such as masochistic self-flagellating, internal persecutory tendencies, and suicidal self-negation, which transpire as modes of self-punishment for abnegating the Golden Idol, the very object we crave as mortals who experience, feel, and suffer. Negating God (the sublime object of ideology) is tantamount to the most unforgivable form of obscene sacrilege, so much so that it becomes *sin*, a prohibitive sentencible by death. Here the moral of the story becomes: Never question the Ideal. This is the supreme instantiation of ideology: You are not allowed to think! Moreover, you don't want to. And if you dare, be prepared for the paranoiac "remainder" lying dormant in the gaps, not to mention the residue of melancholia that lingers beneath our traumatic anxiety distracting us from our (unconscious) loss.

17 Ibid., p. 130.

Regardless of religious identificatory variances, these inner dynamic conflicts spur further ideological battles between every part-aspect of oneself, or sub-selves, so to (metaphorically) speak, that have an endless stream of microagents with their own fantasy preferences that retaliate and dialectically protest with one another as political reactionaries; which can further lead to an internal war between hegemonies that inform split-off aspects of the self until they are brought together under some unity principle, what we may attribute to God as the unifying unifier. But this unity principle has a tough row to hoe when libidinal, destructive, and ideological mechanisms interpenetrate one another and suffuse the human condition with competing agendas. The individual is ultimately left with the anxiety of mollifying a torturous wholly other—the Holy Thing that institutes the Law, yet allows for us to bask in the ecstasies of our *jouissance*, namely, the painful realm of excess where a perverse enjoyment occurs when we transgress our own moral prohibitions (ones so-called instituted by God), only to be left with self-reproach, insatiability with no meal, and a foreclosure of certainty, for our object of desire is unknowable and inaccessible, as it is unconsciously barred and lies outside the scope of symbolic articulation. No wonder why humanity is neurotic.

Interpassivity and illusions without owners

In depicting how the pleasure principle operates in culture, Robert Pfaller argues that illusions with no proper owner or author largely structure the way our individual and social practices are defined, and hence determine how we think and behave without us being properly aware of them as such. This cultural phenomenon assumes that illusions exist independently of those who carry them, yet they are simultaneously the disavowed illusions of others the subject unconsciously identifies with. In other words, the masses live in a fantasy world fashioned for them by anonymous others that have no discernible source.

Media, Hollywood, politicians, the church, the ideological State apparatus—all function in ways to solidify illusions we do not question and live by everyday. Moreover, we desire and expect them to, and do not want them to disappear. For example, television, online forums, and social media have replaced respectable journalism and peer-reviewed newspapers as credible sources of news, when they are largely epistemologically corrupt and disseminate inaccurate information that is accepted at face value by a mindless public; film and movie producers fulfill the fantasies of viewers by depicting totally fabricated and unrealistic situations as "really real;" church and state have their own propaganda machines, whether this be informing the congregation on how to get into heaven, or the citizenry on how wonderful their government serves the polis, while all along engaging in pedophilic cover-ups and illegal back-door shenanigans; and politicians will say anything to get a vote by attempting to portray themselves in totally inauthentic and dishonest ways simply because that is what they think is expected of them by society. Here the populace become like Pavlovian dogs waiting for the bell to ring, where they can hardly wait to have their fair trade coffee furnished by (the chimera of) ethical capitalism, or get home to watch their favorite television "reality" series, attend sporting events, and perform their daily rituals, such as playing with their electronic devices, download a new apt, piddle around while surfing the Internet or on social media, or waiting for that next text-message or email to arrive, as though life depends upon that next information bite. These routine distractions are laced with illusions yet we know they are not entirely what they claim to be; but the fantasy itself carries with it a modicum of enjoyment we immerse ourselves in despite knowing otherwise.

Within myriad contexts, such as in popular culture, mass media, and religion, masses act in compliance with such illusions despite knowing better, as if society is supposed to run in a certain way that is immune from truth, alterity, and the existential duty to think critically about what one experiences. The mantra "Yes, I know, but still ..." encapsulates this form of disavowal, where knowledge is suspended for the illusion of otherwise. The scriptures of ideology tell them what to think, how to act, what to say and do, and relieve them of their onus for which they passively acquiesce through blind obedience and consumer fetishism. Here people become conditioned sheep in the meadow who interpassively assign over any personal powers of decision-making to an abstract power that structures their lives through hegemonic social fantasies that are unconsciously enacted as though they are staged for a virtual audience. In interpassivity,[18] we attribute to the mythical other any requirement we may have to participate in or adopt through forms of displacement. Others and objects are assigned the role of the active participant while

18 See Pfaller (2014), pp. 17–34.

the interpassive subject merely observes its own delegated enjoyment through being represented by something or someone else. Yet interpassivity that is initially thought to be merely subjective, that is, confined to the idiosyncratic experiences of the individual, is in fact upheld by *objective illusions*: others apart from actors must believe in these illusions, and such realizations function as substitutions for the subject's own disavowed and displaced interiority.

Let us apply this concept of illusions without owners to obsessional religious actions. Religious doctrines and rituals, regardless of the type of religion, have always been others' convictions without having been our own. They are the Other's desire superimposed on the populace of any society, in which any culture involuntarily adopts as transcendental illusions that one never really thinks about critically until they reach the age of reason, yet they form the cultural edifice and social fabric of a given set of expectations one is coerced into believing because almost everyone around them thinks and acts in this manner. This is most salient in childhood where questioning adult authority is not permitted without suffering certain consequences. The belief in God is always *belief in the Other's belief* in its existence, and faith is always the entanglement and acceptance of the idea of God's existence that is given over by the literal or symbolic Other as social illusion. In other words, one never stops to think; rather they just conform to social expectation, including adopting various sectarian beliefs and practices as a "sacred seriousness" that sustains the suspension of having to think. In Pfaller's words, *"whenever sacred seriousness reigns, there must be a denied illusion that is kept suspended.* Sacred seriousness is a sign indicating the presence of an illusion of the other. It is its symptom."[19] Here we may observe a key ingredient in ideology: unreflective belief (in the Other's illusions) is elevated to the realm of faith as the suspension of belief for the illusion itself. No longer capable of owning any responsibility for one's own thoughts, illusions without authors become an objective social truth. There is always a deferral to some other source, some other signifier that becomes the authority which justifies the belief or faith in the idea itself. Something or someone else is always accredited to be the reason why we think and behave the way we do, even the illusion itself.

19 Ibid., p. 100, italics in original.

This insight is illuminated by observing acts of obsessive-compulsive religious sacraments whereby most ordinary votaries have no clue what the rituals actually mean or signify, as they are concealed through a collective appearance of meaning the typical worshiper lacks any understanding of whatsoever. People just go through the motions: the compelled act is merely a displacement or substitution of what the act is supposed to symbolize despite the fact that the devotee does not truly understand what the rite accomplishes other than deferring or assuaging a free floating anxiety that has no locus or owner. The compulsion itself is merely in response to generated anxiety without a discernable source. Pfaller concludes that the obsessional ceremonial rituals of religious actions are intensified when displacement or substitution take the form of a miniaturization as the symbolic act, such as through prayer, reciting scripture, rehearsing a verse, touching a rosary or crucifix, and so on, when these manifest nonsense practices are designed to imprison subjects in the illusion of ownerless others revolving around imaginative fantasies without a discernable image. Here God becomes that imageless image.

Freud famously showed how these obsessional displacements onto substitute acts and ancillary compulsions serve to distance the subject further away from the real issue, namely, that of any substantive justification for the obsessional ritual itself, when in reality it is merely a "displacement from the actual, important thing on to a small one which takes its place... so that the petty ceremonials of religious practice gradually become the essential thing and push aside the underlying thoughts"[20] associated with its originating purpose. The miniature symbolic displacements onto something else as a form of distancing from the real significance of the object in question allows much of humanity a reprieve from justifying their illogic through cultural practices that promote such illusions to flourish and thrive as an appeal to custom. We may especially observe this notion of displaced symbolic miniaturization in reformed religious rituals and beliefs, where countless denominations offer their own theological reformations and reinterpretations of scripture, church structure, revamped ceremonials, modified belief systems, and so on that act as a displacement of psychical values in the service of compromise functions.

In Freud's view, when neurosis as individual religiosity is supplanted for a collective (universal) obsessional neurosis that appeals to

20 Freud (1907), p. 126.

the narcissism of minor differences, as seen in all the various sects and reformed congregations and factions that pride themselves on reformulated identities, this re-microstructuralization speaks to the nature of institutionalized social displacement. Here reformed belief and praxis are the replacement of original fundamental values that define a particular religion in the guise of its own self-deluded notion that it is the original thing, when in fact it is merely the appearance of historical substitutions. Furthermore, when obsessionality over minor differences in reformed beliefs that restructure religious rites becomes the locus of identity, we are carried further and further away into renegade illusion.

Pfaller perspicaciously points out that societies have a certain affective dependency on their illusions to the degree that their culled enjoyment makes it a *need*. This need intensifies emotional ties to the illusion, but of an ambivalent nature. When one is not free of their emotional dependency on an illusion, it may serve as a quasi-functional addiction to repetition compulsion, the very sum and substance of obsessional neurosis sustained by perpetuating substitute activities, which temporarily serve to neutralize ambivalent internal prohibitions that are exteriorized onto a Deity. Here the God introject becomes the substitute (misrecognized) source of external prohibition as divine law, one that serves as a placeholder for stifling inner impulse and natural desire on the one hand, and instituting fear and punishment fantasies on the other. Yet this always leaves residual internal conflict and ambivalence, for many sacrifices are made unconsciously. The pious are plagued by an unconscious sense of guilt due to their dispositional sin they aver to deny, as well as the compulsion to show penance and make reparation for (fantasized) transgressions against their own interiority they mistakenly attribute to an extrinsic omnipotent agent they themselves have manufactured in their minds. Pfaller nicely recapitulates Freud's treatise on the psychological processes of religious life:

> if religious practices, like obsessive actions, are compromise formations, and thus originate in a defensive conflict, then ambivalence is at the beginning of religious activity and obsessional neurosis. This corresponds with the elevated 'sacred seriousness' of the former and the compulsive character of the latter. Without ambivalence, there would be no sacred seriousness and no religion.[21]

---

21 Pfaller (2014), p. 130.

Here ambivalence generates the engine of displacement as a series of defer-
rals transposed onto miniaturizing activity, namely, telescoping minimizing
efforts at reduction by focusing on other details rather than the original
matter at hand. In effect, the interpassive subject as spectator to the Other's
illusions constantly refashions its (disowned) ambivalent internal discord
through refined ruminations and nuanced activities directed toward restriction and curtailment that serve as a symptomatic substitute for focusing on
one's original psychogenic conflicts, which are dislocated onto God.

Pfaller notes that "suspended illusions form a culture's pleasure
principle,"[22] which inadvertently lead to unhappiness caused by these
various illusions themselves. In effect, displacements can only go so far:
substitutions are never the real thing, and they can only be suspended so
long before the psyche is confronted with its subverted operations of substitution, the meaninglessness of obsessional deferral, and deceptive truth that
bears no genuine article. The practice of prayer and religious ceremony is a
good example of miniaturized displacement as the pressing rumination on
details that lose sight of the original issue: here what is substituted is an original gratification that must be denied and converted into its opposite via
disavowal, restriction, and prohibition as a form of undoing original desire,
which is then relocated on miniaturized prescriptive actions as if they are the
most important thing. As Freud points out: these "ceremonials are concerned
with the small actions of daily life and are expressed in foolish regulations
and restrictions in connection with them."[23] Here we may observe the overdetermined forces of compromise formation where a certain pleasure is
derived from the substitute act connected to the original repressed object of
desire: prayer mitigates anxiety and keeps one connected to the mental
object, but it simultaneously produces obsessional worry that leads to habit-
ual rituals designed to prolong anxiety and ambivalence as a by-product of
repetition compulsion. Prayer or going to synagogue/temple/church/mosque
becomes an obligation or duty one must do rather than what one really wants
to do, hence ensuring the continuance of such ambivalence despite that they
may feel good in doing so. Although we may say that suspended illusions of
others without proper owners provide the basis of a culture's pleasure principle, they are ultimately unsatisfactory as they are unsatisfying. Illusions
never deliver: they are mere facades people feel impelled to construct and

22 Ibid., p. 137.
23 Freud (1907), p. 125.

engage in through the persona of maintaining social appearances while chasing pleasure. World cultures that are incapable of recognizing their own illusions only lead to the perpetuation of ignorance and displeasure.

God as attachment figure

One of the most celebrated findings in contemporary psychological research is the centrality of attachment in human development.[24] Attachment is a universal biosocial instinct influenced by the contingencies of the maternal environment comprising innate motivations to procure safety via proximity to selected love objects during early childhood, most often one's parents or their surrogates. Object attachment is a unique and special form of affectional bond to a select few identified caregivers and is characterized as a process of emotional connection based upon affective ties, relational longings, and primary identifications with love objects. Attachment processes are normative in every human culture, are highly influential on neurological development and the regulatory system, right hemisphere brain lateralization, affect regulation, and the development of personality.[25]

Attachment patterns become organized at the representational and behavioral levels. Representational models or schemas of self and others are constructed and serve to facilitate internal cohesion of the self, judge the

24 Inspired by the pioneering work of John Bowlby and Mary Ainsworth, there has been a spate of research in infant observation, child development, cognitive and social psychology, evolutionary biology, neuroscience, psychopathology, clinical assessment, psychotherapy, and ethnology that support attachment theory as a viable explanatory model of human development. Contemporary researchers such as Mary Main, Judith Solomon, Carol George, Erik Hesse, Peter Fonagy, Mary Target, Karlen Lyons-Ruth, Beatrice Beebe, Alan Shore, and Arietta Slade are just a few notable academics and clinicians who have made substantial contributions in this area (see Mills, 2005 and Cassidy and Shaver, 1999 for an overview).

25 Contemporary attachment theory is premised on developmental science and the outgrowth and extensions of the seminal work of John Bowlby. Bowlby's classical model of attachment rests on the interrelatedness of three main constructs: (1) Activation of the attachment behavioral system; (2) The role of self and object representations; and (3) Strategies at defensive exclusion. For the field of developmental psychology, the attachment system is an evolutionarily informed process that motivates and regulates internal goal-directed behaviors and intentions aimed to promote and procure proximity to love objects for the purpose of protection from encroaching threats that may disrupt desired levels of security. A variety of internal and external conditions may affect the system including perceived alterations in the environment as well as the dispositions and behaviors of attachment figures, which leads to a dynamic tension between the mother's and infant's individual needs. Low activation levels are correlated with positive internal states and feelings of safety, while high activation levels are mobilized during the presence of intense negative affect, anxiety, alarm, fear, or dread. When the attachment figure is perceived as being unavailable or inconsistent, apprehension, anger, and sadness are typical accompanying emotional reactions.

accessibility and willingness of figures to provide functions of protection, warmth, and care, and to guide future appraisals and goal-directed behavior. Beginning in infancy, we develop such internal working models of self and others that are both positive and negative in content and form. Healthy representations are equated with feelings of lovability and security in the child, while dysfunctional representations proliferate when the attachment figure is perceived negatively, which leads to various defensive exclusions or strategies that allow the child to cope with negativity, intrusiveness, and incongruity that jeopardizes one's psychological sense of safety.

Lee Kirkpatrick argues that the idea of God and other deities are perceived by believers as attachment figures; that experiential claims of having a relationship with God meet all the defining criteria of attachment relationships; and that these perceived relationships psychologically function as real attachments.[26] Across sample populations, these normative characteristics or properties correspond to (a) feelings of love, acceptance, and nurturance; (b) images of God as beneficent, kind, and protective; (c) mirrors the emotional bond that accompanies healthy and secure connections akin to the infant-mother dyad; and (d) can resemble a hybrid form of both genders reflective of genuine attachment processes. Here God becomes a haven for safety, a secure base to gravitate toward, and that the cultivation of certain religious attitudes, perceptions, and actions are a means of enhancing proximity and contact with God. Furthermore, when people have experienced developmental trauma, insecure attachment histories, separation, severe stress, crisis, parental unavailability, and loss, they are also likely to view the God introject as a compensatory, surrogate attachment figure. The overall conclusions of empirical studies that support these findings provide evidence that a person's relatedness to a God object is based on naturalized foundations.

Personality development is predicated on human relatedness, without which the self would not exist. This necessarily requires a process of internalization and introjection of the Other that affects psychic structure and its unconsciously informed organizing principles that transpire within a relational ontology. But what happens if a child views the God introject as an ambivalent (if not malevolent) attachment figure? As noted previously, God by definition is a paranoiac presence by virtue of its purported omniperfections. The very notion of an all-powerful being that sees what

---

26 Kirkpatrick (1999), p. 804.

you are doing at all times, knows your thoughts, judges your worth, and can be cruel at whim, is enough to terrify anyone let alone a child. Elaborate theological rationalizations for evil and random suffering in the world are not cognized or entertained by the unassuming mind of a child; they are unreflectively accepted as things that happen to others and *can happen* to oneself. Depending upon how the attachment system develops, the God introject can influence the formation of structural deficits of the self due to the incorporation, amalgamation, and build-up over time of negatively internalized experiences that are attributed to God as an attachment figure.

When religious upbringing and/or cultural inculcation is sufficiently focused on people's potential for transgression, non-virtuous behaviors, prohibitions, punishment, and sin, it becomes predictable how this will impact on disturbances in self-representation, cohesive self-states, affect regulation, self-integrity, and the capacity for secure object relationships. In my clinical work with people who have attachment deficits, I have observed how toxic introjects can leave unabated unconscious conflicts that perpetuate the structural disfiguration of the self.[27] When negative introjects become too dangerous or menacing, these inner experiences are often dissociated and become encoded and organized on subsymbolic levels of representation dominated by emotional schemata and unconscious fantasy constellations. Toxic and parasitic introjects are acquired during emotionally charged situations (such as fear), which are highly specified and selective experiences of psychic reality that are mnemonically encoded, unconsciously organized, and dominated by the fixed presentation of negativity that coalesce on various levels of representational schemata. They often transpire during the sensory-motor and preoperational stages of cognitive development, are registered and organized through sensory-somatic processes, cluster into affective schemas, and often predate the formal acquisition of language. Because of their prelinguistic acquisition and emotional organization, they are largely compartmentalized and segregated from linguistic intervention.

Children do not think in terms of sophisticated narratives, nor do they have the facility for actualizing advanced levels of metacognition where abstraction, symbolism, allegory, myth, and metaphor signify complex emotional phenomena expressed through linguistic informational meta-representations. Rather they are most susceptible to influence by basic

---

27 I provide extensive case studies and clinical vignettes in my book, *Treating Attachment Pathology.*

pleas to emotion where concrete experiences acquire affective significance and prereflective semiotic meaning. If the God introject is tinged with paranoia by virtue of the omniproperties God is purported to possess, which is precisely what is communicated to children or insinuated when God is said to be a supreme being and creator of the universe, then a logical consequence is that it potentially predisposes a child to feel insecurity in attachment relationships where God is held to be the exemplar model. In isolation, it is likely these experiences only affect a person in a mild manner, as anxiety and ambivalence are part of the normal course of events in psychosocial development; however, those who come from hyperreligious environments may be more vulnerable to the negative aftermath of religious indoctrination, which can contaminate unconscious fantasy systems that inform structuralization processes necessary to the development of the self. When there is a lack of higher-order defenses in a child, the content of toxic introjects may be concretely absorbed as unadulterated truth and registered as inexpressible, preformulated trauma that is not acknowledged as such. Unconsciously, the impact of such developmental traumas are dissociated, affectively filtered, and somatically converted on unconscious symbolic levels so that the conscious mind is afforded a respite from the ramifications of such self-awareness. Here the unsavory impact of these microdynamics are not formulated in conscious awareness, and hence remain sequestered as prereflective unconscious experience, yet their resonances are felt within the deep structural interior of the soul.

When we speak of the development of the attachment system in relation to one's parents or primary caregivers, the field of psychoanalysis has cogently shown that regardless of individual or cultural differences we must assume in all children a fundamental ambivalent fulcrum where both good and bad experiences are encoded during the course of normative development. It is psychologically impossible for any child under any developmental condition of upbringing in a family or social milieu not to have negative experiences in relation to their parents; we only hope that the good outweighs the bad and that there is at least a good-enough familial environment that paves the way toward subjective happiness and social adjustment. These ambivalent attachment patterns (even if constricted to fantasy life) naturally extend toward the God posit as an imaginary object relation. Here the God object carries both idealized and fearsome qualities, that is, psychological properties that are at once projected and assumed based on our unconscious apprehension of what God represents to humanity, a collective symbolic that no child can elude in one's education and exposure to the social world.

The immorality of fostering illusions in childhood

The publically sanctioned promulgation of myths, folklore, fairy tales, and legends are part of every culture and is subliminally responsible (at least proportionally) for engendering certain illusions in childhood. Notwithstanding the various lessons such parables or allegories intend to convey, they deceptively portray fictions as real to an immature mind. In mythoi and folktales, however, children are readily told that such things are only stories designed to deliver certain messages or teachings, while discourse on God is not. In fact, children are invited (even encouraged) to enter into a world of make-believe and asked to pretend that such things are real in order to learn something important, as are adults when they read fiction or watch a movie for entertainment or pleasure.[28] Our inner relation to such cultural phenomena has profound emotional, moral, and aesthetic value to the point that they inform our identifications and the social mores of any given society. But when it comes to the subject of

28 Philosopher Kendall Walton (1978a, b) has argued that engaging fiction is a form of pretending or game of make-believe where the fictional story is taken as truth because it preys upon and draws in the emotional lives of the spectator. Robin Le Poidevin (1996) has elaborated (in a tasteful way devoid of parody) upon how this applies to the God construct and how society engages in a collective game of make-believe that carries instrumental psychological benefits. He states:

> We make-believe that there is a God, by reciting, in the context of the game, a statement of belief. We listen to what make-believedly are accounts of the activities of God and his people, and we pretend to worship and address prayers to that God. In Walton's terms we locate ourselves in that fictional world, and in so doing we allow ourselves to become emotionally involved, to the extent that a religious service is capable of being an intense experience. The immediate object of our emotions is the fictional God, but there is a wider object, and that is the collection of real individuals in our lives. In the game of make-believe (for example, the Christian one), we are presented with a series of dramatic images: an all-powerful creator, who is able to judge our moral worth, to forgive us or to condemn, who appears on Earth in human form and who willingly allows himself to be put to death. What remains, when the game of make-believe is over, is an awareness of our responsibilities for ourselves and others, of the need to pursue spiritual goals, and so on. (p. 119)

The problem with this account is that true belief cannot entertain a fictional world of this kind as it would trivialize God's reality if faith and worship were merely a game of make-believe that imitates something that is supposed to be real. Religious practices would lose all significance if they were not believed to be reflective of or correspond to God's actuality and truth in existence, and hence would pervert the very fundamental tenets of any religion that takes God's ontology as given. In fact, it is only on the condition that belief is not make-believe that it can be taken seriously, or the game or story would end, and devotional practices would have been abandoned long ago.

God and theistic religion, no such practice applies. God is not portrayed as fictional or a subject of play, but rather as a real entity, force, and presence that has direct influence over others and the world including the child who is being brainwashed to believe in such untruths.[29] Here we may say that all of humanity is gaslighted by disorientation and abuse of truth and reason.

When parents and authority figures (e.g., family members, caregivers, educators, clergy, the church-state) see the uncertainty and worry in the eyes and concerns of young children, often their first instinct is to mollify the fear itself by fabricating a story or uttering soothing reassurances that insulate them from the cold hard facts about reality. We may call this *the event*—at once a crucible as both a container and ordeal. Based in dutiful concern for the child's emotional safety, and often viewed as an act of sympathy, in the event of propitiating a child's anxiety we institute a primal *lie*. This lie has cumbersome unconscious ramifications, for it stimulates fantasy processes that may not have otherwise been activated. Adults know the truth of uncertainty and ambiguity, where knowledge is suspended or impassable, and they are often uncomfortable with the intensity of children's anxieties, which they wish to soothe by manufacturing a convenient fable that alleviates all party's discomfort with the situation. While understandably well-intentioned, it may not be inappropriate to reproach this practice as being immoral for fostering illusions in childhood. The psychological reverberations are felt throughout a person's entire life, especially if they bring a modicum of psychic pain.

It is a human propensity to avoid conflict as well as create it. Most people cannot bear witness to the horror of unextinguished helplessness in a child's face, which we immediately identify with as our own through empathy, something dissociated and repressed from our childhoods, so we invent a lie to pacify this primordial anxiety we too felt and wished were removed from our early developmental experiences of the world. A certain emotional immediacy is accentuated and attached to the God introject that forms in response to the event, an affective colorization that germinates alongside the false idea that is inserted by the outside world. The intrusiveness of the event is an initiation that carries a psychological weight unlike no other, as it is our first encounter with a fantasy object superimposed by powerful others and offered as the truth of all reality,

---

29 At least with cartoons and comic books, they know it's not true.

when it is in fact an illusion that is designed to deceive a child by establishing a distortion of known facts, hence the institution of a lie as false consciousness. This false consciousness not only becomes the ideological and emotional bedrock attached to the God introject, it further inhibits a child from later being able to judge the truth of the matter for what it really is due to the internal resistances and defensive systems that are forged in early life, which preserve the integrity of the fantasy object.

In order to illustrate how the God introject has pernicious consequences on psychic organization, I wish to turn our attention to the case of Andrea, a characterologically depressed, body-dysmorphic, eating-disordered adolescent. Andrea was subjected to many developmental traumas at the hands of her primary attachment figures, including her mother, father, and aunt. She was raised in a Catholic home environment, but was subjected to many excessive superstitions, fears, and threats of punishment from God by her mother and aunt who were fundamentalist Christian converts. The patient was told from the age of four onward that the Devil exists and looks for souls to possess, that God reads her mind at all times and knows all of her impure thoughts, and that He will eventually punish her for all her sins. As a result, she was terrified as a child, grew up thinking she was innately bad and evil, developed a clingy-dependent insecure attachment to her mother, was phobic of anyone and any situation outside of her immediate home environment, and subsequently became paranoid, obsessional, and depressed during her latency years, only to lead to a suicide attempt when she was 16. Andrea had developed many rituals to keep evil spirits away at night, such as surrounding her room with bibles, crucifixes, candles, and religious paraphernalia, but to no avail. Her obsessive-compulsive rituals, prayers, ruminations, and internal methods of warding off evil possession and punishment had led to profound suffering to the point that her belief system concerning the nature and question of God was arguably delusional.

It is generally uncontested that the abuse of any teachings hurt people. Psychoanalysts are not neutral when it comes to valuation practices, despite aspiring to observe a neutrality or indifference (*Indiferenz*) when presented with patient material under the rule of analysis. In witnessing Andrea's suffering, I passed a value judgment in determining that the Judeo-Christian principles that were inculcated in her, whether accurate or not, were a destructive force in her psyche that needed to be exorcized.

In my view, my *patiens* largely suffered from the nefarious, maiming elements and insidious invasions of the *event* that her mother and aunt afflicted on her psyche at a tender age: these were damaging, emotionally charged invariants that were internalized as parasitic introjects, mnemonically imprinted, and rigidly laid down within the deep structural configurations of her unconscious mind. She acquired her paranoiac epistemology during the preoperational phase of cognitive development years before she was neurologically capable of developing her capacity for critical thinking, which had since remained dominated by austere emotional schemata and unconscious fantasy systems that were recalcitrant to the intervening mediation of reason.

After initially working with Andrea without questioning her religious beliefs, instead focusing on her experience of them and the pernicious impact they had produced on her adjustment, I decided to address the logical premises and propositions of what she actually thought about God in order to bring them into critical therapeutic dialogue with the healthier portions of her ego. Although we spent several sessions discussing various aspects of her religious beliefs and their negative consequential effects, I will never forget my intervention when she told me that she believed in the Immaculate Conception and Annunciation to the Blessed Virgin Mary. "Ah, a virgin impregnated by a ghost. Sounds delusional to me" I replied. She paused in disbelief then immediately burst out laughing, and then said how ridiculous it was that anyone could think such a thing, including herself.

This session opened up a critical space for exploring the conditioned aspects of her faith and irrational fears based on the uncritical acceptance of religious dogma, which had pervaded her senses as paranoiac knowledge due to the ominous threat of punishment, guilt inducement, shame, and persecutory fears ingrained by her family members. We came to understand how her early affective experiences fueling her paranoid fantasies of persecution and possession were encoded as "emotional truths" that she as a young child could not possibly combat due to the toxic introjectory power of internalization. Although I cannot go into every detail of this case here, suffice it to say that this decision to critically engage the grounds and justifications of her propositional attitudes and beliefs led to drastic changes in her adaptation and social functioning. I am still left with self-reproach in thinking that if I had only challenged her illusions and conditioned religious distortions sooner, I may have spared her from extra suffering.

A recalcitrant cultural neurosis

The "fairy tales of religion" Freud castigates with disdain is chiefly due to the assault on reason he cannot support, where an appeal to tradition or custom, divine revelation, the historical reiteration of ancestral teachings and dogma, and uncritical thinking by the masses remains inexcusable when a *Credo quia absurdum* is the fulcrum justifying belief. An interesting social prohibition we observe historically is how it is forbidden to question God's existence, let alone the religious precepts associated with it, a phenomenon we may still observe today in non-democratic and developing countries where people are imprisoned and even put to death for so-called heresy. And this is certainly prevalent in Muslim countries.[30] This social fact broadcasts the *insecurity* of its claim to authentic truth, for if it were genuine there would be no need to suppress dissent because all the data one would need to deduce for themselves to determine the verity of religious doctrine would be transparent, for only a "fool hath said in his heart, *There is no God*".[31]

Freud highlights that such beliefs are illusory because wish-fulfillment speaks to their motivations absent of any verification principle. But we ultimately believe in what we want to believe in because that which is most sacred in our fantasy lives is beyond the need for evidence, beyond rationality itself—in Tertullian's words, "it must be believed, because it is absurd."[32] These pretenses are enchantments qua enactments of self-deception, Sartrean bad faith (*mauvaise foi*), or *pretendings* humanity is inclined to perpetuate through systematic indoctrination nurtured by unconscious resistances that have become culturally and politically solidified, which largely carry practical and utilitarian value. Consider the commandments against murder, theft, adultery, and envy, just to name a few. These mandates were invented to serve a pragmatic purpose safeguarding material and emotional safety for those living in communal proximity to one another, and to curb the repetition of resentment, hostility, and violence man would perpetrate against one another if there were no such prohibitions, which is the backbone of social justice and punishment for

---

30 Currently, there are at least seven nations, many with developing economies under Islamic political rule, who subject atheists to state executions. According to the report, "Freedom of Thought 2012," by the International Humanist and Ethical Union (IHEU), these countries include: Afghanistan, Iran, Sudan, Pakistan, Saudi Arabia, Maldives, and Mauritania (see Evans, 2012).

31 (Psalm 14:1; 53:1).

32 Tertullian, *De Carne Christi*, 5. Cf. Freud (1927), p. 28, fn.1.

criminal transgressions. With no external constraints or impositions placed on human nature by society, certain segments of the human race would surely mistreat, exploit, pillage, hurt, and kill others, hence perpetuating chaos and cycles of revenge and helplessness, further jeopardizing a sense of domestic harmony and social balance crucial to the equilibrium of civilization. This occurs every day in every society. With large numbers of the world population currently bathing in rage, aggression, poverty, criminality, social injustice, war, and daily adversity, what would it be like without divine decree? But this decree is clearly of human origin, as is currently reflected in the fact that no social prohibitions exalted in status emanating from divine command have made much difference in dissuading the proliferation and tenacity of psychopathology in the masses. Our communal existence is still saturated with neurosis and *pathos* with or without God.

Freud concludes that by identifying with the collective (universal) neurosis of religion, with its obsessional restrictions and wishful illusions coupled with disavowal, the individual believer is spared the encumbrance of erecting a personal neurosis that most people cannot escape from. The acceptance of the collective illusion is in fact a displacement of neurotic anxiety that is channeled through consensual cultural belief (or faith) encouraged by masses. By today's standards, psychological science would contend that these motivations facilitate and answer to the need for affect regulation stemming from primordial anxieties that threaten our functional adaptation to society. Yet these bonds of affection tied to religious teachings are recalcitrant and are not likely to be given up so easily for rational arguments alone. Perhaps this cultural conditioning speaks to the memetic evolutionary processes that underlie the need for the human species to construct a fantasized (ideal) universe in order to psychologically survive in an impersonal (real) universe that has no agency or intentionality, nor does it owe us anything. Unlike a bargain with fate or a pact with a presumptive God, we are entitled to nothing from life, let alone divine comfort or redemption. Yet religious education that is globally entrenched fortifies the collective neurosis that sustains these delimitations from actualizing pure reason. These are the material fantasies of the universal psyche pining for More than what we are dealt by the frosty hands of nature. Logos (λόγος) speaks another truth, one that has no veils, pretenses, or fairy tale illusions, only a rational appeal to our modern intellect. Yet reason is hardly gratifying by itself. Like the extant world, it is concerned with facts and critique: it merely *is*. That is why the fantasy principle intervenes on human reason and constructs a savory alternative to rational inquiry, what we typically call faith. Here we may hear the voice of Luther—*die Hure Vernunft*: "reason is the whore of humanity,"[33] the number one enemy of faith. But as Freud would say, "Men cannot remain children forever."[34] We must all grow up and face life on its own terms.

On the psychodynamics of the God introject

From a psychological standpoint, God is the cultural projection of our own fantasies of grandiosity onto an ideal and infallible object that has unlimited power to create and destroy. This is the basis of all monotheisms that influence the social teachings of organized religion. Taken to the extreme, the story goes, organized religion can enslave people in superstition and ignorance, and thus engender unnecessary sorrow: only through its renunciation can humankind truly be liberated. These are the views of the "new atheists" who recapitulate a psychoanalytic sensibility. Anthony Grayling summarizes the matter succinctly:

> The major reason for the continuance of religious belief in a world which might otherwise have long moved beyond it, is indoctrination of children before they reach the age of reason, together with all or some combination of social pressure to conform, social reinforcement of religious institutions and traditions, emotion, and (it has to be said) ignorance—of science, of psychology, of history in general, and of the history and actual doctrines of religions themselves.[35]

Theistic creed turns people and society into fearful, neurotic, submissive beings who suffer extra guilt and mental agony based on conflicted childhood dependency yearnings that have not been appropriately sublimated. Freud argues that we need to dispense with such illusions because it curtails existential possibilities for personal growth that spring from the natural cultivation of mature consciousness. Furthermore, society is truncated by perpetuating such infantilism that serves to imprison people in futility and naïveté, which affects people's overall adjustment and social

---

33 This quotation is attributed to Martin Luther by E. M. Cioran (1998) in *The Temptation to Exist*. Also see Luther (1546), pp. 374–375.
34 *The Future of an Illusion*, p. 49.
35 *The God Argument*, p. 13.

productivity. To paraphrase Daniel Dennett, it's time for the spell to be broken.

Freud (as well as contemporary atheists) passes the value judgment that society would be better off accepting discernible truths based on scientific facts and by abnegating illusory desires, superstitious paranoia, and neurotic dispositions that are the deposit of early anxieties that are inculcated in childhood. Given that these belief systems are usually laid down very early in life and reinforced by familial upbringing and institutional indoctrination, where limited cognitive brain development is only able to grasp the concrete and preconceptual operations of constructs and their functional consequences,[36] it is not surprising that these compartmentalized teachings become crystallized into entrenched emotional-fantasy structures devoid of capacities for hypothetico-deductive reasoning or abstract logical thought. The affective impact on a young mind is particularly formative and forceful in establishing a dominant fantasy system intractable to later critical analysis precisely because it has such an emotional resonance.

We may speculate how these early doctrinal experiences tap into unconscious anxieties that are both frightful and compensatory; that is, they are rooted in a basic paranoiac reactionary defense designed to combat the terror of an external omnipotent source that threatens to invade the incipient mind. In psychoanalysis, we refer to this as projective identification.[37] The nascent self or ego splits-off various portions of its internal fantasy structure and places it in the mental object(s) of its projection, which it then proceeds to identify with and (re)incorporate back into its internal constitution. The process of externalization is always followed by reinternalization, insofar as every act of splitting and projection leads to an identification and reintrojection of its original

---

36 According to Piaget, and generally espoused by contemporary cognitive-developmental psychology, children engage in naïve cognition dominated by "preoperational" thinking; thus they are unable to think critically or rationally synthesize causal attributions and belief systems that an adolescent or adult would be able to perform under normatively adequate developmental circumstances. Hence, they become conditioned to believe in God based on cultural teachings, ideology, and emotional prejudices.

37 This term was described by Melanie Klein (1946) as a process of discharging certain portions of the ego *into* an external object, the aim of which is to control and consume certain aspects of the object's contents in order to make it part of the ego's own internal organization. For Klein, the ego exists at birth and is plagued by anxieties characteristic of psychosis, which it attempts to fend off and regulate through primary defensive maneuvers of splitting, projection, and introjection, the essential building blocks of object relations and psychic structure.

content displaced through fantasy, although the original content may be modified as reconstruction. Projective identification ensures that the intrapsychic processes that govern mental functioning are transforming as they are transformative: every projective act leads to an internal redistribution of psychic functions through differentiation, modification, and reorganization as mental objects are reappropriated and reconstituted through the dynamics of reincorporation. In fact, this process, as we have said, originally begins with the infant's relation to its mother, not the father, as she is the primary love object for both sexes and is the most significant attachment figure in infancy.[38] As the child matures, its relations to its objects (people) are transferred from the parents to others within its communal milieu, and eventually onto God as a social construction.

In the case of the God introject, the mental object produces paranoiac anxiety, as well as depressive guilt, which must be neutralized by unconsciously altering the fantasy system. For some people the God introject may remain an anxious, persecutory, or depleting internal presence, or it may be transfigured as an ideal object; however, there is likely to be a dialectical vacillation between the positive and negative valences the introject introduces into psychic economy. A particular division occurs when psychic agency splits the mental object into an ideal pole, where it becomes compartmentalized and dissociated from the rational faculty in favor of sustaining an idealizing fantasy. What we may hypothesize about is the degree of autonomous functioning attributed to the introject itself. Here the God object attains an independent status in the unconscious mind with various degrees of freedom that operate on the psychic register as-if it is an entity that presents itself to the mental apparatus as an external object, when it is in fact an internal object subjected to an elaborate matrix of fantasy relations.[39] In this regard, the God introject assumes the

38 Although Freud equates theism, and particularly Christianity, with the belief in an idealized and infallible Father who will bring us salvation from our childhood dependency and helplessness, central to this thesis is the notion that anthropomorphic properties attributed to God could easily be based on an idealized maternal attachment figure where all the basic psychological requirements for nurturance, love, acceptance, attunement to physical and emotional needs, affective responsiveness, trust, protection, and safety and security are fulfilled. Recall that this is the foundation of attachment theory in ethnology, contemporary biology, and human developmental science.

39 See my detailed discussion on the autonomous nature of unconscious agency, representational schemata, and fantasy construction in Chapter 4: Unconscious Semiotics, in *Origins: On the Genesis of Psychic Reality*.

presence of a microagent or self-state that masks as an external entity with various dispositional properties through various modes of re-presentation the mind feels compelled to repeat. This illusory misrecog-nition (*méconnaissance*) of the object as external rather than internal leaves an emotional immediacy of the felt presence of a macroforce we attribute to a godhead as powerful Other.

The God introject may be experienced on the phenomenological level as a fixed presentation (*Vorstellung*) introduced by an extraneous agency in the mind, when on the ontic level it is the alienated contents of the pro-jective fantasies that maintain a dissociative organization through uncon-scious schemata. In fact, there is a confusional element in pin-pointing the source of the intuition itself. This is why for some people the experi-ence of the God introject is felt as emanating from without rather than from within. In other words, its source is intuited or felt to be ego-dystonic. But in others, the feeling itself fortifies a conviction that the introject is a natural ego-syntonic occurrence that emanates from within as a divine implanted faculty or *sensus divinitatis*. Based on both the felt-spatial derivatives of externality and the quality of ideality attached to the introject itself, this endows the experiential object with a unique quality and position within psychic reality.

We may say that the felt-characteristic of an omnipotent exogenous force produces anxiety and paranoiac pressures that must be neutralized through the attribution of divinity and ideality to the introject as a sort of reaction formation via reversal. By inverting and undoing the original encroachment onto the psychic apparatus through a mechanism of reversal, the psyche subverts the persecutory impact of a looming or immanent annihilation by adopting a more positive positionality (in fantasy) toward the introject as an autonomous agency. Although this defensive maneuver may be adaptive to psychic survival, it nevertheless becomes a delusional nucleus that subordinates the mind to irrationality because this fantasy has such a powerful emotional stronghold over the unconscious ego that wants to preserve the notions of ideality and infalli-bility of the internal object regardless of the price to be paid.

When analyzed more closely, a further splitting takes place within the ideal pole that insulates it from critical scrutiny, negation, or intrusive inter-rogation, hence denunciating the need for factual justification, which is the role of the rational faculty. Here the ideal object as divine entity is pre-served at all costs as an unquestionable reality or truism that is insulated from the demands of empirical reality and logic. At this time, the question of the reality principle is suspended in the mind, instead adopting a surrogate fictive reality that carries pragmatic regulatory functions favoring psychological adaptation. The idealized pole of the introject becomes the crux or axis fueling the fantasy system itself, where it is invested with a qualitative degree of psychic energy endowed with numinous properties that must remain preserved. These numinous energies are recalcitrant to negation because they are emotionally vibrant, full of qualitative intensities, and fulfill basal longings supplied by unconscious desire.

We may speculate that the believer unconsciously maintains an idealized internal relation to the fantasy object, and must make reparation for any past violence imposed on the God introject based on early primitive fantasies directed toward the ideal object (e.g., negation, contempt, hatred, envy, etc.), for which in turn, if one is successful, will be forgiven and given love. Hence the unconditional act of love, worship, and devotion to the introject will solicit the object's reverence and acceptance. Instead of being conquered or engulfed by an overwhelming omnipotent force, the puerile economics of mind converts such danger (through an inversion mechanism) into a benevolent, loving-comforting protector. Although there remains an ambivalent relation to the God introject, the overvaluation of the idealized pole of the reified (internal) object as unsurpassed value sustains an intrapsychic emotional presence that is at the very basis of unconscious belief. Here the so-called presence of God is a reincorporated (albeit created or constructed), idealized internal object that informs the affective fabric of psychic reality. What I wish to emphasize here is the emotional supremacy of the inner felt-relation the subject has to the internal object that is mistaken for an external agency thought to implant the feeling itself as a *sensus divinitatis*. The microdynamics of this unconscious organization within the fantasy constellation may potentially explain, at least in part, the so-called claim of self-certainty the believer contends to have in relation to the divine.

It is very difficult for people who have internalized the religion of their parents and cultural milieu to reject it outright without undergoing some form of inner battle for justifying its refutation because it unconsciously corresponds to negating one's parents (or symbolic cultural equivalent) and their values. And because the self is partly constructed based on the internalization of the Other (namely one's parents, the symbolic order, etc.) and its secreted microvaluations, retraction of these beliefs is simultaneously a repudiation of parts of oneself, hence a self-negation. Here the psyche faces both self-renunciation and shame, a most unpleasant confrontation that is more easily dispensed with through denial, dissociation, repression, avoidance, and escape from rational critique. Depending upon the nature and intensity of one's identifications, this may constitute a profane self-attack as an assault on the very fabric of one's being because it is an annulment of oneself as the dissolution of the unconscious identifications that structure personal identity; or less traumatically, it may be experienced as a felt internal tension that requires sublation in order to dissipate certain unconscious intensities that are looking to redistribute themselves through a form of displacement onto other internal objects. This is why overcoming these psychological prejudices is both a catalyst for critical thinking as well as a developmental achievement. To confront the realization of God's non-existence is to overcome a massive internal resistance that must mourn the loss of the fulfillment of a wish.

Mourning absence

Mourning object loss and lost fulfillment is common to human experience, especially in relation to loss over not having particular childhood wishes and life desires placated. But most people are not readily in touch with this. Here mourning is not only in relation to the absence of a lost object, it is in relation to the absence of what *can never be* present, but we feel it *should be*. When the God introject is felt to be empty or missing, or decentered from the perch of idealization, for those who are self-aware of this absence there is often an internal depletion that accrues accompanied by feelings of being forlorn and dejected. We may refer to this experiential void as a felt-emptiness of non-being, our inner relation to lack. This *absent-presence* in our psyche is an inevitable consequence of mourning, one we attempt to remedy by replacing loss with permanence, non-existence with unending presence we nurture through our hopes and fantasies. This qualitative experience of the absence of being is equally felt as a *present-absence*, for this is dialectically constituted as the presentation of lack, of deprivation in being. When we can no longer evade the realization that there never was nor ever will be a divine presence, we are simply left with mourning absence. But unlike normal mourning, the love object is not simply gone. It never was.

Many people with religious hunger, which I would argue is not the same as spirituality, have the need to believe in God in their search to assuage this absence—this lacuna, which is felt as a lack or hole in being. But in the despair of solitude, in the residue of emptiness that comes with insight and mourning object loss, comes the reactionary compulsion or urge to replace lost presence with a loss of absence—the negation of its negation. This peculiar resistance to mourning is in the service of preserving the object, of safeguarding against its disappearance, hence securing its presence within our psychic eternity. This defensive process is simultaneously (both dialectically and paradoxically) an unconscious attempt to mourn and accept our own impending death, the finitude that is closing in on us all, the call of nothingness.

In increasingly large portions of contemporary society, and particularly amongst the intelligentsia, we have lost God, hence any faith in the concept itself, once an untouchable cornerstone of culture. I am not talking about Nietzsche's God, whom we as society have killed in our nihilism through the abnegation of any absolutism, foundation, or ideal,[40] nor Hegel's, where ethical self-awareness is lost in "unhappy consciousness" in search of a "beautiful soul;"[41] but rather the concept itself becomes vacuous when unseen and unfulfilling absence persists, especially when there is nothing else offering to replace it. No longer can we cling to the imaginary, to the phantasmal, which requires the subordination of reason, a stifling of the will, and a life-denying subservience to a destructive suffocation the soul faces when the longing for another world free of discordance is prized. But neither do we find such heaven here on earth, for the idea of God is bankrupt, relegated to the landfill of bad conscience. Here sober reason and sterile science offer no comfort. Yet antiseptic science is not likely to take the place of religion anytime soon; it neither inspires values nor enduring aesthetic works of art, literature, or architecture. Hence the compulsion to invent God serves as an antidote to natural deprivation and lack. But such an invention, too, carries its own burdens.

40 See Prologue, *Thus Spoke Zarathustra*, "God is dead!," p. 12.
41 I am referring to Hegel's (1807) discussion of the divided self that can never live up to its own self-imposed ideals we attribute to God when we are so humanly flawed and fallible. See Sec. C. The Revealed Religion, *Phenomenology of Spirit*, where he anticipates Nietzsche by nearly a century when he proclaims "'God is dead'," p. 455. Also see my commentary in *The Unconscious Abyss*, pp. 152–156.

The belief in God is not merely due to a failure of mourning an absent ideal object—the substantive wish of humanity, but rather a *refusal* to accept its absence, which is self-deluding. This refusal typifies a special form of denial that in psychoanalysis is known as disavowal: we as humanity are empirically confronted with a lack of evidence of any supreme extant being, let alone existential quantifiers or properties attached to this so-called absent, hidden, or invisible divine person, but we refuse to accept it. This hybrid form of denial, which is a combination of negation infused with supple logical extrapolations, allows most of the world a respite from thinking critically about their epistemologically pre-supposed object of faith, which in turn allows a certain wary degree of fortification to insulate the divine object of fantasy from the negative encroachments of interrogating reason, hostile disbelief, radical skepticism, and/or the doubting Thomas's of the world.[42] Disavowal takes such a psychic threshold in world masses that any critical challenge to these invested fantasies are typically met with rancor, disdain, dissociation, and corollary denial in the heels of a protective function. The assault on the belief itself, let alone on the refusal of mourning, is a provocation people are willing to sacrifice their lives for. In some cases, as we may currently observe in radical Islamic fundamentalist groups, critical interrogation of belief is experienced as a supreme negation of believing nations, hence warranting a fight to the death. Whether Muslim, Christian, or Jew, this is the Hegelian battle for recognition neither side is willing to concede or renounce.

Unless one was raised in an environment entirely sheltered from the God question, it is not likely that one can evade a psychological confrontation with its subject matter. And even if it is remotely possible or occurs in a tiny fraction of the world population, it would be psychologically impossible, I argue, to elude having to personally answer to the question of God's existence. When this issue is denied, dissociated, repressed, avoided, or displaced throughout social development, hence leading to certain characterological defenses that inform adaptive functioning and personality formation, it often visits upon a person as they grow closer to death. Either a barter with existence is offered, such as a suspension of agnostic doubt—even a hypomanic denial embraced as hope, or the

---

42 Of course the disciple Thomas was the most rational of Jesus's coterie to question to whom he was speaking to provide proof that he did indeed rise from the dead.

ordinary unhappiness of consciousness watches in somber acceptance as the depressive curtains of reality close for the final time. Because God serves a psychic purpose, accepting its absence is tantamount to grieving, yet the world cannot afford such mass bereavement.

Mourning the God introject is more like grieving the loss of a psychic function rather than the loss of a physical object, such as a loved one. As Freud notes, mourning can be a natural reaction to the loss of an "abstraction" such as an "ideal."[43] If we think of mourning as a psychological process that must embrace sorrow and work-through loss as an organic encounter with grief that transmutes over time, then most people who contemplate atheism will be forced to reconcile this psychic tension, while theists may possibly forgo this unpleasantness altogether in their conscious lives, although unconsciously one is never spared. But in mourning God—the absence of the Ideal, there is no painful remembering of the lost loved object who is no longer present, only our identification with an Ideal Value that is now gone. What is lost is the symbolic function God signifies. Here consciousness can no longer entertain the *belief* in divine idealization, what we may equate with a psychic loss, a loss that must be mourned.

In some ways, such mourning is similar to letting-go of the idealized fantasies one once held toward their parents in childhood, when they were imbued with superlative qualities that belied their more realistic fallible characters with all the imperfections in disposition and behavior belonging to any adult. Most people go through life unaware of these unconscious fantasies where grief-work transpires underground. But here mourning emerges in reaction to *retracting the fantasy relation* one had once established toward the symbolic functions the God introject stood for and represented in psychic economy. This loss comes with a modicum of shame (for believing the illusion to begin with) and guilt (for forsaking the ideal in light of reason), and for some people, melancholia. These are the compromise formations the mind generates as it grapples with bereavement. What differentiates this type of loss from others is that it is solely *internal*, where something is lost from within the self, not from the outside world. In fact, such a loss is compounded by the assault on the Ideal, where an unsymbolized killing of the Other transpires through its brute negation. In such mourning, we are confronted with the microdynamics of

43 Freud (1917), p. 243.

de-idealization, giving up the fantasy object, working-through the loss of the psychic functions it serves, and eventually letting-go of the emotional pain attached to the loss of the illusion as the psyche yields to reason. This process approximates mourning the death of value itself, value that is neither attainable nor possible in any corrigible reality. But the aftermath or *après coup* is a profound sadness all the same, for this opens our gap in being and exposes us to our unrelenting lack of cohesion and wholeness.

It is not uncommon for people who have a spiritual crisis or who have lost their faith to undergo depression. This is a clinical fact. In such conditions, the ego has often taken up a form of over-identification with the ideal object, which has been transmuted and incorporated into psychic structure. The critical agency that stands for perfection and divine judgement, which is personified by the God introject, is now unconsciously turned on the self. The depressive casts all kinds of aspersions on himself, from moral reproach, self-hatred, unworthiness, unlovability, intense aggression and sadism, to the need for punishment and suicidality: identification with the God introject is now replaced by a harsh destructive superego. Here we may speculate that the violence done by negating God and for abandoning the ideal object triggers a reactionary fantasy system via identification with the aggressor set on revenge that is now turned on the self. Now that God is "truly" dead, so is the internally divided ego in jeopardy of facing psychic death.

In spiritual depression, the unconscious reverberations of divine object-loss are transformed into an ego-loss through identification and emotional fixation with the dejected (dead) introject that eclipses the rational faculty of the ego.[44] Because the assault on the God introject is initiated from the standpoint of a critical analytic function belonging to secondary process thinking (namely reason) in alignment with the reality principle, there is simultaneously an unconscious resistance to the repudiation of the ideal, which leads to emotional conflict. Here the mourner may be tempted to blame oneself for the object's loss rather than accept its natural absence. This reflects a fundamental *ambivalence* in mourning the loss of the God posit, for our infantile wishes suffer a disappointing and painful decay.

Because the subjective nature of personality is at bottom an unconscious agency that organizes intrapsychic forces and internalized objects

---

44 Compare to Freud (1917), p. 249.

(contents) based on life experiences that are wholly contingent and idiosyncratic, God often unconsciously resonates within the pristine or beatific parts of the feeling soul, that is, what we cherish in ourselves most deeply. Here our ego ideal—what we would like to become, unconsciously communes with an ideal ego, namely, the perfection the God introject highlights. Mourning this loss is having to give up an ideal self and ideal Other, and disconnect from the values that are most significant to us, values that define who we are as the better half of our natures.

When mourning the loss of God takes its proper place in psychic economy, mourning or melancholia is given up for more reality-based appraisals of self and world free from internal persecution and self-renunciation brought on by the feelings of emptiness associated with the forsaken object. Here normal mourning is overcoming the loss of the *reality* of the ideal object and simultaneously giving up the *illusion* of an ego ideal it can never simulate or become. The laborious work of mourning involves the gradual severance of attachments to this illusory object evinced by the lack of any evidence in its actual existence. Therefore the attachment to the lost object gives way to the reality that it never existed in the first place.

A person who does not naturally have a burning desire for God will likely be spared a large degree of mental agony that another person is bound to bear in mourning the loss of the fulfillment of a wish. Freud points out that: "If the object does not possess this great significance for the ego—a significance reinforced by a thousand [semiotic] links—then, too, its loss will not be of a kind to cause either mourning or melancholia."[45] In other words, those who have had no attachment to the God object are not likely to be bothered by its real absence. But for those who have had ambivalent relations with a God introject, the psyche will likely require some course of working-through to ease this resonance of psychic loss.

The process of mourning absence requires a loosening of the attachment bond to the fantasy object, which is often indecisive, slow, and uncommitted, until a certain *releasing* occurs as the natural culmination of mourning. This releasing is usually precipitated by an immersion or deepening into the fantasy system, which is reluctant to loosen its stronghold over the unconscious ego; yet this gradual undoing or disentangling

45 Ibid., p. 256.

leads to a dissolving of the emotional connection to the ideal object inherent to a proper letting-go process, hence freeing the soul of its restrictive comportment or fixation to the God object. Here we must give up our infantile inner world where grandiose and supersensible fantasies maintain their attachment and unification with ideality, a wish that stomachs the onus designated to the mourner.

In the process of psychoanalytic work, this ambivalent attachment to a divine internal object, which provokes feelings of love and hate within a state of dialectical tension—whereby one side seeks to cling to the introject while the other to detach, can always be associated to a real figure in a person's life, most notably a family member, significant other, or combination of such as condensation. The more difficult element of the working-through process is letting-go of God as an attainable fulfillment of value, or more perniciously, in rendering the introject *valueless*. On one hand, the value attached to the internal object is entirely fantasized, while on the other, devaluing its significance to the psyche means abnegating its symbolic and emotional functions, which are never easy to endure. This is why humanity clings to its symbolic utility. Even if we mourn that which is not present, we are still left with the desire for its presence simply because we cannot mourn desire itself, which is being-in-relation-to-lack. This is the toil of humanity.

Mourning psychic absence may be combatted with a variety of defenses designed to ward off emotional emptiness, especially when the enjoyment of living is curtailed by the realization of transience. Our transient existence demands that we take hold of that which is truly present in the moment, albeit we may rebel against mourning its impermanence. As Freud reminds us, in mourning, the loved object no longer exists; but with the God introject the object was never really present except as an internal object or idea laden with emotional properties that fulfilled various psychic functions. To give this up would understandably provoke resistance and antagonism to the demand itself for renouncement. This is evident in various species of the God delusion. Freud is clear: "This opposition can be so intense that a turning away from reality takes place and a clinging to the object through the medium of a hallucinatory wishful psychosis."[46] In other words, because the attachment is so strong, the existence of the lost object is protracted in the mind, which the work of mourning

46 Ibid., p. 244.

must wrestle with. This is often a painful process of unraveling, separating, and letting-go of the connection to the loved object, which entails a gradual detachment of psychic energies facilitated by the impersonal facts of loss and absence. When the work of mourning finds some resolve, although often incomplete, the ego is more liberated and uninhibited in its activities. Whether the subjective qualitative experience of mourning God is akin to grieving the loss of a perfect parent or attachment figure, an ego ideal/ideal ego, or the death of pure valuation itself, it often works on the psyche unconsciously where fantasy systems are disrupted and seek compensatory modes of gratification the internal object no longer achieves.

The denial, failure, or refusal to mourn the absent object is what sustains the defensive function in the genuinely believing theist, which is organized as a circumscribed delusional nucleus. Those who have grappled psychologically with mourning psychic absence must come to terms with the natural conditions of our existence, which may lead to creative bouts of rebirth and enjoyment in living when the ego is freed of its mourning, although an unconscious affective sense of dissatisfaction is often left in its wake. This is the after effects of any disillusionment suffered at the hands of cool existence. But this is the human situation we encounter: just as we are thrown into stanch nature by accident—without any choice or consultation in the matter whatsoever, life falls short, is full of inadequacies, and offers no spiritual promised land other than what lies directly before us. Although life is full of meaning, the teleology of nature is internally derived and executed, simply a purpose without a cause. In fact, the transience of life gives life more meaning and value precisely because it is scarce and temporally kerbed. As Freud reminds us, "Limitation in the possibility of an enjoyment raises the value of the enjoyment."[47] It is incumbent upon us to seize life's enjoyment while it is here, an enjoyment that is possible only in the moment.

When one is taught or led to believe that there is something more and better than what one has and experiences during their lifetime, then it becomes emotionally painful to renounce this transcendental illusion. Mourning psychic absence is experienced as a form of psychic loss, for the adored and idealized object is gone, which feels like it has been taken away by death due to one's conditioning based in childhood. But such loss eludes the type of mourning in a traditional sense where the physical

47 Freud (1916), p. 305.

object has disappeared, for here the object was only presented as an idea that was not present in any tangible corporeal manner; therefore mourning is in response to giving up or letting-go of the relation or attachment to the idea qua idealized value the God object symbolically signifies to that person. Although it is not in actuality, strictly speaking, a loss, it is nonetheless felt as a loss, what God once was and now no longer can remain. Hence the loss is of an internal object that never existed as anything other than a psychic property and function of ideology and cultural habituation. Most of humanity refuses to accept this rational conclusion. Internal defenses fortified by common beliefs inherent to the religious practices of modern civilization create a bulwark against this truism. In the end, negating God is butchering hope, and nobody likes that. The result of humanity is a failure to mourn natural absence for the fantasy of divine presence.

The phenomenology of faithlessness—the brute acceptance of nothing hereafter—leaves a dull internal ache, the feeling that Something is missing, indeed something No-More. This is the spoiler to existence. When one mourns the loss of Something No-More, there is still a pining for Something Else regardless of how one comes to reorganize their internal experience, for we endeavor to resolve the riddle that we are condemned to repetitiously relive, like Sisyphus and his eternal boulder. There is nothing more than *this*, yet the torment of uncertainty and apprehension of ultimate finality—death—is too intolerable to bear. So we invent *more than this*. "There must be Something More." God becomes the Infinite (*Ein Sof*),[48] the inversion of what God truly (dialectically) symbolizes—An Ending. Rather than the boundless infinity of *apeiron*, which is the spaceless and timeless aspect to nature and Being, we must accept our mortal sense of limit (*peras*), the bounded finitude in which we are abandoned. We all *must* die, but we love good endings.

The atheist can find no justifiable rational argument to believe in a transcendent supernatural being that has a sense of personal agency, let alone any claim that such an entity possesses omnipotent powers of supremacy, omniscience, creationism, and so forth, which is uniformly attributed to a theistic God. Put simply, these are grand fantasies of invincibility fuelled

---

48 In the kabbalist tradition, *Ein Sof* literally means "Endless," God's radical transcendence. Daniel Matt (1995) informs us that Jewish mystics adopted the negative theology of Maimonides when attributing *Ayin* or Nothingness to the first sefirah, which comprise the ten sefirot. See *The Essential Kabbalah*, p. 7.

by fear and ignorance instilled in childhood that stand in relation to our most cherished unconscious wishes and desires to be *unconditionally loved* and accepted by our original love objects or attachment figures, and by extension, humanity itself, free of all the ills that define our human condition. Unfortunately, everything is conditional. The ideality of Heaven—of unadulterated perfection—is defensively transmuted into an illusorily constructed, abstract invisible deity. Philosophers have been quite ingenious in salvaging the professed existence of God from the bog of indeterminacy, including demoting God to nature itself, panpsychism (à la Spinoza), nothingness or non-being, as well as pure abstraction, what we may refer to as an incorporeal intelligible,[49] or what Whitehead, who himself was an atheist, calls the non-temporal concrescence of all eternal objects.[50] In the tradition of Thomism, the ex-nun and comparative theologian Karen Armstrong even goes so far as to make God Being itself (*ipsum Esse subsistens*).[51] This misappropriation of God as "being itself" is further echoed by David Bentley Hart's muddled metaphysics.[52] We may even revert to relativism: God is whatever you define it to be. But unlike Saint Anselm's depiction of God as an insuperable being, a being greater than which nothing greater can be conceived,[53] *you simply cannot think something into existence.*

The Prime (Unmoved) Mover, Uncaused Cause, Absolute Spirit, or Pure Reason as pure thought thinking itself into existence is merely an omnipotent grandiose fantasy of our desire to affirm (through the faculty of understanding) that which we cannot directly experience or know. But if "*I think it*, it must be so!" The fallacy one is seduced by is that of assuming that an object of thought is equivalent to its substantive material existence. This is the Hegelian resurrection of Anselm's thought experiment: We know the *Ding an sich* by virtue of the fact that we posit it. But just because we posit it doesn't mean it's real, let alone make it actual. It exists only as an idea. Even Hegel's dictum that "essence is appearance"

---

49 This is David Bakan's (2001) term derived from Maimonides' negative theology, which was developed based on Aristotle's notion of form and the Active Intellect.

50 Alfred North Whitehead (1929a), p. 7. Also see my neo-Whiteheadian critique of concrescence as a naturalized account of process and reality without God (Mills, 2002b).

51 Armstrong (2010) tells us that "God is not *a* being at all" (p. iv), rather "Being itself" (pp. 11, 141), what she attributes (wrongfully I might add) to Heidegger's notion of *Sein* as the equivalent of God (see pp. 279–280), hence making God pure metaphysics rather than making God, as Tillich does, the ultimate ground of being.

52 *The Experience of God*, p. 30.

53 This appears in Chapter 2 of his *Proslogion*, and further qualified in Chapter 15.

fails because God has not appeared as a Being-in-itself, let alone For-itself.[54]

As human animals, we must concede that when we reach for religious experience, or try to snatch the spiritual from our lived moments—that is, what we may label or signify as spiritual, there is an inferential leap of reason to posit the concrete ontology of God based on inductive disposi-tions, rather than remain on the level of agnostic symbolic experience, simply because the human mind is psychologically oriented toward seeking the fulfillment of its objects of desire. Here the ultimate object of our desire (as the ultimate cause and purpose structuring the cosmos) is our communion of consciousness with the fantasized (illusory) selfobject of our internal (relational) experiences that beget the meaning-making powers of our rational passion, the passion for ideality that gives life structure, temperance, and value.

Because we have properly determined that the God hypothesis is a metaphysical question, there is no logically demonstrable or scientifically verifiable basis for justifying the belief in a transubjective, suprapersonal entity or cosmic being encompassing the universe; however, there is a plenitude of empirical reasons to attribute such an idea to our deepest psychological needs and desires for wish-fulfillment. Freud tells us that the God construct is a symbolically exalted Father who holds the promise of salvation from our childhood helplessness and conversion of our suf-fering into the ultimate fulfillment of our ideals. And this is why Freud believed that the great theistic traditions were repetition compulsions borne of a world plagued by obsessional neurosis. Here the conception of God is the ideal projection of our primary conglomerate attachment figures based upon our familial identifications, whereby our ideal self and object relationships are concretized in the immaculate abstraction of pure wish-fulfillment. And in Hegel's terms, religion becomes a concrete uni-versal of spiritual embodiment in the cultural institutions that define our collectively shared humanity. But unlike Hegel, I would say that these universals are the productions of imagination as value-idealizations col-onized by our collective unconscious wishes instantiated in social custom and practice, the future of a delusion.

---

54 For Hegel, "appearance is essence" (*Phenomenology of Spirit*, § 147), for that which appears is actual. This further means that nothing can exist unless it is made actual, for "essence must *appear*" in order for anything to be (*The Encyclopaedia Logic*, § 131). God has not appeared, *ergo* God stakes no claim to existence.

The reification of Ideality is humanity's invention of God. The ideal personifies the perfect Subject we all unconsciously want and desire to incorporate, as well as be placed under or incorporated (hence included) by [Lat. *subjectus*, brought under, from *subicere*, to place under]. This wish for the divine object of our fulfillment must be mourned in order for the ego to reattach to a real internal object, yet this confrontation meets with a profound resistance as it signifies the death of the wish. This is tantamount to a working-through process of therapeutic healing, of accepting inevitability and replacing fantasy with real possibility. Although it may be said that a wish never dies, only its fulfillment, the refusal to mourn the loss of the fulfillment of this sacred wish maintains an internal state of depletion that does not allow for the expansion and substitution of objects. Even though I admit that I feel an emotional void and wish it were otherwise, I cannot deny what my senses and my intellect tell me are desirous longings for a fictitious reality I must mourn, because it does not exist. We sustain the need to believe because it gives us comfort through hope. Conversely, sustaining loss merely keeps use mired in sorrow, whereas the intermediate attitude of embracing a naturalized spirituality may allow for a psychic transitioning from mourning to actualized freedom.

Chapter 4

Spirituality without God

Although statistical consensus differs,[1] and despite religious variances, it is generally accepted that most of the world population believes in some form of religion, which more often than not includes some notion of God. Here we must reiterate that religion is a global defense that gives billions of people a sense of purpose and meaning and allows them to function in the face of existential absurdity, without which life would be unbearable, pointless, or futile. Arguably, to take that away would result in psychological and social calamity. A valid argument (albeit unpopular) could be

1 What is interesting to note is that there is statistical variance and a lopsided distribution in theistic belief throughout the world. Maitzen (2006), for example, highlights an interesting polarity. As he notes:

> The populace of Saudi Arabia is at least 95 per cent Muslim and therefore at least 95 per cent theist, while the populace of Thailand is 95 per cent Buddhist and therefore at most 5 per cent theist. The approximate total populations are 26 million for Saudi Arabia and 65 million for Thailand. Presumably these samples are large enough to make the differences statistically significant and not merely a statistical blip that would disappear if we took an appropriately long view of the matter. If those data are even roughly accurate, the distribution of theistic belief is at least highly uneven between those two countries, and they are hardly unique in this respect (pp. 179–180).

Also see *CIA World Factbook* (2004). Whether we want to generalize this distribution to the rest of the world based on the small populations of Saudi Arabia and Thailand are another matter altogether. A substantial recent epidemiological study of world atheism or nontheistic belief shows that as many as 500 to 750 million human beings worldwide are skeptical about or do not believe in God (Norris and Inglehart, 2004; Zuckerman, 2007), although we may never have an accurate picture due to methodological and sociological difficulties inherent in measuring such phenomena. According to the Pew Research Center (2012), as many as 1.1 billion people have identified themselves as "religiously unaffiliated," accounting for about 1 in 6 people (16 percent) worldwide. However, when you closely examine the surveys used to compile this data, atheists, agnostics, and those who do not identify as belonging to any religious group are lumped together into one basket; and even among this pool, many people identify themselves as believing in *a* God or higher power, albeit not a traditional one, and/or they participate in religious ceremonies due to heritage or culture, more than three-quarters (88 percent) of which are concentrated in Asia, the Pacific, and Europe.

made that because most of the world population are either illiterate or uneducated, they are not intellectually capable or enlightened enough to live life on its own terms free of this type of psychological need for self-protection from the truth of reality. Instead illusion through fantasy replaces the harsh confrontation with one's defenses, without which it would surely bring internal tumult and atrociousness if one were forced to tackle head on their own irrational beliefs in favor of faith that provides some solace.

Should we strip away the defense with the education of atheism via *logos*, philosophical inquiry, critical thinking, and rational science? Perhaps the answer is obvious. But is it possible? We are not talking about the educated Western public, let alone the intellectual elite, such as those who hold academic prestige, popular esteem, and are typically wealthy. The world masses have no such privileges or luxury. Contemporary humanists who are educated, well-informed, and disposed to think critically about the God question are a small number in comparison to the rest of the world.[2] Although there is a new consciousness burgeoning within many parts of the world that have abandoned the idea and belief in God,[3] especially among the youth, this does not eradicate the prevalence of belief in God in some form throughout the rest of the world that is now over 7 billion in population. Pippa Norris and Ronald Inglehart observe that the future trends of believe and disbelief are growing worldwide, although in disproportionate ways: there are more people now who espouse traditional religious belief than ever before in human history based on the world population explosion.[4] Of course they come from the

---

2 Secular humanist organizations are represented worldwide in at least 31 countries (American Humanist Association, 2013), but there are likely to be substantially many more (Cf. Adherents. com, 2013). Those who identify themselves as Humanists are estimated to encompass as many as 5 million people worldwide; but because there is a lack of criteria or consensus in providing a universal definition, it is logical to assume that many more million exist. Having said that, a few million people is a drop in the bucket in comparison to the world masses.

3 In their book *Sacred and Secular*, Norris and Inglehart (2004) provide a broad epidemiological exposition of disbelief worldwide, which is prevalent in North America, Britain, and various reformed European, Scandinavian, and Nordic countries, as well as in some regions in Asia. Zuckerman (2007) identifies the Top 50 countries containing the largest percentage of peoples who identify themselves as atheists, agnostics, or nonbelievers. The Top 10 in order of highest percentage are: (1. Sweden (46–85 percent); 2. Vietnam (81 percent); 3. Denmark (43–80 percent); 4. Norway (31–72 percent); 5. Japan (64–65 percent); 6. Czech Republic (54–61 percent); 7. Finland (28–60 percent); 8. France (43–54 percent); 9. South Korea (30–52 percent); and 10. Estonia (49 percent).

4 *Sacred and Secular*, p. 25.

most socially challenged, unhealthiest, and compromised regions on earth where belief in God is directly proportional to societal impoverishment and insecurity. An interesting correlation is that countries with high percentage rates of nonbelievers are among the healthiest, wealthiest, best educated, and are from free societies whereas the nations with the highest rates of believers are from the least. The upsurge in secularization is limited to highly industrialized and technologically advanced countries with low birth rates in comparison to their counterparts from non-industrialized or developing countries that are among the poorest nations on earth with exponentially high birth rates such as Africa, India, and China. Not surprising, high degrees of atheism are associated with increased individual and societal health and security while countries with high degrees of religious belief and low rates of atheism are correlated with poverty, social instability, gender inequality, and lack of education and democratization. Although atheism is increasing worldwide, it is barely discernible to most of the world.

It is historically understandable why the notion of God would have been socially acceptable and customary for many societies in the past to embrace, for it served as a viable solution to life's dilemmas based on a lack of knowledge. Today it becomes harder to sustain this social illusion due to the progressive advances in education, science, social awareness, consciousness-raising, and the dissemination of informational technologies in globalized culture. But most of the world is not sufficiently literate or educated, trained to think critically, nor encouraged to have free inquiry. Nor are they willing to abandon certain historical religious practices that have traditionally given unique definition to their cultural identities despite the fact that they are based upon misunderstanding or a lack of information and reiterate irrational beliefs due to entrenched social conditioning and custom. Not to mention the uncomfortable barbaric fact that you can be murdered in Middle Eastern societies for saying otherwise.

Non-industrial and developing countries in particular are enslaved by ignorance, hardship, authoritarianism, patriarchal religious subjugation, paucity of resources, lack of institutionalized education and democracy, abuse by powerful men, universal domination of women and children, and pervasive psychological distress due to attachment deficits, developmental trauma, ingrained systemic violence, and abject poverty. Until these oppressive conditions improve, I cannot envision a world where belief in God is abandoned. And even if they are, I still cannot foresee a world where the logical abnegation of God is probable simply because belief and faith provide psychological defenses the rational intellect alone cannot furnish nor champion. Theist beliefs are affirmative, therefore they provide a (deceptive) *sense* of subjective certainty, while the agnostic has to live in ambivalence and uncertainty and the atheist in negation.

Even if my assessment of the God posit is correct, truth or reason by itself is no match for a wishing humanity. The God fantasy is culturally embedded in worldhood and recalcitrant to change. Probabilistic odds alone suggest it will never disappear from majority social consciousness. What compels people to look beyond the confines of their personal existence to transpersonal or supernatural principles may correspond to a calling that is stymied by psychological analysis alone. The masses will likely never rise above this mode of thinking because organized religion produces exalted human emotions. Even many atheists are unhappy about this unsavory state of affairs, because they have to confront their own non-being directly, while the believer gets a convenient ticket to bliss and salvation. And they will be the first to tell you so, usually with acerbic humor concealing a forlorn melancholia suffused with deeply felt envy. If not, their professed intellectual superiority (as enlightenment) usually belies a narcissistic vulnerability and sadness that is difficult for them to admit.[5]

It is precisely because God does not exist that humanity had to invent It. Humanity simply cannot live up to its own self-imposed ideals informed by Lack—the absence of fulfillment, so we must locate an imaginary invisible space where meaning, truth, and value are said to exist outside of ourselves. In Lacanian terms, religious masses live in the Imaginary register where God is superimposed by the Symbolic order and sustained by unconscious eruption breaching the thresholds of the Real. Rather than accept the brute facticity that we are ultimately responsible for making our lives into what we are capable of becoming, much of humanity must defensively transfer this responsibility onto a displaced

---

5 Here I am reminded of a sagacious quote from Žižek (1997): "the more you perceive yourself as an atheist, the more your unconscious is dominated by prohibitions which sabotage your enjoyment." What this means is that even if you are fully justified in your logical dismissal of the God posit, unconsciously there will be massive resistance to such denial due to an insatiable pining that spoils other aspects of psychologically enjoying life. An interesting epidemiological fact is that despite the overwhelming connection between high rates of atheism and increased societal health and security, the only palpable exception is with suicide (Zuckerman, 2007). Suicide rates are highest among secularized nations and lowest among countries and populations that are religious. We may speculate that this is due in part to the religious prohibition against suicide, particularly among Christianity and Islam, but it also speaks to much of humanity's need to defend against emotional pain through faith practices.

imaginary idea we call God. Because we are desirous and appetitive animals—with our hopes, dreads, and limitations, our given nature is informed by an unrelenting absence that unconsciously pervades through our feeling soul—the heart or core of our felt sense of inner self, our being-in-relation-to-lack.[6] This pervasive lack dialectically generates an unabated craving that constantly requires objects to satiate its appetite, including all modes of spiritual hunger.

Secular humanism today

Secular humanism is a worldwide phenomenon based on universal egalitarian commitments to value inquiry, human rights, and moral conscientiousness based on reason and scientific knowledge rather than supernatural premises grounded in religious faith or doctrine. According to the American Humanist Association,

> Humanism is a rational philosophy informed by science, inspired by art, and motivated by compassion. Affirming the dignity of each human being, it supports liberty and opportunity consonant with social and planetary responsibility. Free of theism and other supernatural beliefs, humanism thus derives the goals of life from human need and interest rather than from theological or ideological abstractions, and asserts that humanity must take responsibility for its own destiny.[7]

Many supporters view humanism as an ethical sensibility, life philosophy, or worldview that provides meaning and fulfillment through the pursuit of human value and the good life devoid of metaphysical assumptions about a supreme being that hinder the attainment of personal and societal happiness. Although humanists are as varied in their beliefs and attitudes as any

---

6 In *Origins: On the Genesis of Psychic Reality*, I systematically articulate how mind desires because it stands in relation to absence or lack. Thus, our conscious wishes, urges, and bodily drives emerge from an unconscious primal desire, the desire to fill the lack. In the most primitive phases of psychic constitution, mind is an active stream of desire exerting pressure from within itself as drive, clamoring for satisfaction, what Freud would call "pleasure." But unlike Freud, who sees pleasure as tension reduction, mind may be said to always crave, to always desire. While a particular drive or its accompanying derivatives may be sated, desire itself may be said to never formally stop yearning: it is condemned to experience lack. Unlike Lacan, however, who describes desire as "lack of being," and Sartre, who initially views human existence "as lack" or nothingness, here unconscious desire is *being-in-relation-to-lack* (see p. 133).

7 *The Humanist: A Magazine of Critical Inquiry and Social Concern*, p. i.

social group, they share a common skepticism toward the existence of God and instead focus on present-day matters involving the promotion of positive human relations bolstered by critical thinking, concern, and compassion for others.

Founding pioneers focused on humanism as an alternative to religion that emphasized a core ethical commitment to human values, equality among genders and peoples, Unitarian and Universalist principles, and educational and social interventions promoting human fulfillment as life's ultimate purpose. As in Greek and Roman antiquity, the need to pursue happiness, affection among friends, find harmonization in nature and the universe, and seek truth and wisdom in present experience is preferred to the fantasy of an afterlife as the goal of existence. Free thought and inquiry, confidence in humankind, liberty, equality, moral integrity, freedom of choice, mutual recognition and aid, social consciousness, ecological awareness, and political action tend to be primary values endorsed by humanist proponents. From its history, we may see that the preponderant focus behind this movement is on an *ethics of being* rather than the nature of the spiritual, hence eschewing the footsteps of religious tradition, one that is still fraught with debate in redefining the parameters of what is considered religious or spiritual.

Contemporary humanists claim that their worldview is closer to truth than religious proclamation, one based on naturalized epistemology, objective science, and the practical welfare of citizens that mirror human reality. Some are militants and wish to stamp out organized religion in every form as it is considered one of the chief kernels of world dissonance and hindrance to prosperity and peace, while others are conciliatory, less confrontational and condemning in their views, hence recognizing that social ideologies and oppressions exist and will not change overnight; and that political compromises must be met in order to introduce ideological reform especially when stepping gingerly around cultural sensitivities that could inflame domestic situations and increase the plight of those they wish to liberate. Others are more passive or indifferent about such matters, thus taking a spectator's approach or stoical stance in analyzing the psychological and political nature of the human animal without getting too emotionally involved. And still others privately hold ethical principles based on rationalism that condemn religion as an anathema against the liberation of the human mind, yet they do not wish to get their hands dirty in professing their opinions publically so as not to offend others, although they speak their mind freely among intimate circles.

The more political advocates of humanism are dismayed by the persistent social oppressions the institutionalization of religion engenders based on its coercive ideologies that adulterate fundamental human rights and the greater principles of civil liberty. More quarrelsome atheists have little patience for political correctness or according "respect" due to religious faith simply because religion has been socially accepted as part of cultural tradition, for the epistemological foundations based on systemic indoctrination are in conflict with critical inquiry, liberalism, and rational modernity. The divisive conditioning the new conquistadors wish to vanquish is the nonsensical gibberish that still continues to brainwash children and enslave societies in ignorance, superstition, and fear, retard capacities for critical thinking, and perpetuate social injustices and harm. Therefore contemporary humanism as a movement feels an urgency to politically and legally oppose religion on moral grounds. Here freedom against the ill-effects of organized religion is seriously viewed as a liberation struggle based on a moral imperative.

Setting aside the narcissism of minor differences of what constitutes "true" or "proper" humanism, a secular sensibility values liberty above all matters, for this reflects an ethical comportment toward humanity as a whole. With its locus on ethics, we may say that the substance of human concern returns us to classical Greek antiquity where the question of the good life was its main interest, hence how to live a moral, aesthetic, and intellectually satisfying life, which is the recapitulation of virtue theory, namely, how to be a good person. In ancient, scholastic, Renaissance, and enlightened paradigms, the good life always entailed thoughtful engagement in philosophy, history, politics, poetry, drama, literature, art, music, and culture as enjoyment of the humanities. From common masses to the intelligentsia, we all covet a good life.

A. C. Grayling frames the humanist emancipation struggle around three separate yet interrelated disputes: (1) the theism-atheism debate, which is about metaphysics; (2) the secularism debate, which is the right and degree to which religious freedoms are allowed to be public rather than private affairs; and (3) the morality debate, that is, the source and content of our values.[8] Throughout this project we have been principally concerned with the first issue by arguing against God as a metaphysical transcendent

8 See *The God Argument*, Ch. 12.

entity in favor of viewing the God posit as a psychological object socially constructed to assuage human desire and mitigate suffering, despite the suffering it generates in its wake. As an unconscious defensive process, the human mind pines for a glorified ideal it is condemned to experience as being-in-relation-to-lack. We may generally say that humanism as a social movement is more focused on value inquiry, ethical demeanor, freedom of lifestyle, and real or perceived infringements on liberty than on the question of spirituality. Indeed, many secularists cannot buy into the language of spirituality due to its burdened history, although we are only metaphorically referring to the mental ingredients of the psyche, mind, or embodied soul. Here I believe it is important for secular audiences to revisit the language and phenomena of spirituality as it speaks to our deep psychological craving for sacred inner experience and emotional resonance that touch us affectively on a human gut level. Rather than based in an idea of God or a deity, spirituality is uniquely cultivated by each person as authentic self-relation toward our being in the world.

What constitutes spirituality?

Although the complex question and nature of spirituality is beyond the scope of this brief book, we may generally say that the human spirit is an animating principle or vital force within the psyche [Lat. *spiritus*, breath < *spirare*, to breathe]. Just as the original notion of the word "soul" (*anima*), derived from the Greek *psuchê* (ψυχή), had no religious connotations to it whatsoever in antiquity, we may wish to preserve a discourse on spirituality that focuses on the animating or life-enhancing factors that invigorate and sustain mental verve. To have soul is to be animate (*empsuchos*) or vibrant, what Aristotle says "by which primarily we live, perceive, and think."[9] This animator in us is what gives life a glow or buzz. Hence to have soul is to be alive. From a qualitative standpoint, to have spirit or spirituality is to *feel* life.

Whether in solitude[10] or with others, our subjective relation to (and relationship with) our own *interior* informs our capacity to create

---

9 *De Anima*, 414a13.

10 Following Whitehead's (1929b) view of religion as "what one does with his own solitariness" (p. 16), Gerald Gargiulo (2004) emphasizes the "essential aloneness" of spirituality that is part of our "everyday transcendence," which is our awareness of our "unlimited mist of possibilities" (pp. 26, 15). In this sense he returns us to the Platonic view of thought as the silent dialogue the soul has with itself. This insight is an appreciative reminder that we are all ultimately alone in our own process.

meaning, connect to people, and engage life in fulfilling ways. Our relation to interiority progressively evolves over time and persistently
demands that we analyze ourselves in authentically honest and confessional ways, both as we find ourselves in the present and as we wish to
be. There is an innate restlessness to the psyche that seeks more than the
complacency of the here and now, for it *wants* what it is *not* and pines to
redefine itself. This means that we must vigilantly look and intrusively
probe for the divine, see what is hidden in presence, excavate, resuscitate,
and transform the past, nurture and savor the present, and ponder the
future mine of possibilities we feel destined to fathom and grasp. This
search is born of unease and suffering, as I know of no one who is
granted peace or redemption without enduring anxiety and existential
labor. We must listen for the call—that still inner voice that summons us,
the unpretentious heart that speaks the truth and points the way toward
our fumbling path, the doorway to our dying pain.

Spirit[11] is a process of becoming fostered through greater degrees of
self-consciousness as being in the world.[12] When I refer to spirit, I
mean the life-force of mankind, not as an immaterial metaphysical
entity, but rather embodied, intentional psychic activity on a developmental trajectory aimed toward reflective self-conscious awareness, an
enamoring awareness of humanity as a whole—the potential of what

11 For Hegel (1807), spirit is the coming to presence of pure self-consciousness. Spirit or Mind
   (*Geist*) is historically constituted within nature (material embodiment) and dialectically traces its
   own logical and real (substantive) succession as civilization or culture (*Bildung*), hence taking
   into account the burgeoning process of cognition and subjectivity (as universality) within an
   objective world that seeks and progressively achieves pure self-consciousness (as thought thinking about itself and its operations) as its ethical, aesthetic, religious, and rational culmination. It
   is only by looking back at the process that we can see its self-articulated dynamic progression as
   complex holism.
12 Heidegger does not profess to have a grand synthesis of everything, unlike Hegel's philosophy of
   Spirit, yet both Hegel and Heidegger offer complimentary philosophies on the human being oriented toward achieving greater degrees of freedom through self-conscious awareness of humanity's ideals. *Dasein* is Heidegger's (1927) term for the human being, literally translated as
   "Being-there." Dasein's disclosedness as Being-in-the-world is Heidegger's project for a fundamental ontology outlined in *Being and Time*. We find ourselves born into a world already pre-
   given and constituted, where we exist alongside others within established social structures, and
   thereby come to developmentally cultivate various existential capacities for relating to our world,
   others, and ourselves as psychological creatures. We exist *in* a world and *alongside* other entities
   in the world, and within our *own* internal world and *for* our own relatedness to self and others
   equiprimordially *with* and *through* the world that is always temporally transmuting. As Dasein
   (and Spirit) acquires increasing freedom through self-reflection and insight, we as human beings
   come to pursue an authentic mode of living as *care* or concernful solicitude toward self, others,
   and the world, the ethical-spiritual dimension of our shared humanity.

we can become. Spirituality is a sensibility or attitude toward psychic maturation and meaning, something that requires cultivation, experimentation, and (re)inventing novelty in one's creative trek toward individuation, namely, the pursuit of wholeness. One is never truly in possession of it, for it must be born anew, rediscovered, rekindled, refashioned albeit forged. Here spirituality is much like the preSocratic notion of truth as *aletheia* (ἀλήθεια), namely disclosedness or unconcealment, the uncovering and coming into being of something that lay hidden yet is always there. Spirit is revealed or disclosed as self-revelation, hence self-awakening, the "opening of presence,"[13] the light of Being. When our spirit is awakened, our soul is touched—that sacred facet of our interior, for we feel truth has visited us in a most special yet esoteric manner. When this happens organically, it speaks to a certain psychological admission and felt reverberation it has on our personality, whose unique subjectivity is affected on the most archaic levels regulating unconscious organizing principles. In its pith, it changes your being. Here concrete applied meaning is most important, for spiritual truth is ultimately about personal lived experience (*Erlebnis*) as self-realization and self-honesty that transpires within the broader domains of authenticity, creativity, and valuation permeating the genuine lived encounter. Spirituality is inner necessity.

The question of spirituality is a lived existential crusade, one that escapes universal definitions by virtue of the fact that it is based on a felt interiorized subjectivity peculiar to each individual. This leaves us with the quandary of whether it is possible to offer a general definition of what constitutes spirituality and its parameters, as its meaning eludes unified consensus.[14] Whether predicated in religious convention or renunciation,

---

13 Heidegger (1966), p. 390.

14 It is a daunting task to arrive at a universally accepted definition of spirituality, for it is contingent upon what source you consult, and it is usually defined synonymously with religion in the history of ideas. Such definitions may be circumscribed to traditional gospel and customs that accompany any organized form of world religion, or it may be as unconventional as "nationalism" to the broadest definition as "a way of being." Theologians emphasize supernatural belief, tradition, scripture, worship, and doctrine; sociologists and anthropologists emphasize social relations, group organization, cultural rituals, and communal activity; psychologists emphasize intrapsychic, emotional, and group dynamics, as well as unconscious aspects of personal experience; and philosophers emphasize metaphysical speculation, ethics, valuation, and the role and constitution of the lived experience. There are popular definitions, substantive definitions, functional definitions, symbolic definitions, empirical definitions, contextual definitions, hermeneutical definitions, political definitions, systemic definitions, pragmatic definitions, operational definitions, heuristic definitions, and theoretical or conceptual definitions (See Spilka, Hood and Gorsuch,

I will attempt to show that the value of the lived experience becomes the phenomenological criterion underlying spiritual meaning. Whether grounded in devotion or secularism, spirituality (or religiosity, as some may historically prefer to call it)[15] is directed toward the lived experience, and more specifically the *quality* of the lived experience.

If the nature of spirituality ultimately rests on the lived experience, then qualitative experiential manifestations become the phenomenological standard that separates this specific type of sensation or occurrence from religious belief. While belief may contribute to and in some cases even enhance religiosity, it is not a necessary condition for spiritual transcendence. Contrarily, I wish to argue that the lived experience alone may be both a necessary and sufficient condition for leading a spiritual life. In piety and disbelief, the quality of the lived experience becomes the cornerstone in defining the phenomenology of transcendence.

The word "transcendence" has an encumbered history. Here I wish to confine its meaning to the psychological parameters that describe a qualitative state of rising above or surpassing certain felt limitations to reason and experience (Lat. *transcendere*: *trans*, over + *scandere*, to climb), what we may properly attribute to more exalted human emotions that find higher spiritual value, meaning, and purpose in the synthetic unifying functions of moral, aesthetic, and rational self-conscious life. Here transcendence may be defined as the possibility of thought achieving its unitive aim though these modal forms culminating in higher degrees of consciousness, usually accompanied by sublime valuation and intense emotional satisfaction. But what differentiates the spiritual attitude from other kinds of lived experience? In other words, what makes experience per se spiritual? We may generally say that having a spiritual outlook or sensibility evinced in our lifeworld can take myriad forms, the type and quality of which are subjectively mediated and vary from person to person. In an effort to explore the penumbra of these possible forms, with their fluctuating degrees of intensity and valences, let me suggest the following properties (as orienting principles) belonging to anything we may

---

1985; Banton, 1966; and Roberts, 1990, for a review). After delving through the barrage of opinion, one is likely to agree with Yinger (1967) that "any definition of religion is likely to be satisfactory only to its author" (p. 18).

15 Many atheists take objection to the term "religiosity" because of its association to organized religion, however, here I wish to emphasize common human experience that may be said to participate of spiritual and religious sentiments alike.

rightfully call spiritual: (a) the ethical expression of value inquiry; (b) the life of feeling; (c) the subjective organization and resonance of qualia; (d) aesthetic experience; and (e) the pursuit of the numinous, each of which I will examine in turn.

Spirituality, which is mistakenly confused as (albeit enjoined by) religious belief and custom, is often felt and expressed through a shared communal activity of ritual and ceremony around a common set of constructed values and construed ideals, which are ultimately individually forged yet collectively entertained. Although shared by others, spirituality is ultimately an intimately private process of self-relation, yet one that is subjectively universal. Such subjective universality conjoins others in a mutual dialogue and search for value inquiry, which collective peoples may identify with and relate to. In this regard, spirituality is authentic relatedness to self, other, and world, and specifically a *felt self-relation to value*. It is this felt self-relation to value that is most psychologically rewarding due to its unique experiential quality and emotional timbre, which is what makes it so special.

The pursuit of spirituality is a form of value inquiry that resonates within the deep unconscious configurations of each person's soul—their inner being—that potentially stands in relation to a greater collective experience or transcendence of shared meaning and value. The content or meaning of values (namely love, peace, beneficence, and so on) often have universal themes all people deep down truly covet and therefore place on a high existential plane of lived qualia. That is why, in part, ritualized ceremonies, which are common to religious, secular, pagan, and shamanic observances alike, concretize these ideal values and hence symbolically bestow onto them an embodied reality of idealized value that transcends the subjective attitudes of the individual.

We generate metaphysical beliefs based on these experiential feelings of felt-value, and most of humanity have a tendency to universalize them to a so-called transpersonal realm we equate with a greater cause, force, or animating presence in the cosmos, such as a divine Originator, primary Spirit, or ultimate Source, which people typically intuit to be a supreme being—our transference unto God. These are transcendental illusions, but for most people they are necessary ones in order for them to protect and sustain the felt-meaning of lived spiritual moments reflective of a collective (qua objective) valuation system. Ritual and symbolic communal sharing of value lend a sense of hypostatization to this experience, where the natural mystical wonderment of what is felt subjectively yet shared interpersonally is generalized into a metaphysical factor as supreme transcendence. Here God becomes the Transcendent—the symbolization of all Ideal Value—the One.

The transcendental ideal humanity covets and posits is ultimately Value itself, or more specifically, the *process* of valuation that holds the promise of fulfillment, namely, what we hope for as an attainable ideal. When the sublime is intuited or ecstasies experienced, they are conferred with a specific set of valuations and conveyed as the most important of all exalted feelings, hence objects of worship (what we ideally desire) for all humanity. These values are idealized, I suggest, because they cannot be fully attained, yet they signify the state of perfection we wish to possess. In fact, it is the *pursuit* or process itself that confers its own valuative meaning and emotional exuberance. For the believer they remain necessary transcendental illusions to strive toward because they fulfill certain collective identifications and wishes for ultimate fulfillment and betterment of humanity as a whole. The same may be said of secularists in search of spirituality without God.

When people participate in these value systems through some modicum of felt-expression as the validation of one's inner world, this honors their (wishful) belief in the existence of a transcendent reality, and engenders further hope and aspiration to pursue the path of spiritual valuation so they may merge with or form a union with such a glorious transcendental state of being, what we may call a *mysterium coniunctio*. That is partially why some people who have little faith want to believe, and those who have no belief seek to acquire faith.

What does it mean to have spirituality without God? At the very least, it must necessarily involve adopting the ethical as a way of being. More specifically, spirituality requires cultivating a relationship to value through an ongoing inner dialogue of self-relation. Spirituality as embracing the ethical is a gravitational pull toward the good, namely, what is right, what is just, what is coveted and emulated for being worthy of valuing, what the ancients called the pursuit of excellence or virtue. This begins in our relations to others, in forming attachments and affectional bonds, in having empathy and sympathy for others through identification with their emotional lives, and in developing a sense of caring for others and the world in which we live including having ecological self-consciousness and respect for natural environments that grant our subsistence. Here these values are in accord with the spirit of the teachings of monotheism, as they place planetary value on human relations. But we don't need to appeal to celestial authority or fear to promote their value or to motivate good actions. We embrace them not because they are commanded by God, but because they are simply the right thing to do.

Spirituality enlists a *relational principle*, whether this be a general caring or concernful solicitude for others, compassion for those who suffer, the expressed need for cultivating friendships, love directed to those we are more attached to, and sexual enjoyment with those who mutually experience and reciprocate loving feelings beyond the mere call of *agape* (ἀγάπη). Here we may be reminded of Levinas' legacy: our being stands in ethical relation to the being of the Other, not merely as an abstract reference to humanity, but as a concrete obligation of being decent to others, of having empathy and consideration, and valuing the social ties of affection, appreciation and thoughtfulness, and tenderness that come with developing genuine relationships with others as subjects rather than objects; that is, those who are seen as distinct individuals yet participate in a subjective universality that joins people and groups in a common union of affiliation, kinship, fellowship, and shared merit. Above all, it involves a genuine engagement with the desire, comportment, and need to foster well-being in others. We do not need a godhead to identify with and aspire to fulfill these values, for the call of conscience hears its own path toward the holy.

These forms of relationality equally apply to oneself, which means being open to one's internal emotional world as the life of feeling and being. I believe it also entails appreciating the aesthetic dimension to life and the art of experience as an evolving creative process. To cultivate spirit is to open up more novel avenues for creativity and original self-expression yet ones that remain connected to a universal good despite differences in their instantiation. Moral sensibility and authentic attunement to being in the world generates an aesthetic symmetry that we may compare to the stratification of value, truth, and beauty as an integrative function, what the neoPlatonists sought as an overarching, supraordinate metaphysical unity. As it was for the ancients, to have a refined soul necessarily involves a commitment to the pursuit of virtue as a quest for truth, honest self-insight, knowing for the sake of improving one's life and others, and intellectual appreciation for the sheer wonder of being—what philosophy calls the love of wisdom.

Although the existence of God cannot be satisfactorily scientifically or logically justified, this does not psychologically eradicate the need for God. The psychic need for God drives humanity, which must be accepted as an anthropological fact, although the God construct, as I have elucidated, must be mourned. This leads to an impetus for atheists to foster a secular spirituality as a replacement for the God object, which addresses the emotional needs of peoples facing the existential inanity of decay and death while maintaining a sense of transcendence and enjoyment over life. The phenomenological attitude—particularly the pursuit of the numinous—is what really matters, and this is what people are really after when they claim to have a religious disposition.

Feeling and the value of lived experience

William James comprehensively outlines the elements of spirituality in *The Varieties of Religious Experience* where he focuses on the primacy of lived experience and its impact on the spiritual reality of the individual and our collective societies at large. James ultimately defends "feeling at the expense of reason" and locates the value of religiosity in the overall lived quality of one's life.[16] He further tells us that "feeling is the deeper source of religion, and that philosophic and theological formulas are secondary products." If feeling is the locus of spirituality, then the quality of intrapsychic experience is ultimately grounded in the personal subjectivity of one's emotional life. Religious subjectivity may or may not be a part of greater shared feelings of transcendence with others or adhere to communal practices that are familiar pillars of organized worship, but regardless of one's subjective persuasion, feeling is a necessary condition for spiritual experience to emerge.

Feeling maintains an ontological priority in the constitution of religiosity, for without it we may rightfully question whether we can call such lived experience spiritual. Here a categorical distinction can be made between what we call "religious" as that which adheres to an organized structure of devotional beliefs and scriptural observance versus what we call "spiritual" as a feeling state devoid of doctrinal attributions of any

16 James (1902), p. 422.

kind; however, the mode of affect grounds the two categories and fails to adequately articulate how these lived experiences are fundamentally distinct. Recall that the term "religion" etymologically signifies that which conjoins [OFr. *religion* < Lat. *religio*, from *religāre*, to bind]. If the inner organization of affect binds our emotional dispositions to the spiritual encounter, then these events are imbued with valuational properties irrespective of the content of one's belief system. Here it is important to highlight the affective nature of *form* that colors our apperception of the spiritual.

What is common to all religious experience is the feelings or sensations it produces irrespective of belief, and it is precisely this experience that we can identify as a spiritual moment. Thus the ontological distinction (as different facets of being) between affect (feeling) and conceptuality (belief) is realized as a phenomenological one: while mediated belief may or may not augment religious feeling, the *feeling itself* is the proper locus of religious sentiment. Although affect is structurally bound to religiosity, the judged qualia of the emotive moment becomes the decisive touchstone underlying spiritual subjectivity. Here I would argue that, at this level, religiosity and spirituality are virtually synonymous: the essence of religious experience is an *act* of feeling, the animating force of the lived encounter.

Spiritual experience is intimately acquainted with freedom: it is not confined to the dictates of belief, scripture, reason, or ideology. Dewey avouches that "the religious aspect of experience will be free to develop freely on its own account."[17] This points to the transformative power of spirituality as a process of becoming. As a result, religious or spiritual experience is not subject to a fixed set of universal truths, ritualistic conduct, or bound to a pre-established mode of being, but rather it is a teleological and dynamic burgeoning generativity.

Feeling and valuation are necessary ontological conditions for spirituality to transpire and are indissoluble dimensions of holistic paradigms. Here they coalesce within a primal bedrock of the soul, what James says elicits a total reaction upon life:

> Religion ... is a man's total reaction upon life... To get at them you must go behind the foreground of existence and reach down to that

---

17 Dewey (1934), p. 2.

curious sense of the whole residual cosmos as an everlasting presence, intimate or alien, terrible or amusing, lovable or odious, which
in some degree everyone possesses.[18]

Here we may say that James is referring to the metaphysics of experience, that indelible form of wonder and awe at the mysteries of life and
cosmic order that speak to the unconscious core of every person as a raw
affective calling. The life of feeling is that primordial region of the
psyche that is most sensitive to the spiritual encounter. Belief or reason
alone does nothing to move the soul: without feeling, religious meaning
becomes a vacant intellectual exercise. This is why the most exuberant
spiritual moments are emotively laden.

Life as qualia

The phenomenon of life is not a question of biological facticity or organic
cellular organization, nor the complex systems underlying the energetic
stratification of material substance, but rather it is the qualitative vitality
of experience. The quality (*qualis*) of life pertains to a class of events that
is distinguished by its particular kind(s). Here particularity supersedes the
universal: from the perspective of the singular, existing concrete subject
who lacks, life is ultimately about qualitatively filling that lack. If quality
is the internal self-regulatory touchstone for which life itself rests, then
experience can never be a neutral phenomenon. If we accept this premise
that life and qualia are inseparable psychic categories that inform the lifeworld of each person, then we cannot speak of life devoid of valuational
properties without plummeting the human being into the abyss of thing-
hood, of merely existing. Therefore life is an inherent axiological process
punctuated by qualitative contingencies peculiar to the experiential-
hermeneutic subject who lends value or worth to the presence or absence
of such qualities it experiences.

For Dilthey, experience is life, what he referred to as *Erlebnis* (lived
experience), a primordial reality of consciousness that is prereflective.[19]
In other words, what is "lived" is the immediate inner presence of something, an unconscious consciousness. How do we individually define or

18 *The Varieties of Religious Experience*, p. 35.
19 See *Introduction to the Human Sciences*, p. 13.

assign a qualitative attribution to our experiential lives? This involves self-consciousness or reflection, for qualitative experience requires mediatory agency to lend it any value. When the question of life is approached from the standpoint of qualia, the question then becomes one of existential self-definition and the valuation of lived experience.

Qualitative valuation, I argue, is the essence of life. If you lack that, then life is impoverished. Here we should not be surprised by Camus' dilemma: The most important philosophical question is whether one should commit suicide. Without qualitative valuation life is vapid and meaningless. Life is more than mere existence: it is constructed and given value based on qualifications. And these qualifications are e/valuative, hence based upon the critical (analytic) or judgmental (discerning) nature of our valuation processes. The continuation of experiential complexity that underlies the processessential nature of our subjectivity is organized around qualitative variants. It is these qualitative variations that lend a certain zeal to inner experience, which may be the psychological equivalent to an affectively laden animism. But here spirit is not some supernatural force, rather it is a vitalizing principle that animates the psyche—*spiritus*, to breathe.

Life demands a qualitative factor that only the human psyche can generate. This is the meaning-making power of valuation that transcends the banality of ordinary experience under the governance of our biological bodies or sentient thrownness. The work of our vitalizing principle requires us to craft our lived experience, in short, to create and redefine who we are, what we value, what we long for, and what we wish to become.

The qualitative self-organization of the soul (*Seele*), as the experiential complexity that generates lifevalue, is in essence the animating principle underlying the core of our being. This makes life an affective phenomenon, not merely a cognitive (let alone rational) enterprise. It is also not confined to conscious order, for the large majority of psychic processes are unconscious constellations of experience. In this regard, qualia is life—at once both a universal and a deeply singular, personal idiosyncratic expression of interiority, our private felt self-relation to inner being.

Feeling the qualitative permutations of life presupposes an element of self-reflectivity in order for there to be any judgement of valuation assigned to such feeling self-states; and this in turn acquires meaning systems that connect affectivity to valuation. Therefore the trinity of affect, value, and meaning becomes an intersecting desirous-ideational unit of inner experience that properly signifies and defines subjective qualia. And if we further construe the meaning of this meaning to the human psyche, then life becomes purposeful value-laden experience that is crucially significant to our human functionality and worth. Valuation lies at the very heart of life, for life is about quality. Here life acquires a transcendent function, for we seek to experience and realize a future full of qualitative value, one we must make for ourselves. This is why the etymology of the word "experience" derives from the Latin *experiri*, to try. Despite a world without God, we all must try to continuously breathe spirit into life, a life worth living.

Chapter 5

In search of the numinous

I fundamentally believe that deep down, all people are ultimately in search of peace, love, happiness, harmony, fulfillment, and a penetrating feeling of purpose and connection to something in life (even if amorphous or ill-defined),[1] although we may not know what that is in any tangible sense or how to find it. This pull or attraction often comes from an inner voice, as muted and opaque as that may be, what we may refer to as an unconscious call or summons from the beautiful soul—the best part of us—looking to accomplish its ideals. Our psychological symptoms (and every human being has them) as internal dynamic conflicts or compromises are thwarted or failed expressions of these encumbered strivings that may or may not be known to those who pine or suffer. The growing awareness of this need (let alone the striving itself) is emotionally noteworthy and often leads to a shift in one's reflective function and impetus to seek out greater or nobler inner experiences by encountering and crafting life in more meaningful ways. This impetus has been generally referred to by humanistic psychologists as a process of self-actualization. This complex endeavor, which is based on an internal desire, motivation, or compulsion (sometimes brought about by life events that precipitate an inner awakening or revelation of self-reflection) to deepen and expand one's *core*, such as one's emotional resonance states and their expression, or to develop a deliberate cognitive state of mindfulness toward self, other, and world, and to enhance moral, aesthetic, and spiritual value, is what we may signify as the pursuit of the numinous.

There are many different forms of numinosity, from the non-rational *sensus numinus* that has been historically elaborated within academic

---

1 This universal propensity also applies in a lesser degree to the misanthrope and the psychopath who lack these internalized qualities and meaningful attachments to others, as they suffer. That is why they hurt others.

religious studies and its interface with mysticism, to our psychological encounters with natural phenomena. The meaning, depth, and scope of numinous experience are contested among scholarly circles, hence emphasizing many variants in content, form, and typology, but they often refer to affections that are deemed beautiful, ecstatic, moving, intoxicating, magnificent, splendid, inspirational, and so forth. Some varieties illuminate the value of lived experience while bracketing metaphysical claims, while others point toward a transcendent realm of union with an absolute reality that may champion both philosophical and theological tenets. Although I believe numinous experience is itself a form of spiritual authenticity, we do not need to get bogged down in debate over its metaphysical origins in order to appreciate the psychological functions it serves and the qualitative value it brings. It may be generally said that our encounter with the numinous often involves a form of unitive experience with the collective, namely, a greater feeling of unity or connectedness to humanity and cosmos as a whole. We may view this experience solely from the vantage point of naturalized psychology or human phenomenology without importing onto-theology, and it is from this perspective that the secular quest for spirituality is often initiated.

Where does this leave us? If we view self-actualization as a burgeoning process of becoming, a journey not a destination, then each person is their own microcosm transpiring within the internalized psychosocial matrix in which we are situated. In other words, we are our own becoming and fashion our own actualization experiences. Psychoanalyst and religious scholar Dan Merkur argues that unitive phenomena involve an underlying mystical union of incorporation and inclusion that all people possess,[2] but he differentiates between autosuggestion, self-deification, and pathological instantiations yet ultimately adopts a favorable position grounded in negative theology (*via negativa*),[3] although he has been faithful in explicating naturalized accounts of mysticism without venturing

---

2 See Merkur (1999), pp. 22–23, 25, 34. This sentiment is best captured by his statement:

> A great deal of everyone's everyday thinking is unitive. Much of what passes for rational thought is either explicitly or unconsciously unitive. Most of us do not ordinarily think of ourselves as mystical; but mysticism is nevertheless universal in our species (p. 35).

3 This position is outlined in his recent book, *Relating to God* (Merkur, 2014), pp. xi, 44–45, 156–158. Also see Keith Haartman's (2004) influential work on the psychoanalysis of unitive ecstasies in the Methodism of John Wesley in *Watching and Praying*, pp. ix–x, 20, 42–44, and Ch. 5.

into metaphysical waters. But regardless of such caveats, we cannot avoid making metaphysical commitments. Here the presence of *unio mystica* employs its own divinity principle since the contents, affects, and relational intensities produced are radically subjective and private, hence psychical. What anchors unitive thinking in this tendency toward incorporation, linking, synthesis, integration, and unification is, I suggest, that human consciousness is (at least in part) oriented toward transcendental acts of processing perceptual and fantasized events through a priori cognitive faculties,[4] hence modes of thinking and emoting that are largely unconscious. And part of unitive experience is the *feeling* of the transcendental—our psychic positioning toward meaningful value, even though we have argued there is no definitive transcendent, other than that which is conceived through human ideation.

The spiritual quest is ultimately personal and solitary, although it often includes others (by necessity) in forms of relatedness and communion that are deeply intimate and psychologically rewarding; yet this aesthetic supplement is secondary to the internal work of the soul in dialogue with itself. There is a certain uncertainty and obscurity in initiating this task, as one cannot simply go out and purchase this ready-made commodity, for it must be renovated continuously, sometimes contemplated while other times stumbled upon experimentally, or spontaneously enacted out of our unconscious creativities or potencies. While the variety of spiritual experiences generate various psychic penumbras, they are often spurred and inspired, whether consciously realized or not, by our being in relation to finitude, namely, our being toward death.

The oceanic feeling

Not only is feeling an ontological constituent of religiosity, it further becomes the pivotal attribute underlying the phenomenology of spiritual value. Here the quality of the lived experience becomes the overarching criterion for spiritual satisfaction. Religious or spiritual feeling may enjoy many possible enduring forms with varying degrees of meaning and

---

4 I say "in part" because, although we seek greater degrees of psychic integration, the mind is also dialectical and preserves complementation and difference. To say that mind integrates and unifies all bifurcations, polarities, and complementarities is to miss the point that unitive experiences may only involve a certain moment or movement in the dialectic that is attuned to its experiential immediacy, not its totality.

intensity, but is there a certain type of feeling that supersedes others? This leads us to focus upon a particular aspect of spirituality that may be said to lie at the heart of religious sentiment. It is what Freud called "the oceanic feeling," named after his friend Romain Rolland's appeal for him to understand the true source of religious conviction. Freud states:

> It is a feeling which he would like to call a sensation of 'eternity,' a feeling as of something limitless, unbounded—as it were, 'oceanic.' This feeling, he adds, is a purely subjective fact, not an article of faith; it brings with it no assurance of personal immortality, but it is the source of the religious energy which is seized upon by the various Churches and religious systems... One may, he thinks rightly call oneself religious on the ground of this oceanic feeling alone, even if one rejects every belief and every illusion.[5]

The oceanic feeling is an emotionally aesthetic event one may rightfully call sublime—so idiosyncratic and arcane that it may lay beyond that which words can define. This core experiential event, however, is the sensation of a particular emotive tone, namely, the feeling of unity or Oneness. Here we are justified in calling this phenomenon mystical,[6] yet the experience of "oneness with the universe"[7] also has metaphysical overtones. This *unio mystica* of oneness with cosmic totality is character-ized by the loss of personal boundaries through the felt suspension of agency, a surrendering of one's sense of identity with a totalizing col-lective that obliterates all notions of singularity and difference. Like enveloping space, the engulfing presence of Being is oceanic and all con-suming, where particularity is dissolved and becomes incorporated into a momentary feeling of absolute unity.

What distinguishes the oceanic feeling from belief is the felt nature of the *apeiron*—the infinite or eternal: oceanic intuition is boundless while doctrinal belief is delimited—hence bound to set ideation belonging to *doxa*. Here we may further highlight the ontology of religiosity as felt-sensation phenomenologically realized as unbounded experience. More

---

5 *Civilization and Its Discontents*, p. 64.
6 See Robert Segal's (2011) cogent analysis of Rolland's emphasis on the mystical origin of reli-gion as the feeling of oneness with the world versus Freud's psychological claim that mystical union originates in infantile delusion where the ego has not yet differentiated or formed a sense of separation from its external environment (pp. 2, 4).
7 Freud (1930), p. 72.

specifically, we may say that oceanic experience is our subjective emotional relation to the *sensation* of an indefinite cosmos as unlimited expanse, that which goes on forever, the feeling of infinity. Here we may locate the kernel of our unconscious wish to transcend our personal mortality as a fusion with an endless cosmos.

Because such a sensation is so epistemologically private and foreclosed from objective verifiability, its realized meaning resists universal consensus or generalized understanding. This unbounded experience may be tied to natural phenomena such as an awe inspiring sunset, music so moving that it makes you weep, or the beauty and mutual recognition of falling in love—all leading to an elevation of consciousness that transcends the parameters of self-interest or a personal sense of self. The oceanic feeling may be said to be spiritual based on the elevation of consciousness alone, a feeling that evokes the deepest sense of personal satisfaction as a transcendental act. When understood for its total worth, the oceanic experience becomes an aesthetic expression of the soul intimately conjoined with the nature of the moral—what may be conceived in these moments as an ultimate goodness underlying the structure of the universe.[8] I simply prefer to call this the beauty of *wonder*.

Freud himself admits, "I cannot discover this 'oceanic' feeling in myself. It is not easy to deal scientifically with feelings."[9] But it is precisely this feeling that constitutes the spiritual experience. Freud goes on to dismiss the feeling as a regression to the symbiotic stage of infantile development where the ego boundaries of the infant are not yet individuated and thus are merged with the undifferentiated unity of the mother-child matrix. On his psychogenic account, this feeling is rendered a deposit of unconscious desire, a need to remain tied to the maternal union experienced as the limitless "bond with the universe." Yet he goes on to say that "there is nothing strange in such a phenomenon, whether in the mental field or elsewhere" for "in mental life nothing which has once been formed can perish—that everything is somehow preserved and that in suitable circumstances (when, for instance, regression goes back far

8 Here I do not mean to imply that value exists in-itself as an objective datum of the universe independent of the human being, as some proponents of moral realism will have, nor the rather pedestrian view of Ronald Dworkin (2013) who equates religion without God as a form of mind-independent value that structures one's life and underlies the physical structure of the universe that furthermore has an objectively inherent beauty; rather these judgments and experiential realities are necessarily contingent upon human consciousness.

9 Freud (1930), p. 65.

enough) it can once more be brought to light."[10] Although an argument can be made that one should not hold onto such puerile desires, for the mark of a mature ego is one that relinquishes the need for the fulfillment of such a basic wish, the feeling is nevertheless important here. In fact, here Freud may be accused of committing a genetic fallacy: just because developmental precursors condition later experience does not invalidate the experience itself. Even if we grant Freud the presumption that the oceanic feeling is merely an unconscious artifact, it nevertheless is experienced as such, which serves spiritual needs the psyche cherishes as the reality of the life within. From this standpoint, one's spirituality does not stand in isolation from the common values we all share or aspire toward. This is the shared meaning of humanism, an ideal worthy of worship.

Life as art

Nothing can deny the reality of the interior—the life of feeling—something secret, something sacred. Feeling is the ontological basis of spirituality and thus is the necessary condition for all religious experience. A person who does not feel is spiritually languid and suffers internal deprivation, the affliction of a sick soul. Because the order of feeling maintains an ontological priority, it may well be a sufficient condition for leading a spiritual life. In all qualitative variations of religiosity, the value of the lived feeling becomes the essence of spiritual fulfillment.

John Dewey reminds us that experience is aesthetic:[11] life is art and one must live it artfully. The aesthetics of living is enhanced by the spiritual encounter, an experience we may duly call beautiful. The quest for spiritual fulfillment is a process that enjoys many adventures of change, veering from the mundane into the sublime. And for James, "Religion ... *is the feelings, acts, and experiences of individual men in their solitude, so far as they apprehend themselves to stand in relation to whatever they may consider the divine.*"[12] Here James circumscribes religious experience to a relativizing tenet, indeed a totalizing self-instituting assertion of freedom as the beatific self-appraisal of the holy. Religious experience cannot stand for a single principle, and because we all have "differing

10 Ibid., pp. 68–69.
11 *Art as Experience*, pp. 3–19.
12 *The Varieties of Religious Experience*, pp. 31–32, italics in original.

susceptibilities of emotional excitement, [with] different impulses and inhibitions,"[13] religiosity is relegated to the domain of radicalized subjectivity. Whether bathed in belief or feeling, in the end the personal subjective quality of the lived experience becomes the fundamental phenomenal criterion for judging spiritual sentiment.

One's spirituality is an extremely intimate enterprise. Ultimately we must decide whether the subjective value of our own quest is justified, and for this we will have to appeal to the overall quality of our lives. The answer may be *prima facie*, available to the bona fide associations of each individual, but sated or not, the question of spirituality existentially moans for a response. The real question is, What enhances the quality of your living? How about others? Does your relation to life bring you overall fulfillment and well-being—the *eudaimonia* of which Aristotle spoke? This is Aristotle's word for happiness attained when individuals fully realize their lived potential expressed through their inherent capacities. This striving for self-actualization symbolizes the essence of what it means to be fully human.

The love of nature

There is a certain immediate affective response to our encounter with nature. We are drawn to it in its imposing presence, are astonished by the sheer magnitude of its diversity, and accept its beauties and dangers in all its visceral majesty and disgust. Although nature itself is impersonal, showing wholly indifference to the variegated species of life, our relationship to nature can be much more personal and particularized. Fascinating the ponderous soul since antiquity, our love of nature is reflected in the great works of philosophy, poetry, art, architecture, literature, and science that have infiltrated every domain of society throughout human civilization. And the new environmentalists, animal rights advocates, and the guardians of Gaia are astutely aware of our global need to foster a sustainable world where natural habitats, ecosystems, and the biosphere are preserved and protected from human exploitation threatening to destroy our planet.

The romanticism of nature that defined the transcendentalism movement, from Emerson's *Nature*, to Thoreau's *Walden*, underscores how the spiritual may be found in solitude as "an original relation to the

13 Ibid., p. 265.

universe."[14] Being in natural environments, from forests to mountains, country sides to seas, produces an unconscious resonance that connects with the primal earthy dimensions of our animal sensate beginnings, where affective bodily rhythms, melodies, and the prosody of intrapsychic states mirror the topography of our external surroundings. Early sensory and affective organizations tend to cluster into patterns of inner experience that form the foundation in which we construct our personal sense and appreciation of the world.[15] Our earliest experiential relations to sensible objects where desire, sentience, feeling, form, and image often coalesce in an embryonic unconscious language, where difference is contained within symbiotic unification, the particular within the universal given as the whole of nature. Here our relation to nature in its particularized forms and in its given totality conditions the backdrop of meaning we extend to our being in the world, one that is both radically subjective and individualized yet participatory of a greater collective process as shared universality.

Just like seasonal light features and the absence of sun affects our mood, as does the dazzling variety of hues on the color spectrum and the audibleness of certain sounds, being in nature returns us to our basic equiprimordiality of being at home with our inner world. This return to the organic, to original form, echoes internal natural regulatory processes we equate with stillness, peace, comfort, tranquility, seasonal change, beauty, awe, inclusiveness, unity, love, and so on. From primeval landscapes since the dawn of prehistory to the wonder of life in all transforming ecological environments, the presencing of nature discloses the givenness of our world that transcends a known particular purpose, for we are merely thrown into the blind teleology of existence. The intricacies of natural forms and patterns in all matter and animal bodies, from elemental particle physics to the colossal celestial masses that populate our universe, delight the senses and stimulate a wonderment that allows for aesthetic satisfaction. The visual world of images weds our inner sensuous, affective life to a vibrant corresponding external reality, not merely as a bland cerebral processing of informational events, but as the synthetic binding of feeling to Being.

Just as the sounds of natural phenomena such as crickets on a summer night, pouring rain, thunderstorms, forest life, ocean waves, trickling

---

14 Emerson (1990), p. 3.
15 See Marilyn Charles (2002). Cf. Mills (2010), pp. 232–233.

brooks, and so on soothes the senses and induces blissful sleep, we cannot help but be drawn to natural aesthetics and the ensuing flow of emotional resonance states that subsequently unfold. From the cosmic panorama of deep infinite space to the enigma of fractals, our fascination with botany, animal species, geography, land masses, bodies of water, and their myriad inhabitants speaks of our profound attraction to the phenomena of nature. In the poetic words of Whitman, "A morning-glory at my window satisfies me more than the/ metaphysics of books."[16] Perhaps the natural instantiation of Being itself is where we may find our divinity principle.

Environmental self-consciousness is itself a form of spiritual communion with nature, as a coextensive ethical relation to the Earth. The religious and secularist alike cannot deny the inherent spiritual expression of our relation to natural environments, as it broaches multifarious overlapping feelings of beauty, admiration, aesthetic taste, peacefulness, emotional warmth, moral consciousness, and so on united in an ideal or conceptual appreciation of the interdependency of psyche and world as a dynamic complex holism. This spiritual awareness occurs when spending time outdoors and may be cultivated in a variety of ways, as any ecologist, conservationist, forester, bird watcher, or gardener will tell you, or it may be more directly pursued through physical activity in specific natural ecosystems, such as hiking or canoeing, including thrill seeking behavior designed by extreme sports enthusiasts in search of a natural high or peak experience. Here the love of nature involves a concrete engagement with the material world as an authentic expression of the soul.

Happiness

In the *Nicomachean Ethics*, Aristotle provides the first comprehensive treatise on virtue in the history of Western philosophy. Here he introduces many notions that point toward living a good life, among which is the pursuit of happiness. As psychological creatures we seek something that is good, as this is what we ultimately aim to achieve in our thoughts and actions, hence happiness is good. But what is happiness exactly? Living well and doing well is often associated with being happy, but this is far from a sufficient condition. Conventional wisdom tends to

16 Walt Whitman, *Leaves of Grass*, Song of Myself, Part 24.

equate happiness with pleasure, which is both desirable and experientially fulfilling, but pleasure may be a fleeting moment that does not fully capture the phenomenology of happiness. For Aristotle, happiness is the ultimate purpose and end goal of human existence. As such, happiness is an idealized category of experience and emotional attainment that may participate of many features, some of which are more primal and conducive to the senses, while other dimensions are psychologically refined and develop from a more mature standpoint of cultivated human consciousness.

It would be very insincere, if not nihilistically deflating, to argue against the value of enjoyment in life, as most of us live for this qualitative aspect of existence. But slavish concession to base consumption and the immediate pursuit of gratification or hedonism is not what Aristotle had in mind. Happiness entails much more than pleasure, although we may say that without pleasure, enjoyment, and satisfaction in life, one could not be rightfully happy. Most of humanity faces this challenge, namely, finding happiness, especially when there is so much suffering in the world. This is why Aristotle conceived of *eudaimonia* as a nurtured process rather than something you find through a step-by-step method endemic to modern mentality hungry for quick fixes and self-help cures. In fact, we may say that the question of happiness has become a profound psychological emergency fueling the spiritual crisis in contemporary American culture desperate to embrace new age experimentation, including forays into Eastern spiritual practices like yoga, meditation, Zen, tantric sex, Feng Shui (or in more earthy fashions, the use of crystals, aroma therapy, etc.), obsessions with health, nutrition, wellness, and exercise, such as the craze of eating organic foods and utilizing personal trainers instead of initiating psychotherapy, or conversely, the resurgence in drug indulgence such as the recreational use of marijuana and psychedelics. We may rightfully conclude that all these forms of experimentation are attempts at cultivating or recovering some semblance of the spiritual.

For Aristotle, happiness is among the things that are most prized, the result of excellence derived from a special activity of the psyche aimed toward achieving the best ends.[17] Here happiness may be said to be a movement or action, not a condition or a procured thing, but rather a striving toward the ultimate self-actualization of a psychological *telos*.

17 *Nicomachean Ethics*, Bk I, 1099b1, 26.

Among these ends are the cultivation of virtue and noble character in one's journey toward having a complete existence. In this regard, happiness is the exercise of virtue that culminates in a fulfilled life, hence it is a natural goal rather than a temporary state that is not garnered until the end of our lives. As an ideal, "happiness is an activity of soul in accordance with complete excellence,"[18] which contains both intellectual and moral wisdom, but it may be argued that this ideal can never be properly attained, only approximated, for we are always in a process of becoming, and hence by definition are incomplete because we lack. It is the *pursuit* of human excellence that is the main point, one we may only broach imperfectly yet value as one of the greatest goods attainable by man.

As a coveted end in-itself, happiness may be said to be a mixture of qualitative pleasure or enjoyment in living along with an overall sense of contentment. And for Aristotle, to be content is to look back at one's life and feel one has adequately achieved a sense of excellence in pursuing the good, where intellectual and moral refinement has been adequately attained through the activities of a contemplative and practical life. Here one must not only think and meditate on the good, truth, justice, beauty, wisdom, and so on, but one must also *act* in accordance with such worthy principles. Therefore, happiness requires cultivation of the intellect, contemplation of goodness, development of honorable character, and ethical comportment in the service of leading a meaningful life. If we may interpret the meaning of happiness following this general formula, then perhaps we are justified in thinking that the pursuit of virtue is what is truly "divine," namely, that which is present within us as *valuation* living in the soul.[19]

Perhaps it is enough for us to say that happiness is to be found in becoming good. This is the expression of spirit, for ministering to value is what qualitatively gives life its luster. The satisfaction and contentment that comes with this type of success means making the right choices as an exercise in liberty and habituation. Such choices are informed through the multiple identifications we adopt based on our values and ideals. Here it may be said that the celebration of the human spirit is to be found in the striving and actualization of what we can potentially become, namely, happy.

18 Ibid., 1102a1, 5.
19 Cf. Ibid., Bk X, 1177b1, 27.

Friendship

A human being cannot be happy without friends. This is why Aristotle elevated φιλία (friendship) to the pinnacle of happiness as the union of enjoyment and virtue (*arête*), "a single soul abiding in two bodies."[20] This is spirit in its highest form, what is "most indispensable for life."[21] Here friendship is a special breed of kinship that is coveted most of all, for it typifies a coalition between minds and personalities valued for their intrinsic worth, simultaneously a relation toward value and expression of the good.

While there are many types or forms of friendship, from pleasure to utility and/or mutual benefit, guest-hospitality, neighborliness, interpersonal reciprocity, companionship, and social collegiality motivated by a broad range of private and political interests, what is most prized and cherished is true or primary friendship based on a joint bond that intimately engages the emotional, intellectual, and moral dimensions of the other grounded in the mutual pursuit and appreciation of virtue for its own sake. This is an ideal for which most will never achieve.

The presence of the spiritual in friendship is based on its intimate, animating, and evolving organic nature, which is neither effortless nor automatic, for it needs continual nurturing to be sustained. Friendship is not an imposed obligation, nor is it based on extrinsic circumstances such as being born into a family or having relatives, but rather it is elective and selective. This makes friendship a matter of choice and not merely a social institution that one participates in by virtue of our thrownness. This is why you cannot have many primary friendships, as it takes hard work to maintain such commitments to others we selectively choose to value and give to. They are also not easy to find because many psychological variables often come into play that make mutual enjoyment and compatibility of fit a requisite. One should consider themselves lucky if they can count their friends on one hand in their entire lifetime.

Central to the development of these selective relationships is a special form of attachment, one based on love (*philia*), which we typically designate as non-erotic, more like the brotherly affection of *agape* as positive regard for the well-being of our fellow man, but based on love nonetheless, one that is deeply personal and emotionally gratifying.

---

20 This quote is attributed to Aristotle by Diogenes Laërtius in the third century ACE in his biographical work, *Lives of the Eminent Philosophers*, Bk 5: The Peripatetics, Aristotle 9.
21 *Nicomachean Ethics*, Bk VIII, 1154b1, 1, 5.

Friendship is an exemplary form of interpersonal relations where affectionate ties support a mutually reciprocal appreciation and respect for the other as distinct selves but also conjoined through collective identification and feelings of shared meaning.

What constitutes the basic ingredient of an authentic primary friendship is the unconditional acceptance of the other. Like trust,[22] such acceptance is earned. It is not a generic attitude one flagrantly casts toward abstract humanity; rather, it is selective, acquired, and enduring only after confidence and trust have been repeatedly established over a period of time. It may be argued that it is very difficult to have this type of relationship with anyone at all, as it is too high of a standard to achieve, let alone with someone who is perceived to be unequal or lacking in character and virtue. While certain differences in personality, taste, aesthetics, and social attitudes may be proportional or even overlooked, a person's inherent character and moral sensibilities are adjudicated along with their honor. If people do not match on this level, true friendship is impossible.

Intellectual companionship is another mark of compatibility among equals, as we seek to acquire universal knowledge and engage the greater questions that concern the human mind. Here friends aspire to know, learn from each other, support and encourage their development, and stimulate and inspire the other to become and achieve their potential. This is often based on shared identifications even if the specific content and subjective nature of their values vary. This usually involves a simpatico in individual psychologies where concord or harmony is fostered as well as mutual play, for without playfulness, joviality, and laughter no one can be said to be truly happy. And if such cheerfulness and mirth transpires over libation, then all the more is the elevation of spirit, for there is nothing better in the moment than a good laugh over a drink.

True friendship involves empathy for the other, for we are motivated to feel for their joy and pain as a primary way of relating and being toward their personhood. Through the establishment of mutual trust and acceptance, friends confide in their secrets, relaying hopes and sorrows, where one speaks freely and openly marked by honesty and without the need to censor certain thoughts or verbalizations, including sharing in one's psychological struggles, disappointments, suffering, and emotional

---

22 In the *Eudemian Ethics*, Aristotle highlights that the mark of a stable friendship is attained through the development of reciprocal confidence and trust (*pistis*). See 1237b8–14. Cf. *Nicomachean Ethics*, Bk VIII, 1156b30.

vulnerability without fear of judgment or reproach. This empathic stance conveys an internal beauty as each feels felt, understood, accepted, and loved by the other. Here true friendship is the mirror reflection and extension of the ideal self. This means that we suffer when they suffer, celebrate when they have good fortune and success, and feel their felt-relation and attunement to our subjective modes of being, as they do ours.

Although friendships can be competitive and exhibit rivalry, this is often expressed in a good natured spirit of sportsmanship without direct envy and with upmost respect for the value of the other as an individuated self. There is a lack of jealousy among best friends, as we gain from their gain and vicariously feel satisfaction, pride, and enjoyment in their accomplishments. Friends who are able to demonstrate affection, be open in discourse, and convey empathic expressions of affective attunement, acknowledgment, and support during times of vulnerability are the closest, for when our defenses are weakened and we are emotionally fragile, the unconditional acceptance of true friendship is reaffirmed through the mutual recognition and validation of the other. This also echoes an ethical stance of reciprocal love and supersedes the mere principle of friendship through the very acts of *demonstrating*—hence exemplifying—such ideal embodiments of virtue. When genuine care is displayed and received, primary friendship acts as a psychological container or holding environment for spirit to feel, heal, and thrive. Here we may say that true friendship provides necessary transitional space and fulfills attachment needs and selfobject experiences that may be compared to the God function, with the exception that the divinity of friendship is actualized in reality rather than remains interred as an internal relation to a fantasized object. But what do we have when primary friendship exceeds mere friendship? In other words, can friendship surpass itself? Here I can think of no better form of therapy than the embrace of friendship and romantic love.

Being in love, eros, and ecstasy

Sexuality is spiritual, as two souls conjoin through their bodies. Sexual relations with your partner, especially when one is in love, is one of the most spiritual and intense emotional experiences one can have. As feelings of elation bathed in physical pleasure, love introduces a seemingly moral merger of minds embraced in mutual adoration and desire, to the point that we may rapturously call it beautiful. This union of value is represented by the cosmic sexuality of Tantra, the cult of ecstasy that occupies special sentiments of Hindu religion, ritual, emotive symbolism, and art. This is why Indians adorn their temples with graphic scenes of lovers in myriad sexual positions, such as the copulation reliefs at Khajuraho, and why Tantric sex is practiced for its prolonged spiritual integration of body, mind, and soul.

It is no coincidence that visions of excess and religious ecstasy often refer to the great unconditional love of God, as in Bernini's orgasmic depiction of *The Ecstasy of St. Theresa* of Avila, for love is an ideal state of ultimate being. This is why so many people(s) from a variety of faiths experience their God and religion as expressions of absolute love—pure beatitude. But being in love in the romantic sense carries its own exalted feelings of bliss that many people, perhaps the majority, would likely say is what they desire most of all. The notion of having another—of possession and being possessed, of losing one's sense of self and separate boundaries of identity, of incorporation or engulfment, of suspending one's personal needs, of valuing the other more than yourself—all of which are part of giving oneself over to the ideal love object. These are ways spiritual transcendence is experienced by religious votaries when describing the numinous.

When one is in love there is a playful sense of carefreeness, or more precisely, a lack of caring where there are no longer concerns about your immediate personal existence, where you are on the verge of transcending your body as a sense of (or the feeling itself of) suspending your consciousness in that moment. Daily consciousness is reformulated and expanded through the heightened emotional immediacy of realizing what matters most to your valuing soul, where the adored love object becomes divine and most coveted. This is fortified by mutual feelings of reciprocity.

Being in love, or in its initial idealizing stage, "falling" in love, captures a qualitative state of transcendence that is non-volitional nor self-directed, because it just happens to us. Falling in love is something that overcomes you and experientially seizes the very fabric of your being. This seizure is something that suddenly comes over you like a fever, hence compelling you to surrender to its pull or force, where the sense of pleasure and euphoria is excessive. The all-pervading goodness of love produces qualitative degrees of intensity in emotions, such as elation, as well as degrees of valence in *eros*. Sexual passion is always an unconscious goal operative in romantic love even when conscious desire is subdued, for sexuality is the physical expression of love on this most instinctual level. It is not surprising that people often refer to sex while being in love as a "natural high," for there is a notion of suspension or dissociation from daily life in these moments of being "lost" in love to the point that one does not want it to end. This also enters the domain of *jouissance*, the realm of excess in pleasure, to the degree that it transgresses the limits of enjoyment, for we unrealistically wish to bask in it forever. But we could not function if we were always in this state, as it signifies an unenforceable limit situation, the boundaries of which are unsustainable and hence open to a destructive surplus bringing inevitable negative consequences, such as seen in how precipitous affairs ruin many good marriages and fracture families disputing over the custody and access of their children.

People who live their lives on the run, going from one person to the next in the pursuit of sexual conquest, undermine the greater sense of value in developing an enduring loving relationship for the transient thrill of immediate gratification. These individuals often struggle with the capacity to form genuine attachments to others, where giving, providing, and nurturing emotional connections is deficient and lacking, which condemn them to cycles of impermanent relationships or a life of loneliness. Here attachment to others is the most important aspect of having a qualitative life, without which spirit suffers. For the classical world, Eros was much more than base sexual desire, but rather the desire for the good, including rational, moral, and social justice that reflected the political nature of the polis. While sex is an erotic and aesthetic enhancement to the spiritual union of souls, the passion for the good reflects virtuous character so prized among the ancients. This is why the praise and pursuit of the good lends extraordinary value to human ideality, and why the lover of wisdom aspires to live and lead an ethical life.

Broaching the ethical

There is a certain ecstasy that comes from intellectual work, but perhaps this is more emotionally accentuated when we feel we have broached the ethical. The self-revelation of our ideal desires can never be fully sheltered from those who we engage in honest discourse, for our authentic call of conscience can hardly remain silent. When we embrace the spiritual as a moral enterprise, we must mollify the tension between the realistic or practical and the ideal through some form of negotiation or conciliatory stance we often call genuineness or authenticity, namely, the honest self-appraisal we adopt in relation to moral principles and action. This especially applies when we feel compelled to live up to a professed self-ideal.

Philosophers long ago have alerted us to the broad and contradictory array of ethical systems that characterize our moral discourse, valuation practices, and formal axiological categories to the point that one could be easily overwhelmed when determining the right course of moral appraisal. From ancient to modern times, relative, teleological, deontological, and utilitarian perspectives have championed many diverse positions including (but not limited to) ethical absolutism, objectivism, dualism, skepticism, stoicism, egoism, conventionalism, hedonism, consequentialism, nihilism, naturalism, constructivism, pragmatism, intuitionism, eudaimonism, virtue theory, and philosophies of right. There are so many -*isms* that it unavoidably creates a schism in conceptual thought and practice. Although we may perhaps agree that each ethical position promulgates a legitimate kernel of sensibility, it is not so clear that they may have any immediate, discernable degree of spiritual utility.

Each person is thrown into ontic valuation with others that inevitably challenge our own moral proclivities or way of being, including our own self-relation to our evolving ethical consciousness. Regardless of what telic vision we have for our lives, we cannot escape the fact that each of us is continually faced with redefining the personal dimensions of conducting an authentic life, and this necessarily entails a confrontation with the moral parameters that define our self-identity. I am not concerned here with arguing for the existence of ethical properties, which is the position of moral realism, nor do I wish to advance the notion of ethical subjectivism through the negation of objective moral truth.[23] Rather, what becomes important for spiritual inquiry is how subjective moral agency is constituted and engaged.

Regardless of the perennial debate surrounding what constitutes ethical identity, such as one's moral obligations, belief systems, duties, and justified actions, all ethical decisions are filtered through the subjective lens of our own personalities, developmental histories, unconscious conflicts, transference proclivities, and emotional dispositions. It is from this standpoint that

23 In the history of Western and Anglo-American philosophy, "moral realism" is a metaphysical view committed to the objectivity of ethics such as moral facts and properties that exist independent of consciousness (e.g., people's beliefs about right and wrong); while "ethical subjectivism," sometimes equated with "ethical constructivism," is the belief that moral facts and truths are constituted and dependent upon an individual's state of mind.

we must necessarily engage our own internal processes when confronting the ethical. When we engage our moral agency, we have a tendency to suspend other considerations for the primacy of inner experience that speaks to us as an emotional call or summons we feel deep within our interior. Notwithstanding the sober grasp of reason that may inform other reflective capacities, we are often drawn to the emotionality of the ideal that, whether based in illusion or reality, captures us within the affective immediacy of our conscience or moral register, including the impulse to take ethical action. We are always faced with a calculated risk when it comes to self-expression, for every subjective act communicates some form of self-valuation. We feel compelled to speak authentically even if we remain silent, even if we are self-conscious or ambivalent that such authenticity may negate the authenticity of the other. Who has not become conscientious when speaking openly about one's values to others?

Our superego visits us in both passivity and activity, that is, whether we disclose our personal views to others or whether we decide to keep them in abeyance, mindful of their sensitivities despite the fact that our mindfulness may betray our personal moral principles under the rule of not wanting to offend others. In either case, we are under the sway of internal judgments that guide our actions, which in turn lay down "definitive standards for [our] conduct."[24] In this way, ethics obey a *logic of the interior* based on emotional resonance states and affective truths that reverberate within our souls grounded in our primordial identifications with the parental agency or its surrogate within the cultural symbolic, including all related derivatives.[25] Morality no longer remains an external presence: it becomes an internal presence based on internalized negation and absence, that is, the dialectic of prohibition and lack as desire for the

---

24 See Freud (1933), p. 78.
25 Unlike Klein who views the origins of the superego as sadistic expression, for Freud, the superego (*Überich*) is a developmental achievement based upon the complex divisions and modifications the ego undergoes through maturation, differentiations that originally emanate from the epigenetic transformations of the unconscious. The superego is therefore a superior psychic construction based on ethical identifications with otherness, hence truly an agency that stands over the I (*Ich*) and unconscious impulse. Although Freud's views on the superego went through many theoretical modifications, his insistence on its later development out of primitive mind was due to his conviction that the superego was originally conceived as an identification with a set of value ideals internalized and appropriated from parental authority or its cultural signifier. Here Freud wants to preserve the importance of the psychic function of ideality within the moral register we have come to call conscience.

ideal.[26] Ideality always remains something personal and private, hallowed and clandestine, yet capable of transcending personal subjectivity within a collectively shared identification system. But even when ideality is collectively united, it is never devoid of personal ownership or what we commonly refer to as "mine," for this is the affective invigoration that defines our unconscious soul, what Hegel refers to as the "law of the heart."

Ethics is not merely a set of prescribed precepts that inform a procedural code of conduct; it becomes an internalized law—what is both sacrosanct and taboo. Ethics is inner experience—the reverberation of inner truth, even if that truth is transient, dubious, dissolute. When we are attuned to our interior, we seek to express it outwardly in order to make it more real, to validate its presence—to vitalize our immediate self-certainty. This is the call of spirit, the coming into being of pure self-consciousness. Yet it is unacceptable to sequester ethical consciousness to the domain of immaculate thought alone, the dilemma of the "beautiful soul,"[27] where one is split or divided in knowing ideality but unable to actualize it, for we must *act* in order to make it real. When our moral agency is called up, we feel compelled to assert our interior as a matter of principle regardless of the costs, perhaps later justified as a heroic stand for championing our ego ideal. Indeed this compulsion may take the form of a defensive impulse to fulfill our wish to become our ideal ego through the act of self-assertion via negation of others who harbor differing values; hence our ego ideal is validated and our ideal ego advanced in

26 In Hegel's logic of the dialectic (see Mills, 2002a), negation is an act of every movement of thought by entering into opposition with any object we conceive, for oppositions are conjoined and are mutually implicative in all aspects of thinking and being, including unconscious fantasy. At the moment a certain object in thought is negated, it is also preserved within a new state of consciousness, as it is simultaneously surpassed into a higher plane of synthesis. An internal moral stance derived from identification with and internalization of the Other, is based on a dialectical relation that necessarily requires negation of a particular experience (e.g., a specific value, propositional attitude, etc.) that stands in opposition to its complementary relation, which is incorporated as an implicit yearning of what is absent, hence endowed as an idealized object. Therefore, moral presence within the psyche is conditioned on certain prohibitions as well as coveted value judgments that stand in relation to pursuing an ideal, a doubling effect of the dialectic of desire.

27 See Hegel's (1807) introduction of the beautiful soul as an unhappy consciousness, which is the inherent bifurcation of the psyche that has ethical strivings based in its identification with ideality and the divine, but is also a creature of natural desire that is imperfect and cannot live up to such lofty standards despite its purity in contemplating the ethical. Here we have a divided subject that knows the good but is unable to actualize it in its ideality so it remains ensconced in despair (*PS* § 658).

that instance of self-posit. It is here when our identification with ideality breaches other sensibilities and pragmatic concerns to the point that moral proselytizing can supersede. But what I have in mind here is the subjective need to consult one's own ideal interiority. This is the domain of virtue theory, namely, what is good, what is right, what is best, what makes for desirable character, what the Greeks call human excellence.

A person's life is not adequate unless one engages the question of the moral. This requires us all to undertake an honest moral appraisal of our interior. This is arguably not easy, as I am aware of the untold problems in defining clear ground-rules for when, where, and how to act, not to mention the equivocal epistemological foundation of moral action; but I do nevertheless believe that we have an obligation to ourselves to impart the value of self-insight, and in this way aspire toward eudaimonism, namely, ideality—what the ancients called the good life—contemplative, content, just. Notice here that I say "aspire," for an ideal may never be fully achieved, only approached. And this always entails the endeavor to lead an ethical life, albeit imperfectly; for the enlightened soul, according to Plato, is the unification of the passions, reason, and morality actualized through leading a good life. But this necessarily produces a certain degree of *pathos*, for suffering is part and parcel of the striving for the good. From this standpoint, the pursuit of ideality becomes an infinite, poignant striving perennially fraught with conflict.

As did the Platonists to the Idealists, I am of the opinion that we can approximate an ideal, but there is always a limit to attaining it by virtue of the fact that ideality is an embodied (abstract) perfection,[28] which I believe cannot be fully achieved. When we admire or strive for an ideal, it is because we identify with and covet it, and this is in all likelihood because we lack it. Hence absence is an important attribute to the labor for ideality because, with qualifications, we would not desire an ideal if we were already in possession of it; and even if we were, we would continue to desire it in order for it to be maintained. When I speak of ideality here, I am generally referring to the greatest valued principles, such as love, wisdom, truth, justice, beauty, empathy, compassion, and other virtues. We can approximate these things, but I believe, as well as others, that we

---

28 Here I may be similarly guilty of Anselm's conviction that the ideality of God must be actual in reality, hence an embodied instantiation, rather than pure perfection conceived as conceptual thought.

always fall short of attaining them in their most pristine forms, for ideals are ultimately abstract formal concepts. But through particular concrete actions, we can nonetheless attain some form of satisfaction or fulfillment in our approximation or striving toward the ideal. This endeavor for the ideal is a mirror reflection of spirit as ethical being in-and-for-itself.

Aesthetic rapture

If spiritual life is contingent upon the development and refinement of the psyche, which is ultimately about the cultivation of mind, then pursuing an intellectual and moral way of being is part of *spiritus*. But what about the aesthetic dimension to spirit? Is not the mind itself beautiful, if not the most beautiful thing of all, that which creates value and ideality to such a degree that it cannot surpass its own value? This deification of mind is what we typically attribute to God, the source of all divinity. But here divinity rests on the shoulders of human creation, that which we attribute to objects and bestow with ideality by virtue of the fact that we covet them and reproduce artistic representations of what they signify to our interiority as fulfilling ideal standards, even if these representations are imperfect or perceptually ugly.

In his *Lectures on Aesthetics*, Hegel tells us that "artistic beauty stands *higher* than nature. For the beauty of art is the beauty that is born ... of the mind."[29] Here Hegel is underscoring the metaphysical commitment that the life of *Geist* is categorically superior to impersonal nature, namely, that which lacks consciousness, and is therefore more beautiful. Art, and particularly fine art—architecture, sculpture, painting/pictorial representations, music, and poetry—is "divine," the perceptual appearance of "what is godlike."[30] Here we may say that artistic beauty signifies the appearance of God,[31] which for Hegel is an expression of the absolute truth of self-consciousness as *Begriff*, the self-reflective movement of knowledge derived from and forged through the unification and culmination of spirit. In other words, what makes art stand over nature in beauty is that it is ultimately about human subjectivity.[32] Beauty "is the sensory

---

29 Hegel (1835/1842), p. 4.
30 *G.W.F. Hegel's Werke*, XIII, p. 151.
31 Compare to Wicks (1993), p. 349.
32 For Hegel, "what is human constitutes the center and content of true beauty and art" (*G.W.F. Hegel's Werke*, XIV, p. 19).

appearance of the idea,"[33] namely, that which symbolically encapsulates the highest ideals of humanity. And what makes artistic beauty divine is not that it reveals God's presence, but rather it speaks to ideality generated by the human mind. Art reveals this truth through sensory modes of perception where the ideals and values of human culture are instantiated as concrete realizations in the movement of humanity seeking to express and complete itself. Here ideals as rationally apprehended valuations are embodied in representational forms of artistic expression, and hence reflect the higher achievements of mental life that define a given civilization.

The essence of art is *expressivity* derived from mental creativity grounded in affective sentience and teleologically captured through the displacement of mechanical manipulations of raw material onto sensory form. In other words, art is intentional. Regardless of our subjective predilections, aesthetic acumens, and/or criticisms toward objects of art (with regards to quality, form, medium, content, symbolism, perceptual presentation, visceral reaction, and so on), sensation, percept, and affect often coalesce in any aesthetic judgment. In aesthetic experience we inevitably face the question of whether we find the object or event pleasing to us, and this stimulates unconscious echoes that become projected onto the sensory object of judgment. This is why Hegel (as well as many others before and after him have) placed a high premium on the value of feeling and the stir of emotions solicited by the luring aesthetic object. But this emotionality is conjoined in symbiotic meaning with the sensory experience of encountering a sublime object of ideality, a *felt-meaning* corresponding with the presentation of the subject matter of sensation and the inner timbre it generates in the soul. This is why aesthetics is the locus of satisfaction, where we want to become. The thought of its loss is symbolic of death, tantamount to the loss of meaning and pleasure.

Because art is statements about the psyche, aesthetic experience may be said to exist on a continuum of qualitative states of taste and discernment, from the prosaic to the rapturous; or conversely, the hideous and profane. Regardless of the medium or content, art is the concrete manifestation of inner experience. Kandinsky saw the spiritual in the "internal truth of art," which is reflective of both the individual soul and the

---

33 *G.W.F. Hegel's Werke*, XIII, p. 151.

collective whole, "the vital impulse of life."[34] He saw art as the inner need, necessity, or sounding (*innerer Klang*) of humanity seeking an object "realized in feeling," which is ultimately "free."[35] Here the notion of freedom becomes the essence of spirituality, for only an unhindered soul can express itself by adapting form to enunciate inner meaning.

In his *Lectures on Aesthetics*, Hegel proposes an architectonic, structural hierarchy of human aesthetic development beginning with architecture then advancing to sculpture, painting, and music, culminating in poetry. Notwithstanding contemporary criticism of Hegel's philosophy of aesthetics, without trying to make comparisons in artistic valuation, I have always felt that music is at the summit of aesthetic expression, for it conjoins the primordial domains of desire, prosody, rhythmic pattern, emotionality, form, content, and conceptual elucidation contextualized through sound and lyrical articulation. Whether through the instrumental music of the great composers to the improvisational sound of jazz to vocalization, the inner being of the voice of soul speaks to the infinite, namely, the "spirit realm of sound."[36] Music unites the immediacy of sensation with emotion harmonized into a formal order, even if amorphous or lacking in symmetry; and when words are incorporated as voice through singing, spirit is released even more, for language binds meaning in affect, sound, and symbol experienced as a deep emotional reverberation that captures the full dimension of the feeling soul. Singing and song directly convey spirit in festivity, sorrow, and celebration as the aliveness (and emotional pain) of psyche, the rapture of soul.

It may be said that all of the fine arts, as well as art culture in general, solicits an emotional engagement with our interior. In doing so, aesthetic experience is spiritual insofar as it is the expression of the sociality of human subjectivity. As an artefact of mental creativity, the art object embodies spirituality for it reflects the complexity and interiority of human experience as inner pulse, that of unconscious feeling. Art is ultimately about the expression of the psyche that emits metaphysical knowledge, which is both perceived and conceived through human self-consciousness, a merger of the sensuous and the conceptual where the configurations of the social, ethical, and spiritual interlace at the highest level of aesthetic value. And here the notion of art itself is reflective

---

34 Kandinsky (1911), pp. 20, 22.
35 Ibid., pp. 62, 25, 63.
36 E.T.A Hoffman (1814), p. 64.

of a higher valuation as sensuous beauty mirrors an ideal form of humanity.

Transcendence and time

Spiritual experience is imbued with diachronies that punctuate the pervasiveness of lived time. One could have a very immediate sense of temporal presence or a suspended sense of being in the moment that may involve a dissociative or trancelike feeling of timelessness, precisely because you are no longer preoccupied with the present apprehension of temporal events or current concerns that envelop everyday consciousness. The diachronic experience of time is that there is a sensation of interruption with ordinary sequential time: it could be that lived time is experienced as long when it is short, minimal when it is quantitatively enduring, fleeting when it is protracted, or unaccounted for, such as a depersonalized loss of time when one is in a state of psychogenic fugue, meditation, or mystical absorption. Here time is both instituted and constituted in the moment of our living experience as we live it, which may entail a (felt) adjournment of consciousness as withering streams of awareness, or conversely, an attunement and intensity of self-consciousness as heightened self-reflectivity that directs our focus of awareness to a particularized moment of lived experience.

While pondering the infinite, Husserl discovered the double continuity of time-consciousness that apprehends the presence of the past and the future in the immediate present moment of awareness as an intentional act of relating to meant objects.[37] Husserl theorized that the origin of subjective experience sprang from an originating or generative center in which all appearances arise, and that each moment is its own center responsible for engendering time. In *The Phenomenology of Internal Time-Consciousness*, Husserl referred to this center as "a point of actuality, primal source-point" in which time generates itself, "that from which springs the 'now'."[38] Each present moment is held together by its simultaneous relation to the past and the future as a doubly continuous instant preserved in dialectical continuity. The double continuity of new presence,

37 See Husserl (1964). For a nice overview, Cecile Tougas (2013) provides a succinct elaboration of Husserl's notion of subjectivity and the double intentionality of time-consciousness (see pp. 50–65).
38 Husserl (1964), § 36, p. 100.

of the bipolar reiteration of itself in every fresh moment of experience, ensures that the continuously new presence of the "now" becomes the ground of all appearances. Our subjectivity of time always corresponds to a "new now" whether one is reflecting on the past, the present, or an imagined or anticipated future state that has not actually occurred.

Our attunement to presence involves a lived sense of "passing" and "enduring" within our moment-to-moment awareness of meant objects, which is both an act of "transcendence" and "immanence." For Husserl, the ego or consciousness is a transcendental structure that generates forms of subjectivity in and through time where there is no formal division of subject from object. Here subject and object, self and world are conjoined as a whole or superordinate totality only separated by moments, hence abnegating the vicious bifurcation between nature and mind. It is in the bracketed act of *epoché* (ἐποχή) or reduction that reveals the world as a correlate of consciousness, which is performed by the pre-reflective transcendental ego. So when Husserl speaks of time as instantaneously transcendent and immanent, he is also speaking of the psyche in general. That which is given to consciousness is as much a transcendent objectivity as it is subjectively constituted. The feeling or thought of something beyond us or in abundance of us that is temporally present to our immediate lived experience is a form of transcendence, as is the notion of anticipating the coming to presence or innateness of that experience arising in us. Such transcendental immanence, so to speak, is often infused through spiritual or mystical unities as a radically subjective act of meaningful lived qualia.

Time is a succession of phases experienced through our river of consciousness, a patterned fluidity of perishing awareness that contains the coming into being and passing away into nothing of its previous series of moments, what we may call phenomenal diachronies of difference and change within a transmuting process of persistence. There are beginnings and endings, openings and closings, both ephemeral yet permanent. Time is pure flow and unrest, at once continuous yet spontaneous and fleeting, for as soon as you try to pin it down, it is already gone. Each moment is merely a transitory conduit to a new movement or mode of experience within an interconnected chain of moments containing past, present, and future (not to mention their gradations of closest to farthest, undiscernible to palpable, in their sequence) all standing in dynamic relation to one another. Yet there is a universality to time that is ontologically invariant as sheer process.

Time is not merely a theoretical abstraction, for we feel its presence, its coming and going, that which is momentarily here then gone, only to be cyclically present as a dialectic of passing-over into a ceasing-to-be only to enter into a new movement of becoming that is retained through enduring experience encountered as transient intervals of length and intensity. At the same time we may view time as an incorporeal condition, an immateriality of pure event, namely, experience itself. Yet experience is a temporal embodiment. On the one hand time is not an entity, literally no-thing, and in this sense immaterial; yet on the other it exists as actuality governed by natural laws of patterned continuity, duration, perishing, and succession as a flux of appearing modes of becoming. Time is always coming, going, and is *here*, hence developing, transitioning, succumbing, and expiring yet never fully ceasing, as it is born anew as an eternal presence and recurrence within an ordered series of temporal modalities and periods.

Paradoxically, we may even say there is no such thing as pure time independent of mind, as it is merely a formal concept; rather time is constituted through embodied space, hence its appearance is always enmattered yet nowhere to be seen. To be more specific, because mind is embodied activity, temporal experience is only possible through cognition. And here the notion of time takes on its own phenomenological encounters. Time is neither static nor fixed, nor is it a tangible thing that can be appropriated, for it is invisible and indivisible yet it transpires in a series of spacings each of us inhabit in our mental and material worlds; and this is why it is more appropriate to think of our experiential relation to spacetime as a fused event. Here the essence of time is process.

Our relationship to presence and absence, finitude and eternity, flux and permanence, all presuppose our intimate dynamic relation to what I call *temporal mediacy*.[39] Here time draws on the (a) *archaic primacy* of our past as the amalgamation of our historicities, ontological preconditions, and developmental trajectories, the (b) *immediational presence* of the phenomenology of our present (concrete and qualitatively) lived experience as mediated immediacy, and (c) the *projective teleology* of the imagined future as a valued ideal, goal, or purposive aim. These three simultaneous facets of temporal mediacy are operative at any given moment in psychic tandem where the past and future convene on the

39 See my explication of temporal mediacy in *Origins*, pp. 54–56.

present, or immediate, subjective experience. The presentational encounters of past, present, and future we confront as immediacy become our metaphysical relation to time, albeit phenomenologically realized in the here-and-now.

The phenomena of awareness involves our immediate immersion in what we presently desire, feel, perceive, think, remember, emote, cognize, or otherwise experience as an internal temporal relation to intentional objects in reality or fantasy mediated by unconscious agency. And just as Freud reminds us that the unconscious is timeless,[40] the nature of consciousness as such is its epigenetic instantiation and dialectical contrary that fractures its primordial cosmic eternity by introducing temporal enactments in and through qualitative experience, namely, that which we live. Here the intervening notion of self-reflective or introspective awareness introduces a self-consciousness most of us want to retreat from in psychological denial or despair. Our lived relation to time commands us to respond to an encroaching spiritual emergency we often wish to postpone—the fact that we are going to *die*, which is the end of time as we know it. Ever try to buy time? The awareness of our transience—the momentary nature of our existence, versus those who live in disavowal, repression, or a dissociative state of denial over our inexorable demise, brings a certain existential pressure to experience life while it is *still here*, an urgency that we cannot afford to myopically ignore.

Awareness of the evanescent nature of life and experience breaks down this denial of death, for you become more attuned to the fleeting nature of your personal existence and what this psychologically signifies through such attuned awareness. When we start living life from this existential standpoint of attunement toward our impending death, we often hear the call of what is most important. When we acclimatize ourselves to this mode of embracing the triteness of momentary existence, this facilitates a transition to a new state of consciousness where everyday concerns become insignificant in the grand scheme of things. The trivialities of personal esoteric matters become less important when confronting the omnipotent face of our imminent death, where extraneous worries of daily life become irrelevant, vain, or pointless. In this regard, the spiritual path is an exercise in arcane freedom as the pursuit and liberation from the chains of daily life oriented toward attaining something more

---

40 See Freud (1933), Vol. 22, p. 74.

meaningful. This is what we may rightfully call transcendence, whether this is experienced as the communion or unity of consciousness with nature, the felt mystical loss of self in otherness as a merged totality, the joy of relationality with other human beings, ethical self-consciousness, aesthetic sublimity, or any other numinous events available to human experience. Whether we attain such a lofty prize is immaterial, for it is the search that matters. When you give yourself over to the emotional moment as a psychic act of surrender, which is no different than true dispositions of religious faith, you suspend the sense of concern about other judgments and clinch the experience itself as a fusion of self with cosmos, or in more mystical-metaphysical language, as one absolute reality that lacks divisibility. Here time-consciousness is phenomenologically bracketed in this experiential mode of transcendence even if it merely corresponds to our mental life.

The sublime

In the *Critique of Judgment*, Kant offers his immortal views on aesthetics. For a judgment to be properly aesthetic, such as when we find something to be beautiful, we often estimate beauty based on four movements of reflection that make up an aesthetic judgment of taste. That which is deemed to be beautiful is: (1) felt with disinterested pleasure; (2) is generalized to be a universal object of delight to others; (3) perceived as a form of finality without a specific purpose; and (4) that it pleases the subject necessarily and without the aid of conceptual explanation.

Kant's first emphasis on an aesthetic judgment is that it feels pleasurable to the person, but in a personally indifferent manner devoid of self-interest. This way an object is arbitrated to be aesthetically pleasing independent of the subject's personal dispositions toward the object. Here we find something beautiful because of the way it affects us emotionally and subjectively, but not because we are invested in experiencing it that way; rather it *happens* to us and informs how aesthetic representations are reflected in our "feeling of life" (*Lebensgefühl*).[41] This is a psychological observation on how feelings operate in our general scheme of mental functioning, whereby perceptibility of an object is related to one's

41 *Critique of Judgment*, (§1, 5:204).

inner affectivity, yet is simultaneously mediated by imagination and cognitive understanding in formulating an aesthetic judgment.

Next, the experience of the aesthetic object is universalized, namely, it is thought to apply to other's appraisals of its formal properties and is not merely determined to be beautiful based on subjective caprice or esoteric relativized experience in content and taste. Kant alludes to an objective element in our experience of the aesthetic—a universal criterion, one that is adjudged based on its form and necessity, namely it exists in-itself and arouses a pleasing affective reaction independent of the object. Here a confluence of the (a) life of feeling as an inner sense, (b) the intervening domain of imagination in apprehending the perceptible object, and (c) rational understanding find a harmonization in the experience of the beautiful.[42] As discussed before, a prime example of aesthetic experience is our encounter with nature, but here Kant elucidates a specific form of aesthetic circumstance he defines as the sublime.

In Book II: Analytic of the Sublime (§§ 23–29), Kant lays out his thesis that sublimity is not a feature of nature, but rather a projection of the psyche. While objects of nature may be judged to be beautiful and hence produce positive feelings of pleasure, natural objects in themselves are not sublime; rather sublimity is a determinate power conferred onto objects by the faculties of mind. Kant makes the point that the totality of nature, the vastness, the unboundedness that characterizes its might and vital force, evokes outpourings of emotion filtered through imagination in the face of its almighty power. Rather than aesthetic beauty, the sublime is an *idea* mediated through the supersensible transcendence of reason that gives rise to a form of "negative pleasure" based on the "seriousness" of the situation, more like "admiration and respect" for nature's omnipotence. In Kant's words:

> For what is sublime, in the proper meaning of the term, cannot be contained in any sensible form but concerns only ideas of reason.... Thus the vast ocean heaved up by storms cannot be called sublime. The sight of it is horrible; and one must have already filled one's mind with all sorts of ideas if such an intuition is to attune it to a feeling that is itself sublime, inasmuch as the mind is induced to

---

42 Ibid., see (§15, 5:228).

abandon sensibility and occupy itself with ideas containing a higher purposiveness.[43]

This higher purposefulness is the exaltation of the psyche in its creative encounter with making meaning of its visceral apprehension of the empirical event so "that we can feel a purposiveness within ourselves entirely independent of nature." And for Kant, this negative pleasure arises in the face of the dynamism of the natural world where chaos, enormity, devastation, and tumult govern our experience of sublimity, something which intrinsically produces a "mental agitation" in our judgments of natural wonder.

When Kant focuses on the dynamically sublime, he highlights the psychological disposition of *fear* that is aroused in the presence of the might or superiority of nature in its dominion and intensity over our ineffectual opposition to its powers. In what is generally considered Kant's most memorable passage in the whole third *Critique*, he encapsulates the sublime:

> Bold, overhanging, and, as it were, threatening rocks, thunderclouds piled up the vault of heaven, borne along with flashes and peals, volcanoes in all their violence of destruction, hurricanes leaving desolation in their track, the boundless ocean rising with rebellious force, the high waterfall of some mighty river, and the like, make our power of resistance of trifling moment in comparison with their might. But, provided our own position is secure, their aspect is all the more attractive for its fearfulness; and we readily call these objects sublime, because they raise the forces of the soul above the heights of vulgar commonplace, and discover within us a power of resistance of quite another kind, which gives us courage to be able to measure ourselves against the seeming omnipotence of nature.[44]

What is nicely emphasized in this passage is the raw emotional impact stirred by the pure impersonality of the brute force of nature. The overwhelming immensity and engulfing presence of Gaia's powers, which has no intentionality to it whatsoever, stimulates our own unconscious upheaval. The mind's subliminal reaction is not to cower in terror, but to

43 Ibid., (§23, 5:246).
44 Ibid., (§28, 5:261).

transmute this immediate fearful situation via reversal as reaction formation, the transference or inversion of energy. In short, there is an annexa-
tion of power. Fear is converted into enchantment and sublation over
nature once one determines that a certain level of security or safety has
been achieved. This is a very special qualification, as it is only on the
condition that one's personal being or bodily integrity is not imperiled, or
at least proportionally protected from mortal harm, that one can have a
feeling of transcendence over the hazardous situation.

The feeling of sublimity involves at least three positions or movements:
(1) fear; (2) mobilization of courage; and (3) the transcendental act of mind.
We are scared yet marvel of nature's physical independence as might, a
blind unintentionality yet teleologically constituted as disorder within
organic order. When we feel secure in our relation to the tenuousness and
commotion around us, there ensues a felt-resistance to vulnerability, a
bravado which further involves a self-relation as an appeal or will to courage
to rise above the throes of our emotions. Notice how Kant underscores the
fascination we may have with courting danger, which makes it all the "more
attractive for its fearfulness." There is an immediate unconscious seduction
we are drawn to (or pulled toward) in our subdued apprehension of naturalized unbridled power, simultaneously experienced as an awful appreciation
for the tempestuousness we encounter. This is when sublimity is affectively
perceived as an aesthetic experience conceived in our cognitive relation to
nature. Here the sublime is the felt-experience (as illusion) of conquering a
piece of unconquerable nature. We may see this sentiment mirrored in the
Romantic conception of imagination captured marvelously by the German
artist Caspar David Friedrich in his 1818 painting, *Wanderer Above the Sea
of Fog*, a depiction of a man in trench coat and cane standing on a rocky
precipice with his back to the viewer overlooking a mountain range enveloped in a volatile ocean of fog crashing all around him. There is an aura of
invincibility to the image, of self-reflective man gazing out over the heavens
in precarious harmony with the lability of nature.

In his analysis of the sublime, what Kant truly offers us is a psychological theory of our inner world mediated through unconscious dynamics.[45] More specifically, the experience of the sublime is the sole product

45 Walter Davis (2001) provides an original critique of Kant's notion of the sublime as it is applied
    to the psychoanalytic exposition of our traumatized relation to our inner nature we must vanquish
    through reversal and externalized displacement of our psychic contents onto an object we must
    then deracinate, the terrorized other within.

of *fantasy* as the projection of our grandiose self-states of ideality, power, and mastery over feral nature, particularly the nature within. Here it may be said that the phenomena of sublimity evokes archaic, preverbal and prereflective unconscious schemata that stand in relation to primordial fantasies of omnipotence, idealization, and perfection, including narcissistic configurations of our self-in-relation to unconscious objects.[46] For Kant, this internal relation as our tenacity to resist the overwhelming engulfment of nature's magnitude and ferocity is an act of valor, yet one that imaginarily suspends the reality principle in favor of an idealized self-relation to self-value. Here the essence of the sublime is the contemplation and enactment of inner courage. In other words, this mental or intentional stance matters more to the subject's sense of self (e.g., one's ego or self-esteem) than it does to heed the parameters of objective reality that warn us of impending danger. In Kant's words, we find "in our mind a superiority over nature" as our ability to judge ourselves independently of this otherness through virtue of being human—with dignity capable of summoning inner fortitude, and to *feel* our own sublimity as *mind itself* apprehending its otherness, namely, the external world.[47] But this externality is merely a stimulus for our own introspection we are forced to confront. What becomes sublime is not only our inner experience of transcendence over nature through the fantasy of supremacy, but through our "mental attunement" or self-consciousness of our "superiority to nature within us,"[48] that is, the ideal subject of our subjectivity—the felt-mastery over our otherness and alienated shapes of being. Hence our inner trembling borne of irrationality and discord is counteracted (or perhaps merely neutralized) through the act of generating rational meaning. And for Kant, this ultimately is an ethical self-relation to our interior as a valuing moral agency.

The sublime is a confrontation with our interior in the face of potential danger, the danger within, namely, the demand placed upon us to make a choice—to act, which summons the courage to be. It is an imagined

---

46 George Hagman (2005, pp. 26–27) argues that this is why we give aesthetic experience such supreme value, because it embodies the ideality we once felt (or wished we felt) in relation to our parents in infancy. Although he avoids reductive explanations, the potential difficulty with this assessment is that it assumes that all aesthetic experience is the recapitualization of an earlier developmental period (in reality or fantasy) in history, and hence runs the risk of attributing *all* aesthetic experience to the charge of committing a genetic fallacy.

47 *Critique of Judgment*, (§28, 5: 261–262).

48 Ibid., (§28, 5: 263–264).

relation but very real. In the face of turbulent nature, the soul is moved to confront its otherness in its absoluteness, and with this comes an appeal to take a stand over the inner vulnerability that often remains concealed when danger is absent. This appeal is an emotive elaboration that connects the subjectivity of the concealed self to a supreme inner value that is evoked during such felt-experiences with environmental phenomena, namely, the bravery of moral self-consciousness—what the self wants to express as its *essence*. This experience, which is both ambiguous and paradoxical, transports the psyche into the realm of ideality, namely the transcendental acts of higher consciousness that seize upon this opportunity to assert its independence over its primal (inferior) nature. Here the vitalizing principle of soul speaks out even if it remains ensconced in the mind, for the impulse to embrace this dialectical otherness (simultaneously, the other within) is itself an act of bravery.

Kant's analytic of the sublime also celebrates the notion that the beautiful is that you have *survived*, that you have transcended the raw menace of nature (including culture as human nature) as we are exposed to its presence. In this way, his treatise on aesthetics is really conveying our most intimate emotional relationship to life and death. The sublime is that feeling—"I am alive! I am not dead!" Here the sublime is the common sentiment that one has lived through something really scary, hence eluding trauma, itself an ecstatic traumatic, and this is what is sublime. Beauty becomes this particular triumphant experience that raises psyche or spirit above the slovenly complacency to life, bellowing—"I want more. We all want more." What is beautiful is when the dark part of soul loses out to an affirmative brightness that breaks over the celestial skies like Friedrich's mountain man standing over a newly discovered, experiential land.

When Kant intimates that the sublime is beyond the sensible through the supersensible triumph of reason,[49] he also broaches a noumenal reality of transcendence that takes pleasure in contemplating its self-aesthetic achievement. Here we must emphasize that the life of feeling is the catalyst behind the power of the mind to grasp itself in its sublimity as a moral agent that stands over brute impersonal nature actualized through rational thought. The satisfaction obtained in the feeling of mind vanquishing its sensuous world is a felt-relation to value, for as we

49 Ibid., see (§26, 5: 255).

contemplate pure sublimity itself, it is at once an affective-aesthetic attribution that is psychologically grounded in a moral disposition that stands
in relation to what is deemed to be good. And here we may venture to say
that the sublime entails a majestic terror unconsciously encountered yet
triggered by the forces of nature and the ensuing spiritual resonances it
generates within our feeling soul, what is often referred to as the *mysterium tremendum et fascinans*, namely, that which we are attracted to yet
afraid of, the subject matter of the numinous.

Numen

Although *numen* historically refers to a divinity principle derived from
Roman cult philosophy, which Cicero emphasized as an active power,
living force, or presence underlying events in the world,[50] as well as
Virgil who used the plural when he referred to prayer to the gods (*magna
numina precari*),[51] it was German theologian Rudolf Otto who popular-
ized the term in 1917 in his book, *Das Heilige*, which was later translated
as *The Idea of the Holy*. Otto articulates many elements of the *sensus
numinous* that comprises a hybrid composition of spiritual experience at
once encompassing fear, affective intensity, urgency, and sublimity that
results in an appreciation of the sacred.

Numinous experience involves a *mysterium tremendum*, which is the
fear and trembling associated with one's encounter with the mysterious.
Here there is an element of anxiety and danger associated to it, one that
produces a heightened sense of awareness and emotional exigency. On
one hand, there is a sensation of awe, yet on the other there is the apprehension of "awefulness" based on a qualitative state of feeling a mighty
"overpoweringness" that envelops the psyche, which leads to an
intensity in energies that produces an emotional immediacy. This
further generates a feeling of *fascinans*, which is a potent attraction or
fascination that compels the subject toward the numinous object. This
mysterium further engenders a qualitative inner experience that is personalized, whereby the subject stands in relation to and communion
with a *wholly other*. These nuanced elements of spiritual experience are
imbued with an exalted sense of valuation that may be attributed to a

---

50 M. Tullius Cicero, *De Divinatione*, 1, 120.
51 P. Vergilius Maro, *Æneis*, 3, 634.

variety of beliefs in divination and the holy, or as aesthetic experience expressed indirectly and in art.

Otto's portrayal of the numinous not only weds human emotion to a category of valuation, hence a moral enterprise, but also a category of the beautiful as a harmonious symmetry to spiritual experience. What he articulates as holy or sacred is not simply that which is "completely good" as an absolute moral attribute of supreme value, but rather that which has an "overplus of meaning."[52] Here he suggests that *numen* is beyond goodness, for it is a higher instantiation of spirit; but we are justi-fied, I believe, in saying that there is a parallel process that works to integrate both a moral and aesthetic unity, which is a catalyst for this surplus of meaning to occur. Although Otto qualifies the numinous as something non-rational, this does not mean to imply it is irrational, nor can we conclude that it is not subject to logical analysis. In fact, the blending of sense and feeling with the good and the beautiful, which generates a plethora of meaning, not only makes the numinous a rational phenomenon, it becomes an axiological ideal.

As both a category of valuation and a psychological state of mind, Otto attempts to describe a form of spiritual intuition that must be evoked or awakened from within each individual through their own natural path of understanding, for numinous consciousness defies strict definition and may be more properly described as ineffable. Here we may conclude that this attitude toward the numinous is mystical. Although this sensibility is roused from within, he insists there is a *numen praesens* that is *felt* as objectively real and outside the self despite the fact that we cannot grant it independence from consciousness, a point James makes when he refers to a numinous object that has a "sense" of reality and a "feeling of objective presence" that is given as a datum of consciousness.[53]

The *tremendum* element of the numinous is unique to most descrip-tions of transcendence because of the negative emotions it entails. This is distinct from the positive affect attributed to the feeling sensations of sublimity, joy, or ecstasy, however Otto warns us not to equate this dread or trembling with the ordinary emotion of fear, for it is a "quite specific kind of emotional response, wholly distinct from that of being afraid" albeit analogous to it.[54] This is partly due to our "creature feeling" in

52 *The Idea of the Holy*, p. 5.
53 *The Varieties of Religious Experience*, p. 58.
54 *The Idea of the Holy*, p. 13.

relation to an all-powerful *majestas* that leaves us exposed in our insignificance and humility. The ideogram *mysterium tremendum* therefore captures the aweful majesty of this induced emotional state.

The form of the mysterious, in addition to evoking the feeling of a *tremenda majestas*, also produces a seductive facet of attraction or fascination with the numinous object. We may say this is the point of the Hegelian *Aufhebung* where fear is surpassed yet subsumed into a new higher order within the positive polarity.

As with Kant, James, and Dewey, the emotional quality of the lived experience confers a particular form of valuation that Otto identifies as numinous, what traditionally has been relegated to the sphere of religion. Today we may opt for the term "spiritual" as a neutral way of expressing our experience of transcendental consciousness devoid of religious doctrine, although, as stated earlier, we may rightfully conclude that numinous experience lies at the heart of any form of religiosity and essentially shares the same set of emotive and valuational properties belonging to secular spiritual sensibility. Although Otto wishes to make the numinous an a priori category of the holy that is an "inborn capacity to receive and understand" spirit, what is akin to a *sensus divinitatis*, we may part company with his analysis here. When I speak of the numinous, I am referring to a sensation of consciousness that is wholly independent of any association to a divinity principle or supernatural presence sustaining these spiritual events. Rather I am speaking of the exaltation of human emotion as a refined awareness and expansion of consciousness that yolks together what the experiential subject deems to be innately good or of unequivocal value with the self-certain truth and revered beauty of its occurrence, which results in an esoteric and deeply personalized meaning that cannot be generalized to others precisely because this private experience is totally relativized. Here we are not concerned with an extant ontological (divine) object that exists independent of mind, rather we are only concerned with the metaphysics of experience.

To illustrate this point, I wish to draw on my own personal experience of the numinous that has stuck with me ever since it occurred. I was traveling on a plane through turbulent weather (which persisted for almost the entire last leg of the flight) to visit my closest friend in the United States, when, suddenly, the plane began to dive. There was a silent pandemonium that enveloped the passengers, then, in rapid contagion, people began to scream as our cortisol levels skyrocketed. As I recall the immeasurable anxiety and trepidation that gripped us all, there was an emotional rush and imperceptible certainty that death was impending, when all of a sudden a sequential profusion of images flashed before the theater of my mind as if they were emanating from an old-time film projector, except they were in color. What initially appeared to me in sublime vision was my wife's face, followed by the faces of my children in order of their birth, each smiling at me with love and in full acceptance. This instantly produced a majestic sense of calm over me as the pilot commandeered the plane back to safety. The joy induced by recollecting this event still makes me weep to this day.

I would describe this event as an example of the *mysterium tremendum* due to its limit situation and the emotional meaning it generated. Here I am not making an ontological leap of faith or attributing a metaphysical realism to this numinous state of bliss, only that the phenomenology of my ordeal had an elevating consequence on my consciousness. In retrospect, the surplus meaning Otto highlights is likely due to the fact that it was so unique in my life, where a feeling of survival had triumphed over my mortal fear of death, that it could not escape such a glorious classification bestowed by elation. If we were to rationally study such occurrences in people under controlled scientific environments, we would likely conclude that these spiritual events are purely psychological. But that is precisely my point—all human experience is essentially mental. Every embodied psychic event (including all physiological and neural activity) is mediated by mind. It does not matter if *spiritus* objectively originates from within our minds rather than a divine supernatural realm, for what truly matters is the extraordinary nature of the lived affective experience itself that takes hold of a person and awakens another realm of suprasensibility. In this example, we may see how my cherished values and relational attachment to my family unconsciously materialized in this point of crisis, which was colored by aesthetic and valuational properties that neutralized my panic and elevated my fright to a state of spiritual transcendence. In this encounter with finitude, the core of what is most important to me disclosed itself as unconditional love symbolized through the unconscious representation of imagoes. It does not matter one bit what overdetermined factors were at play, only that the experience was meaningful to me. Here we must concede that spirituality is radically subjective and relative, our own private fumbling toward ecstasy.

In contrast, I wish to juxtapose this *mysterium tremendum* experience to the *fascinans*, or what we may call the ordinary numinous when we are attuned to such things. Once again I was traveling by plane to visit my closest friend, this time a night flight to Europe. After a restless night's sleep from Toronto, as the daybreak beamed through the window of the Boeing 787, half-alert I noticed the shape of the wing of the jet, which looked very organic and angular with a thinly tapered end, as though it was designed to resemble the wing of a bird gliding over the earth. Then I observed the top of the world as we soared above the clouds below, which looked like an ocean of white cotton balls with a thin layer of smoky mist undulating over the top, making its way across to my right side only to disappear, followed by a steady flow of pockets of rippling vapor spread thin like layers of smoke—all white. This was in contrast to a vast backdrop of sky, a bit overcast but bright, when I then noticed that the cotton ball clouds had morphed into a rolling tundra that resembled an artic landscape with mountains and jagged spikes of ice and snow, such as a scene out of prehistory before humans had inhabited the planet.

I came to perceive this as a *fascinans*, an ordinary moment—the immediacy of nature, but one that fascinated me more than it usually does. Yet this realization was in the wake of how this great feat of human invention powering above the heavens was in itself wondrous, as if nature was momentarily transcended, mimicking the wings of a bird wavering at its tip, but without turbulence, hovering over the chunky snowy landscape below shortly before our descent into Warsaw. There was nothing personal about the winter artic sky-scene, just an appreciation of the impersonal act of its sheer being, a being ever present, yet hidden from the human eye looking up from earth to sky. Kant would refer to this as an aesthetic judgment of universal beauty, yet one mixed with the sublimity of transcending nature where an indifferent attitude of pleasure arises in the awareness of apprehending the givenness of nature itself.

Another hybrid example of the *mysterium tremendum et fascinans* is when I visited Auschwitz and Birkenau in Poland, the Nazi death factories that housed and systematically murdered over 1.5 million people during 1940–1945. It was December 19 in a rural community outside of Kraków. I was anticipating an abreaction, both dreading yet wanting it at the same time, when I felt a clinical detachment come over me instantly as I stepped into the first compound.[55] It was cold, but there was no snow. I was numb inside—no, I take that back, rather an absence of feeling best describes it, but I didn't know it then. I was frozen but it felt like nothingness. In retrospect, I believe I had rushed through the whole tour, simply wanting to escape. A free-floating trance permeated my visit throughout the entire day, like I was recovering from a hangover. I was unaware of any of this at the time. I can only conclude that my defenses had arranged this so that the details would not overwhelm me.

I've been prone to dissociate since childhood. One of my first formal photographs as a toddler dressed in Sunday's best depicts a sepia tone studio portrait with my mouth wide open staring off into space with an empty gaze like a goldfish in a bowl. It may have been the desperate faces on the walls in Block Six riddled with trauma, the vacant stares looking into the photographer's camera during official processing after they debarked from the trains, having been stripped of their clothes and belongings, separated from family members, and, if they were in the wrong line, deceived into taking showers to refresh from the long excursion they endured cooped up in cattle cars like animals for days. Many were dead upon arrival. By 1943, most of the Jewish children of Auschwitz, after being numbered and photographed, were immediately sent to the Birkenau sector of the camp where four large brick buildings shrouded the gas chambers and crematoria. This was the extermination center for European Jewry, blown up by German soldiers trying to cover-up evidence when the Russians liberated the camp toward the end of the war.

When my wife and I married, we bought a painting from an art dealer who had survived the Holocaust. He had been shuffled around to five different concentration camps, eventually liberated from Mauthausen, which specialized in extinction through labor aimed at snuffing out the intelligentsia. He showed us his number crudely tattooed in indigo on his inside right wrist. He had glazed-over eyes, with the face of a mole. He described how he was pulled from underneath a pile of bodies where the allied soldiers found him alive on his thirty-seventh birthday. He took

55 The infamous gateway to the camp bearing the legend *Arbeit Macht Frei*—"work makes (you) free," was the beginning of their death march once the railroad cars had arrived. The original sign now lies safely in storage at the Auschwitz-Birkenau State Museum due to a thief from Sweden (abetted by two Poles) who had removed it in the middle of the night a few years ago, after which it was returned to authorities.

that as a good omen. Dr. Kuchinsky was his name. He had two PhD's, one in music and one in fine art. He tuned camp commandant Rudolph Höss' piano while in Auschwitz. We learned he died of pneumonia. Ironically, he was attacked by a dog while on a walk, went into hospital, and never came out. He was 98.

The headshots of victims plastered on the walls at Auschwitz were most uncanny. I didn't want to look at their faces, they would become real that way—no longer things if I made eye contact. One of them looked like a chicken with a long twisted neck and a protruding Adam's apple. I wanted to laugh inside—it looked like a cartoon. My defenses kicked in and my antiseptic composure returned. Here I was only a spectator; *I didn't know em' from a load of coal.* But while meandering through another room, the image of a little girl with pleading desolate eyes, holding a stuffy, burned a hole in my consciousness. She looked petrified, like a stone. It could have been one of my daughters. They were the first to be slain. They could not work, consumed precious food, and demanded attention. I will never forget that calcified look. It still cuts.

Almost mechanically, my emotional detachment masqueraded as intellectual disinterest. There was something perverse about attempting to rationalize it, that is, find a reason for why it happened. The barracks, the bureaucratic buildings, the confinement cells, toilets, torture rooms, the reconstructed execution wall, the barbed wire fences, and square wooden signs on posts with the words "Halt!/Stoj!" emblazoned with skull and crossbones just feet before the railroad tracks with large formidable walls and machine-gun towers in the backdrop, sealing off the whole compound. The display rooms of empty gas canisters of Zyklon B, eye glasses, human hair, and personal possessions including shoes, suitcases, clothes, kitchen utensils, children's toys, and prosthetics of all types filled the floors to the ceiling, all encased in glass. Women and children were separated from the men, and, in order not to induce panic, told they would be reunited once they were recorded and cleaned up, only to be used as slave labor, warehoused, tortured, hung, shot, garroted, gassed, killed by lethal injection, slowly starved to death, or whipped like dogs.[56] Gold fillings and teeth were extracted, hair was sent to German textile plants to produce blankets, medical and sterilization experiments were

---

56 A certain sick, sadistic competition between soldiers developed in which the whipping to death of prisoners became blood sport.

conducted by SS doctors; and after corpses were cremated, their ashes were used for fertilizer, or flesh was turned into soap.

Abruptly this place started to morph into a scene from *Hogan's Heroes*, a Hollywood prisoner-of-war set, but it was no sitcom. Then the rubberneck Czech or Pole or Roma or German homosexual whose fossilized face was on the wall (labeled in striped uniform) popped into my mind, like a mug shot gallery, stretched out along both sides to the end of the whole corridor, a photo exhibition of dead people. I suddenly had no desire to see the other camp, but then thought, *I have come all this way*. It is here when I began to realize that I was protecting myself, dissociating from the metaphysics of evil.

As I first came upon Birkenau by car, when I set eyes on it from a distance, I was instantaneously struck by its imposing, disturbing presence. It is a monolith of murder. The ominous 25 feet high "Gate of Death" that demarcates the main entrance and guardhouse, where the freight tracks greeted transports of deportees railed in day and night to be gassed in this massive 425-acre slaughter house, was a horrific visual. The compound was a city with hundreds of barracks. Each dwelling was a sty. They housed over 150,000 people at a time and as many as 20,000 a day were incinerated, their ashes thrown into nearby ponds and fields. The whole experience was as surreal as a slasher film: white frost covered the soil despite the midafternoon sun shining on the creepy grounds littered with buildings in ruin and decay, many having been blown up. Most eerily was the intermittent sound of dogs barking in the distant rural countryside, echoes the prisoners would have heard all night.

Birkenau was the calculated achievement of the psychopathic mind; it was built as a death yard through toil by those who were forced to construct their own burial sites, the largest mass extermination facility in all of human history. Standing on this land, in the flesh, one's reason is embattled by an obscene refusal to believe this was possible, a grotesque reality the mind is not prepared to encounter. *Who could do this to other human beings?* Here, the German psyche is destined to bear the crucible of judgment, and shame, for eternity.

Walking these massive grounds in a Polish December during religious holiday season added another layer of complexity and irreality to this day. It was bitterly cold, so I moved briskly with purpose, as my arthritis was acting up. I wanted to see the site of the gas chambers. The Nazis used *Sonderkommandos*, which were special work units composed almost entirely of Jewish prisoners, to dispose of corpses after being gassed by taking them to the industrial furnaces. Remarkably, their journals and notebooks were discovered under the courtyards and in graves of bones near the first and second crematoria. The ovens were designed by Topf & Sons, a high efficiency customized incinerator equipment manufacturer. Engineers were dispatched to Auschwitz to determine the best immolation method. Their conclusion: one well-fed body, an emaciated corpse, and a child produced the best burning load.

There, standing at this site, I abruptly felt a weird sense of draw, more like a seizure that came over me. I wanted to embrace something, feverishly. I had no idea what I truly wanted, I just felt compelled to internalize this place—to make it part of me, dissociating all along. I needed a symbol to help me metabolize this, to memorialize the innocent dead and unforgivable atrocity that marred the world forever. It was a found object I coveted. My inner self wanted it—the suffering and emotional anguish was every much mine as it was theirs. I was impelled to incorporate this concrete experience into my being, and I instinctively grabbed what I felt my unconscious craved as a natural expression of my internal process. There at my feet, under wet frost, was a porous rock from the ruins of the second gas chambers and crematorium. I picked it up. It was now mine, a part of me—we, us.

Prisoners were forced to roll bodies into trenches, stack them neatly, and sprinkle them with lime. Dissenters would be executed on the spot if they did not instantly obey commands. Dehumanized waste had become an industrial problem. Packing victims into vans and piping carbon monoxide exhaust into sealed compartments on their two-mile journey to gravesites where they were dumped like topsoil at terminus was so horrifying that even Eichmann was distracted from carrying out his assignment of timing how long it took to murder his helpless prey. The terror began at the railroad platforms upon departure.

I felt the urge to walk down the entire railway track leading back to the main gate of the camp where masses were shipped in as many as 50 cattle cars at a time to the unloading area, a hellish place of tears and endings. Their fate was determined by the way they answered an officer's question. Because there was no snow, with open gravel exposed, I noticed a shard of wood from a railroad tie. *A splinter, another piece of nature*. It felt right in my hand. But the next find was remarkable. Further down, astonishingly, I noticed a fragment of terracotta pottery lying stealthily in the rocks. *Could it be unnoticed after all this time?* As I picked it up, I felt a pressing energy to it. This was a real connection for me, not merely impersonal nature. It was a human fragment, like the fractured lives departing the trains, broken, thrown away.

Inscribed on Christ's cross were the Latin initials I.N.R.I., signifying "Jesus of Nazareth, King of the Jews" (*Iesus Nazarenus Rex Iudaeorum*). Crucifixion was an instrument of torture designed to prolong physical torment in a slow and excruciating fashion. After the body is unnaturally contorted and nailed to wood through the forearms and heals, gravity will cause the muscles to cramp and spasm; and in the course of a few hours infiltrate the diaphragm and lungs, hence leading to an agonizing demise accompanied by seizures and terminal asphyxiation or heart failure. The loss of one's bowels was an inevitable consequence of such a gruesome, and public, form of execution.

As I made my way back to the entrance of the camp, I walked into the first wooden building beside the death gate. It was a communal latrine with symmetrical rows of open holes extending the entire length. Here thousands of captives who only had 40 seconds at a time to urinate or defecate were herded in regimented crowds, which happened only twice a day. There, a chip off the cement floor was staring at me, sullied—the human stain.

The mind has an inherent need to symbolize experience it cannot put into words. These found objects summoned me, hence spoke for me, which are now resting peacefully on my mesa, along with other spiritual objects, commemorating what I had dissociated but unintentionally absorbed. It may seem absurd—even profane to describe this experience as spiritual, but it was nonetheless numinous, something I am profoundly grateful for, as it has expanded my soul.

What we find is not out there, it is in ourselves; something sacred, something hiding, yet always present. In looking back at what I was not able to take in or fully comprehend at the time, these acts of gathering were unconscious endorsements of my need to assimilate something greater into my psyche, namely, a world *pathos* I had been staving off that day, a felt meaning of shared suffering with the *anima mundi*—our psychic scar. But my sojourn at Auschwitz also had deep personal significance for me. My wife is Jewish, and by tradition, so are my children, while I am a godless gentile. Perhaps here I incorporated more than just abstract humanity. Yes, I think so; they are me. But as I left Birkenau in a daze with some remnants in my pocket, God was nowhere to be found. And all I can see is that petrified little girl holding her doll.

Individuation and the pursuit of wholeness

Secular humanism, as I advocate for here, is a pilgrimage based on the quest for value inquiry and human fulfillment. As a secular life philosophy, *Weltanschaung*, or comprehensive worldview, humanism is a way of being that seeks to expand our social parameters and conception of truth, justice, morality, and human satisfaction through critical investigation and rational analysis devoid of ideologies. It is arguably the existential tradition that gave philosophical fortification to this movement as an alternative to faith.[57] Its message is clear: We are ultimately responsible to choose our own lifepath in commune (*communis*) with others and create personal meaning within our developmental process of self-making and self-liberation. Although life is meaningful on its own terms, it may offer the masses scant relief when they fundamentally wish for something that naturally will not occur. The truth of our *pathos* is that we are condemned to live *this moment* and only experience *this world*. We have to accept the fact that this *only* existence is our provenance and fate. Nothing lies beyond the natural world. And there is certainly no personal or conscious afterlife. Consciousness and personal identity perish along with the physical death of the body.[58] The inevitability of embracing our own lives honestly and courageously is all we can hope for and expect, even if we find life's tribulations and our own desires cause us suffering. We must simply accept our givenness, itself a *numinosum*.

How do we lead a spiritual life in the face of unfathomable mystery?

---

57 In *Existentialism is a Humanism*, Sartre (1946) tells us:

> Atheistic existentialism, of which I am a representative, declares with greater consistency that if God does not exist there is at least one being whose existence comes before its essence, a being which exists before it can be defined by any conception of it. That being is man or, as Heidegger has it, the human reality. . . Man is nothing else but that which he makes of himself. That is the first principle of existentialism (pp. 28–29).

58 Although one can make a reasonable case that our death is incorporated back into nature or the cosmos, and that we become transposed through the process of decomposition and resultant new growth in the ecosystem—"dust to dust," so they say (Genesis 3:19), or that one's personality is memorialized and hence lives on in the lives of our families, friends, and everyone we have influenced, or through our deeds, writings, and legacy, this should not be equated with personal immortality.

We have to accept the immanence of non-existence, the encroaching certainty that everything must eventually end, especially our short sojourn through life. Death becomes our transition into nothingness, what Becker invites us to live heroically. Dissociation of these non-negotiables as a form of illogic does not take away these pressing matters, as surely as the denial of death cannot sustain its grip over the psyche. How do we contend with the grave disappointment that we have no immaterial soul, that we will not live forever in another perfect world? The vacuous "sterile utopianism"[59] of religious ideology cannot be sustained in today's world. This does not inherently import a cynical nihilism, only a stoical acceptance of reality as we find it. It is not satisfying to accept blunt reality imposed on us like the weather, for we want to disavow these unpleasant truths and displace them through some mental scheme we apply to aid in our understanding and cope with the anxiety of the moment, so we establish a convenient theory of a supreme being because we desperately want to believe in it. The mechanisms of dissociation also allow us the luxury of not being mentally overwhelmed by our utter lack of control or say over the matter. But we all have to face, in contemporary slang, "The Big Bummer." Heidegger's most fundamental insight is what he took at face value, namely, the givenness of the universe we are thrown into, one where there are certain non-negotiables that no one can barter with, redefine through logic, or will into existence simply because our minds wish for it to be so. Religion as a defense against the realization of our looming annihilation by the impersonality of death attempts to neutralize the big bummer that lies at the end of the road on our transient jaunt through life. The dreary fact of finitude, stone-faced and impassive as it is, brings no cosiness, for it simply is what it is: we all end up on a gurney.

It takes courage to live. Life demands a risk, which requires us to take a stand. Theologian Paul Tillich defines courage as "the self-affirmation of being in spite of the fact of non-being."[60] This obliges us to adopt a self-confirming and life-affirming stance in relation to our being toward death, what Heidegger avows "stands before us—something impending."[61] But unlike Tillich, who believes that such courage is to be rooted and conditioned on God's being, the existential humanist embraces

59   Ernest Becker (1973), p. 268.
60   *The Courage to Be*, p. 152.
61   *Being and Time*, p. 294.

the acceptance of finitude and is *inspired by it*, for our being toward death is a catalyst for enjoying life in the present. The self-affirmation of being is continually grounded in relation to our looming non-being as a meaningful trajectory of experience generated and regenerated in each moment. This requires us to courageously seize upon our facticity as being in relation to our impermanence and take hold of and mold the way we wish to structure our lives in the face of our assured finitude.

It takes courage to live life in the face of being when death is merely a blink away. The question becomes, as Tillich asks, How does one acquire this courage to be? His solution is theistic faith. May I suggest an alternative? It is to be found in and grounded in the form of lived valuation or the lifeworld we make for ourselves. This requires us adopting and fashioning a unique sensibility of value we imbue in all important aspects of our being in the world. Rather than faith, which is a plea for postponing natural inevitability, the humanist's sober acceptance that there is no beyond is itself a courage to be.

Because many people (I would say most) live in distress of having to take personal responsibility to create or construct meaning in their lives, to which only we are held accountable, it becomes so much easier for them to focus on personal felt entitlement and/or blaming others or society for not fulfilling their so-called needs, as if the aloof universe owes them something; or on absence and loss, even lost meaning, rather than on what can be gained or generated by the subjective agent standing in relation to the marvel of presence. This belongs to the wonder of being, not as faith, not as a transcendent divine infinity, but as *fascinans*. The wonder that Being even *is* is itself a glorious wonder.

People who are in psychic need of spirituality or long for a spiritual component to their lives without God can no longer afford to dismiss, dissociate, put off, or ignore how one is supposed to live and should live. This is not merely an abstract philosophical exercise, but rather it is a spiritual *quest*-ion that no human who lives an authentic existence can truly avoid, as the psyche is in pursuit of transcendence even if every illusion is denounced and the natural facts of being are accepted by solemn reason. The fact that humans seek transcendence speaks to a fundamental psychological need that is ontologically grounded and phenomenologically necessitated. The pining itself is about the quality of lived experience, the subjective longing to satiate the lack. Therefore the need for transcendence speaks to human desire in search of a soul.

The one variable that unites all these areas of the spiritual—namely, the oceanic feeling, the love of nature, happiness, friendship, being in love, the ethical, the aesthetic, sublimity, unitive ecstasies, and the numinous—is a subjective emotional radiance or felt-connection to the valued and valuing object, whether that be to a human ideal, a person, an object of nature, or an artistic production, because desire, value, and beauty of the ideal resonates within the unconscious soul and informs the epigenesis of mind.

In our psychological refinement as human beings, there is an inner conflict we *must* go through in order to come to terms with mortality, the question of transcendence, and acquiescence to our natural state of affairs without the deception of an afterlife. We may refer to this as the surrender to Being, a giving over of oneself to the naked thereness of the world itself, from the universal to the particular. And this surrender naturally entails a submission to wonder. The spiritual question involves an inner gnawing that is uniquely subjective and peculiar to each individual for it cannot be handed over as ready-made principles of knowledge or prescribed behavior. Knowledge is not the same as inner felt-experience or compulsion, nor do prescribed actions retain the same value as authentic choice, novelty, the discovery of being, and the self-creation of meaning. There is no step-by-step method to follow. Spirituality is generated by each agent in distinct forms fashioned by the values they adopt and aspire to cultivate. Yet the quest for spirituality ultimately culminates in a union with the emotional, moral, and aesthetic communions to what humanity ultimately symbolizes—the idealization of value.

We cannot avoid mortality, our depressing fate, for the "black foe" stands behind the curtain. With this realization comes an inner wake-up call, the existential awareness initiated by anxiety needed to help each of us become and fulfill our possibilities. C.G. Jung referred to this as an individuation process, a self-defined path or creative practice of our own becoming, that is, the personal struggle for wholeness. But what does this mean? At the very least, it assumes a self-defining mission of enriching one's own self-identity and expressing one's personality in authentic ways. This urge or call toward self-definition is accompanied by the inner need for generating meaning (both personal and shared) as a humanizing experiment in becoming a liberated person who has exercised their freedom and actualized to the best of their ability a potential for living a satisfying life. This primal human theme equally applies today as it did in

antiquity, but perhaps it is best captured by the resurgence in the centrality and implementation of the will recapitulated by the romantic, idealist,
and existential movements. Why is this timeless striving so important to
our human psychologies across epochs and cultures? Because we all want
to be free and happy.

The life-affirming path of the human will in search of meaning and
self-realization is a perennial theme that defines the problem of human
existence where we struggle to be unpretentious and overcome anxiety,
despair, isolation, and meaninglessness. The notion of a person's self-
selected individuation process is more of an esoteric journey or aim
geared toward fostering one's possibilities rather than achieving an ultimate destination,[62] and this necessarily entails becoming more self-aware
through introspection and the direct analysis of one's own psyche and the
cultural milieu we inhabit in order to militate against the disharmony,
fragmentation, estrangement, self-alienation, and narrow-focus in which
modern society lives. This means that we must create the existential
fabric of our lives for ourselves by generating qualitative experiences and
nurturing opportunities for fulfillment as the process of our own becoming. Here our optimistic relation to becoming is essential in order to sur-
mount the stasis and disillusionment with the psychopathology of
everyday life that largely saturates sterilized society enveloped in ignorance, consumerism, hedonism, narcissism, apathy, political corruption,
military warfare, and a generalized lack of empathy and compassion for
our fellow man.

The process of individuation demands work and inward exploration,
as well as experimentation by crafting purposeful experiences, not to
mention putting yourself into situations that bring about desired or meaningful results, even if they occasionally garner negative consequences. It
is both a solitary activity and at once a communal one, for we all seek to
establish a personal identity that is unique from others, which differentiates the individual from the mass as the self-assertion of one's personhood, but at the same time stands in relation to a collective set of values,
norms, expectations, and needs for acceptance, validation, and understanding underlying the social motivation for mutual recognition. Here
there is a dialectical vacillation between self and other, the individual and

---

62 J.J. Clarke (1992) offers a nice overview of Jung's individuation process and its embrace of existentialism (especially see pp. 155–156).

the collective, that requires synthetic mediation while simultaneously preserving the notion of difference. This requires us to adopt a dual perspective toward life that is simultaneously oriented toward both self and other within a unifying principle of universality or holism.

Let us first begin with differentiating our self-defining processes and the psychological need for singularity, separateness, and uniqueness. The psychic impulse for difference and distinctiveness is a natural one based on an individual's want for self-expression, competition, value inquiry, and the peculiarity of describing and encountering life. This is a fundamental narcissistic relation to the experience and rediscovery of the self. This is not inherently pathological, for it simply underscores the existentiell preoccupation we have with our own interior. Individuation is a process of self-determination. On the one hand, it is absolutely idiosyncratic and eccentric to the personality of the individual, while on the other it is a universal feature inherent to human nature. The only difference is that only *you* can live your life and give it value, and that is what makes it so special. This is likely why historically the proto-transcendental reference to spirit is both the symbolic personification of an individual's soul and a collective identification with a universal phenomenon as the embodiment of humanity as a whole. As an existential plea for individuation, this means accepting the obligatory necessity of taking responsibility for our lives and making autonomous choices rather than blaming or placing accountability onto others for what is incumbent upon ourselves to accept and accomplish. In its essence, this is our ontic encounter with freedom. We ultimately make our own beds where we lie.

The notion of individuation can be summarized as the human creed for perfecting one's full potential. As Jung puts it, "Personality is the supreme realization of the innate idiosyncrasy of a living being. It is an act of high courage flung in the face of life, the absolute affirmation of all that constitutes the individual."[63] This could have been Tillich speaking. From antiquity through to psychoanalysis, there is an incessant exigency placed upon us all for increased self-awareness and attentiveness to the vicissitudes of the psyche. From the Delphic decree "Know thyself" to Kierkegaard's attack on Christendom, Schopenhauer's suffering will, Camus' absurd universe, and Nietzsche's *Übermensch* who affirms life

---

63 *Collected Works*, Vol. 17, p. 284.

in the face of a meaningless world, Jung is in good company among the existentialists.

On the metaphysical side of our existential ponderings, we ultimately stand in relation to the seduction and promise of something greater, a unifying or integrative function we may rightfully call transcendental, yet one that is not transcendent—meaning it does not exist beyond or independent of mind. And if it does, as it is argued, something that we cannot epistemologically ascertain, it would merely be an impersonal aspect of the natural givenness of objects. Yet this transcendental thrust is a powerful faculty of mind, which, I suggest, is ultimately the mechanism behind unitive processes that wed spiritual experience to ideas and objects. This psychic organization consists of a generic or formal tendency to synthesize objects of experience into logical orderings, categories, causal sequences, patterns, and meaningful wholes as an agentic event. Theologians and religious scholars often confuse or conflate this psychic function with mysticism or claim this is proof of God's ontology, when we may have a cogently rational or logical account for cognizing these phenomena grounded in naturalized frameworks. Although mystical encounters with the divine may be said to participate of unitive experiences that spring from the natural a priori transcendental faculties of mind that are postulated to account for unconscious acts of apperception, incorporation, inclusion, synthetic judgment, and unification that pre-reflectively transpire outside of conscious awareness,[64] we do not need to extrapolate that this formal cognitive proclivity toward information processing supports theological realism nor conclude that unitive thinking is inherently mystical. The mind's ability to integrate, bind, or attempt to form unities of the variances of experience may be viewed as an organic psychological act of making meaning of the world devoid of any supernatural principles whatsoever. Yet the concerning need for wholeness speaks to our being-in-relation-to-lack.

We have an equiprimordial relation to otherness that dialectically informs who we are, that is, the internalization of the Other—the social, linguistic, and cultural ontology in which we are physically and symbolically situated. Our subjective engagement with our own interior is at once an interpersonal relation to others within a greater cosmic rubric of onto-

---

64 Cf. Kant's (1781/1787) notion of the "transcendental unity of apperception" (A 107) and Husserl's (2001) "passive synthesis."

logical inclusion our minds are drawn to consider. Here lies the magic of metaphysics, that of speculative philosophy and abductive logic, namely, the desire to find a rational place where everything logically fits into its own scheme within a supraordinate process. We have called this penchant many things, from the One to the Absolute, the Transcendent, Cosmos, Being, and God, when we are actually illuminating an experiential feeling of the *need for connection* to a whole. For Jung, wholeness as individuation is a remedy for our psychological malaise where spirituality is deemed a necessary panacea. This is why he placed such great emphasis on the pursuit of the numinous. In his words, "A man who has never experienced that has missed something important."[65]

To become a fully functional and individuated self is to acquire a liberated psyche, and this can only be attained through self-knowledge. This requires us to develop an intimate relationship with our own mind and all the various aspects of who we are and what we experience internally. This means being habitually self-observant, introspective, truthful about our inner thoughts, feelings, and fantasies, and attuned to the microdynamics of our interior. This further requires us to suspend our resistances about inner experiences we are sensitive or defensive about and develop a self-reflective function or capacity for self-analysis where our perceptive ego allows for an honest appraisal of our inclinations, will, and personality. In this respect, individuation may be analogous to a form of self-psychotherapy as a voyage of insight, acceptance, and healing.

Because the mind is dialectically constituted, hence populated by multiplicities of dualities and opposing desires that stand in relation to one another, it becomes the task of a liberated mind to integrate these opposites within a meaningful rubric. This capacity for integrating oppositions or complementarities within oneself Jung called the "transcendent function."[66] We may view this psychic pulse as a requisite avenue toward achieving wholeness. Having to embrace myriad aspects of oneself as discrete units of experience held together by a unifying thread of psychic interrelatedness is no small feat, for inner experience is alive and coalesces into quasi-autonomous self-states that demand a sustained existence of their own; yet they stand in juxtaposition to unitive pressures that seek to integrate all internality into a meaningful totality.

---

65 *Memories, Dreams, Reflections*, p. 356.
66 Jung (1916) concludes his essay by saying: "It is a way of attaining liberation by one's own efforts and of finding the courage to be oneself" (*Collected Works*, Vol. 8, p. 91).

As transmutational process (never an achieved finality), we may say that individuation involves a certain exertion toward self-emancipation from the more inauthentic, unsavory, and monotonous dimensions of life despite the fact that we can never fully transcend our fermenting *pathos*. Instead we aim for a more self-actualized existence bathed in enjoyment, fulfillment, and wisdom with the perspicacious awareness that such ideality can never be attained, only approximated. Here we must choose our own unique lifepath or individual way where each person must follow their own organic or natural calling, the life within. This requires a honed acumen for listening to one's inner voice that is oriented toward the better aspects of our nature, such as our ethical side in touch with valuation as humanity's chief preoccupation. In the end it is the pursuit that counts.

Whether unconsciously orchestrated or consciously chosen, the quest for holism becomes much more of a pressing need as you get older and more cognizant of your impinging mortality. Our being toward death is perhaps the most intimate of all experiential encounters, for only "I" can live my own death. There is no stand-in to take my place, no anonymous other. We must live it alone. Despite the fact that mortality is a universal occurrence for all sentient beings, no one else can die for me. This is what makes it completely solitary, inimitable, and exclusive. In the hovering moments of finality, we are all a one-man show. I want to live my own life as fullest as I can, and that means in innermost closeness and sobriety to my own death. No one wants termination, the end of all experience, that is why embracing our impending transience adds more value to the moment and helps us prepare for death. In the end, I want to be able to say, "I had a good life, and I made the most of it the best way I could."

It takes guts to be in full recognition of one's mortality, as it makes us nervous (hence takes nerve) to think we are going to end. That is why most people do not think about their looming death until it visits them in old age, illness, or tragedy. The full realization: "I am going to die"—that is courage, a necessary existential risk we are forced to lean into. This is why savoring the moment and living in the present ceases to be a cliché, for the TV set will be turned off for good very soon. What this recognition compels us to do is to become more attuned and tolerant of the mundanity of the moment, as well as electrifying the urgency of enjoying your experiences now. Enjoying experience right now should be a telic priority if not a fundamental life goal.

No words can placate, intellectualize, or rationalize away our private encounter with death, for life hangs by a hair (*de pilo pendet*). Despite the impersonality of death and our brute rational acceptance of the implacability of finitude, logos cannot prevent the inevitable. Although there is an inherent teleology to both life and death, death becomes our final aim and destiny. In the somber words of Quintilian, everything that is born passes away (*deficit omne quod nascitur*). I personally see no overarching purpose or disambiguation we can assign to death, other than the meanings we generate for ourselves. Just like our birth and our miraculous, astronomical thrownness into a life-supporting universe, it merely happens. Even if we grant death the final cause of existence, understanding does not take away from the human angst it generates. Here death should be respected as an incentive to live life while you can, and this means to maximize the cultivation and incorporation of experience. In our being toward passing, namely, the here-and-now presence of our felt-relation to a future ending, comes the realization that our time here on earth is precious, for death is the end of becoming.

If the aim of all life is death,[67] then we are all preparing for rest, a tensionless state where we no longer feel anxiety and suffer, the culmination and fulfillment of life. God was invented to extinguish our suffering. Here there is no difference: death is the terminus of pain. In other words, death is eternal peace, the end to all negativity and conflict, the cessation of our *pathos*. So how do we prepare for death? By being aware of it, leaning into its immanence, seizing the array of choices we are condemned to face, and making peace with the limited time we have left, such as the activities we wish to take up when we have the chance, and the legacy we wish to leave behind in this flicker of light that traverses the historical progression of the cosmos, which will soon vanish into nothingness. This is why generating and embracing the utmost of experience is all we can strive for.

The spiritual quest does not require a supernatural intelligence to give purpose and qualitative value to life, for this is incumbent on us. Even though we are all headed for a pine box, this does not mean that we cannot find intrinsic worth and meaning in living our lives for the present, not for a fantasized future. Despite that the thrust of our being toward

---

67 Recall that Freud (1920) made the death drive (*Todestrieb*) the centrality of the psyche and the impetus behind the variegations of life (see p. 38). Compare to Horace: death is the final goal of things (*mors ultima linea rerum est*).

death is imposed on us without consultation, we can faithfully choose to live our lives creatively and authentically, as the pursuit of meaning and value, which naturally privileges our relationality to others, for nothing else really matters. The call of finitude is a constant reminder that we are obligated to actualize our possibilities, because we only have one chance at life. This makes every decision we make a priority, and we have no one else to blame for our choices but ourselves.

To be honest with ourselves and others, free of blind ignorance or self-deception; to open ourselves up to the affective interiority of our beings; to experience genuine emotion and spontaneity; to love, work, and play; to tolerate ambiguity through the courage to be; to have compassion and empathy for others' suffering, as well as our own; to contemplate the numinous and follow a moral path; and be committed to becoming a decent human being—What else can we reasonably ask for? We are the authors of our own lives, to be lived and relived. Despite our passions, fallibility, and finite natures, we have no other recourse than to accept our thrownness with humility. We call this humanism—The I that is We, and the We that is I.

About the author

Jon Mills, Psy.D., Ph.D., ABPP is a philosopher, psychoanalyst, and clinical psychologist. He is Professor of Psychology & Psychoanalysis at the Adler Graduate Professional School in Toronto and is the author of many works in philosophy, psychoanalysis, and psychology including seventeen books. In 2006, 2011 and 2013 he was recognized with a Gradiva Award from the National Association for the Advancement of Psychoanalysis in New York City for his scholarship, received a Significant Contribution to Canadian Psychology Award in 2008, a Goethe Award for best book in 2013, and the Otto Weininger Memorial Award for lifetime achievement in 2015 by the Section on Psychoanalytic and Psychodynamic Psychology of the Canadian Psychological Association. He runs a mental health corporation in Ontario, Canada.

References

Adherents.com (2013). *Religious statistical database.* www.adherents.com/rel_USA. html#religions.

American Humanist Association (2013). *Historical Development of the American Humanist Association.* www.americanhumanist.org/what_we_do/publications/Humanism_as_the_ Next_Step/Chapter_8:_The_Development_of_Organization.

American Humanist Association (2014). *The Humanist: A Magazine of Critical Inquiry and Social Concern.* May/June. Washington, DC, pp. 1–48.

Anselm. *Monologion and Proslogion with Replies of Gaunilo and Anselm.* Trans. Thomas Williams, 1995. Indianapolis: Hackett.

Aquinas, St. Thomas (ca. 1256–1272). *Summa Theologiae.* Trans. The Fathers of the English Dominican Province, 1947. www.sacred-texts.com/chr/aquinas/summa/.

Aranya, Swami Hariharananda (1981/1983). *Yoga Philosophy of Patanjali: Containing his Yoga Aphorisms with Vyasa's Commentary in Sanskrit and a Translation with Annotations Including Many Suggestions for the Practice of Yoga.* Trans. Peresh Nath Mukerji, 3rd Ed. Calcutta: Calcutta University Press; rpt. Albany, NY: SUNY Press.

Aristotle. *De Anima* (On the Soul). In J. Barnes (Ed.), *The Complete Works of Aristotle. 2 Vols.* (The revised Oxford Trans.). Princeton, NJ: Princeton University Press, 1984, pp. 641–692.

Aristotle. *Eudemian Ethics.* In J. Barnes (Ed.). *The Complete Works of Aristotle. 2 Vols.* (The revised Oxford Trans.). Princeton, NJ: Princeton University Press, 1984, pp. 1922–1981.

Aristotle. *Metaphysics.* In J. Barnes (Ed.). *The Complete Works of Aristotle. 2 Vols.* (The revised Oxford Trans.). Princeton, NJ: Princeton University Press, 1984, pp. 1552–1728.

Aristotle. *Nicomachean Ethics.* In J. Barnes (Ed.). *The Complete Works of Aristotle. 2 Vols.* (The revised Oxford Trans.). Princeton, NJ: Princeton University Press, 1984, pp. 1729–1867.

Aristotle. *Physics.* In J. Barnes (Ed.). *The Complete Works of Aristotle. 2 Vols.* (The revised Oxford Trans.). Princeton, NJ: Princeton University Press, 1984, pp. 315–446.

Armstrong, Karen (2010). *The Case for God.* Toronto: Vintage Canada.

Atkatz, David and Pagels, Heinz (1982). Origin of the Universe as Quantum Tunneling Event. *Physical Review*, D25, pp. 2065–2067.

Augustine. *Confessions.* Trans. Henry Chadwick, 2008. Oxford: Oxford University Press.

Bakan, David (2001). On the Reality of the Incorporeal Intelligibles: A Reflection on the Metaphysics of Psychology. *Perceptual and Motor Skills*, 93, pp. 531–540.

Balz, Horst and Schneider, Gerhard (Eds.) (1993). *Exegetical Dictionary of the New Testament*, Vol. 3. Grand Rapids, Michigan: William B. Eerdmans Publishing Company. Originally published by H.W. Hollander and Douglas W. Stott (Trans.) as *Exegentishes Worterbuch zum Neuen Testament* Band III, Lieferungen 1–10. Stuttgart, Germany: Verlag W. Kohlhammer GmbH.

Banton, M. (1966). *Anthropological Approaches to the Study of Religion*. London: Tavistock.

Becker, Ernest (1973). *The Denial of Death*. New York: Free Press.

Biderman, Shlomo (1981). Religion without God in Indian Philosophy. *Religious Atheism?* Belgium: E. Story-Scientia.

Boehme, Jacob (1620). *Forty Questions on the Soul*. In *Sämtliche Schriften*. 11 vols. Will-Erich Peuckert and August Faust (Eds.). Stuttgart: Frommanns Verlag, 1955–61; originally published in 1730.

Botterwick, G. Johannes, Ringgren, Helmer and Fabry, Heinz-Josep (2001). *Theological Dictionary of the Old Testament*. Vol. XI. Trans. David Green. Grand Rapids, Michigan: William B. Eerdmans Publishing Company. Originally published by Simian-Yofre (1987–1988) as *Theologisches Worterbuch Zum Alten Testament* Band VI, Lieferungen 1–6. Stuttgart, Germany: Verlag W. Kohlhammer GmbH.

Boucher, Geoff (2014). Ideology. In Rex Butler (Ed.), *The Žižek Dictionary*. Durham: Acumen.

Calvin, John (1845–1846). God the Creator. *Institutes of Christian Religion*. Trans. Henry Beveridge. Edinburgh: Calvin Translation Society.

Carroll, Sean (2012). *The Particle at the End of the Universe: How the Hunt for the Higgs Boson Leads Us to the Edge of a New World*. New York: Penguin.

Cassidy, Jude and Shaver, Phillip R. (Eds.) (1999). *Handbook of Attachment: Theory, Research, and Clinical Applications*. New York: Guilford.

Charles, Marilyn (2002). *Patterns: Building Blocks of Experience*. Hillsdale, NJ: The Analytic Press.

CIA World Factbook (2004). www.odci.gov/cia/publications/factbook/index.html.

Cicero. *De Divinatione*. Trans. W.A. Falconer, 1923. Cambridge, MA: Loeb Classical Library/Harvard University Press.

Cioran, E.M. (1998). *The Temptation to Exist*. Trans. Richard Howard, 2nd Ed. Chicago: University of Chicago Press.

Clarke, J.J. (1992). *In Search of Jung*. London: Routledge.

Collins, Francis S. (2006). *The Language of God*. New York: Free Press.

Craig, William Lane (1979). *The Kalâm Cosmological Argument*. London: Macmillan.

Craig, William Lane (2007). Theistic Critiques of Atheism. In Michael Martin (Ed.), *The Cambridge Companion to Atheism*. Cambridge: Cambridge University Press, pp. 69–85.

Craig, William Lane (2013). Creation and Divine Action. In C. Meister and P. Copan (Eds.), *The Routledge Companion to Philosophy of Religion*, 2nd Ed. New York: Routledge, pp. 378–388.

Davis, Walter. A. (2001). *Deracination*. Albany, NY: SUNY Press.

Dawkins, Richard (1976). *The Selfish Gene*. Oxford: Oxford University Press.

Dawkins, Richard (1989a). Review of Maitland A. Edey and Donald C. Johanson, *Blueprints: Solving the Mystery of Evolution*. *The New York Times*, April 9.

Dawkins, Richard (1989b). Is Science a Religion? *The Humanist*, 57, pp. 26–29.

Dawkins, Richard (2006). *The God Delusion*. New York: Mariner Books.

De Masi, Franco (2007). The Paedophile and his Inner World: Theoretical and Clinical Considerations on the Analysis of a Patient. *International Journal of Psychoanalysis*, 88, pp. 147–165.

Dennett, Daniel (1995). *Darwin's Dangerous Idea: Evolution and the Meanings of Life*. New York: Simon and Schuster.

Dennett, Daniel (2006). *Breaking the Spell: Religion as a Natural Phenomenon*. New York: Penguin Books.

Descartes, René. *Meditations on First Philosophy*. In J. Cottingham, R. Stoothoff, D. Murdoch (Trans.), *The Philosophical Writings of Descartes*, Vol. II, 1984. Cambridge: Cambridge University Press.

Dewey, John (1934). *A Common Faith*. New Haven: Yale University Press.

Dewey, John (1934/1958). *Art as Experience*. New York: Capricorn Books.

Dilthey, Wilhelm (1923). *Introduction to the Human Sciences*. Trans. Ramon J. Betanzos, 1979. Detroit: Wayne State University Press.

Distin, Kate (2011). *Cultural Evolution*. Cambridge: Cambridge University Press.

Durkheim, Emile (1915/1965). *The Elementary Forms of Religious Life*. New York: Free Press.

Dworkin, Ronald (2013). *Religion without God*. Cambridge: Harvard University Press.

Emerson, Ralph Waldo (1990). *Ralph Waldo Emerson (The Oxford Authors)*. Ed. Richard Poirier. Oxford and New York: Oxford University Press.

Evans, Robert (2012). Atheists Around World Suffer Persecution, Discrimination: Report. www.reuters.com/article/2012/12/10/us-religion-atheists-idUSBRE8B900520121210.

Everitt, Nicholas (2004). *The Non-Existence of God*. London: Routledge.

Frances, Bryan (2013). *Gratuitous Suffering and the Problem of Evil*. London: Routledge.

Freud, S. (1896). Further Remarks on the Neuro-Psychoses of Defence. *Standard Edition of the Complete Psychological Works of Sigmund Freud*. Trans. and Ed. James Strachey, in collaboration with Anna Freud, assisted by Alix Strachey and Alan Tyson. Vol. 3. London: Hogarth Press, pp. 159–185.

Freud, S. (1907). Obsessive Actions and Religious Practices. *Standard Edition*, Vol. 9. London: Hogarth Press, pp. 116–127.

Freud, S. (1916 [1915]). On Transience. *Standard Edition*, Vol. 14. London: Hogarth Press, pp. 305–307.

Freud, S. (1917 [1915]). Mourning and Melancholia. *Standard Edition*, Vol. 14. London: Hogarth Press, pp. 239–258.

Freud, S. (1920). *Beyond the Pleasure Principle*. *Standard Edition*, Vol. 18. London: Hogarth Press, pp. 7–64.

Freud, S. (1923). *The Ego and the Id*. *Standard Edition*, Vol. 19. London: Hogarth Press, pp. 3–66.

Freud, S. (1923 [1922]). A Seventeenth-Century Demonological Neurosis. *Standard Edition*, Vol. 19. London: Hogarth Press, pp. 83–92.

Freud, S. (1927). *The Future of an Illusion*. *Standard Edition*, Vol. 21. London: Hogarth Press, pp. 3–56.

Freud, S. (1930). *Civilization and Its Discontents*. *Standard Edition*, Vol. 21. London: Hogarth Press.

Freud, S. (1933). *New Introductory Lectures on Psycho-Analysis*. *Standard Edition*, Vol. 22. London: Hogarth Press.

Fulmer, Gilbert (1976/77). The Concept of the Supernatural. *Analysis*, 37, pp. 113–116.

Gargiulo, Gerald J. (2004). *Psyche, Self, and Soul*. London: Whurr.

Grayling, A.C. (2013a). Oh God! *The New York Review of Books*, Jan. 10, LX (1), p. 63.

Grayling, A.C. (2013b). *The God Argument: The Case Against Religion and for Humanism*. London: Bloomsbury.

Guth, Alan (1997). *The Inflationary Universe*. New York: Addison-Wesley.

Haartman, Keith (2004). *Watching and Praying*. Amsterdam/New York: Rodopi.

Hagman, George (2005). *Aesthetic Experience*. Amsterdam/New York: Rodopi.

Harris, Sam (2004). *The End of Faith*. New York: Norton.

Hart, David Bentley (2013). *The Experience of God: Being, Consciousness, Bliss*. New Haven, CT: Yale University Press.

Hartle, J.B., and Hawking, S.W. (1983). Wave Function of the Universe. *Physical Review*, D28, pp. 2960–2975.

Hawking, S.W. (1988). *A Brief History of Time*. New York: Bantam.

Hegel, G.F.W. (1807). *Phenomenology of Spirit*, Trans. A.V. Miller, 1977. Oxford: Oxford University Press.

Hegel, G.F.W. (1812/1831). *Science of Logic*. Trans. A.V. Miller, 1969. London: George Allen and Unwin Ltd.

Hegel, G.F.W. (1817/1827/1830). *The Encyclopaedia Logic*. Vol. 1 of *Encyclopaedia of the Philosophical Sciences*. Trans. T.F. Geraets, W.A. Suchting, and H.S. Harris, 1991. Indianapolis: Hackett Publishing Company, Inc.

Hegel, G.F.W. (1830a). *Philosophy of Spirit*. In *Hegel's Philosophy of Subjective Spirit*. Vol. 3: *Phenomenology and Psychology*. Trans. and Ed. M.J. Petry, 1978. Dordrecht, Holland: D. Reidel Publishing Company.

Hegel, G.F.W. (1830b). *Enzyklopädie der philosophischen Wissenschaften im Grundrisse*. Heidelberg: C.F. Winter. Ed. F. Nicolin and O. Pöggeler, 3rd Ed., 1969. Hamburg: Felix Meiner.

Hegel, G.F.W. (1832–1845). *G.W.F. Hegel's Werke*. 18 Vols. Eds. Georg Wilhelm Friedrich Hegel, Philipp Marheineke, Philipp Konrad Marheineke, Johannes Karl Hartwig Schulze, Johannes Schulze, Eduard Gans, Leopold von Henning, Leopold Dorotheus von Henning, Heinrich Gustav Hotho, Karl Ludwig Michelet, Friedrich Christoph Förster, Ludwig Boumann, Karl Rosenkranz, 1970. Berlin: Duncker & Humblot/ Suhrkamp Verlag.

Hegel, G.F.W. (1835/1842). *Introductory Lectures on Aesthetics*. Trans. B. Bosanquet. Ed. M. Inwood, 1886/1993. London: Penguin.

Hegel, G.F.W. (1978). *Hegel's Philosophy of Subjective Spirit* [*Hegel's Philosophie des subjektiven Geistes*]. Vol. 1: *Introductions*; Vol. 2: *Anthropology*; Vol. 3: *Phenomenology and Psychology*. Ed. M.J. Petry. Dordrecht, Holland: D. Reidel Publishing Company.

Heidegger, Martin (1927). *Being and Time*. Trans. J. Macquarrie and E. Robinson, 1962. San Francisco: Harper Collins.

Heidegger, Martin (1966). The End of Philosophy and the Task of Thinking. In D.F. Krell (Ed.), *Basic Writings*, 1977. New York: Harper & Row, pp. 369–392.

Hitchens, Christopher (2007). *God is Not Great: How Religion Spoils Everything*. New York: Twelve.

Hoffman, E.T.A. (1814). *Beethoven's Instrumental Music*. Sämtliche Werke, Vol. 1, Ed. C.G. von Maassen. Trans. Bryan R. Simms, 1908. Munich and Leipzig: G. Müller, pp. 55–64.

Howson, Colin (2011). *Objecting to God*. Cambridge: Cambridge University Press.

Hume, David (1739–1740). *A Treatise of Human Nature*. London: Penguin.

Hume, David (1755). Of the Immortality of the Soul. In E.F. Miller (Ed.), *Essays: Moral, Political, and Literary*, 1985. Revised Edition. Indianapolis: Liberty Fund, pp. 590–598.

Husserl, Edmund (1900). *Logical Investigations, Vol. 1.* Trans. J.N. Findlay, 1970. London: Routledge.

Husserl, Edmund (1964). *The Phenomenology of Internal Time-Consciousness.* Trans. J.S. Churchill. Bloomington: Indiana University Press.

Husserl, Edmund (2001). *Analyses Concerning Passive and Active Synthesis: Lectures on Transcendental Logic.* Trans. A. J. Steinbock. Dordrecht: Kluwer.

Irenaeus of Lyons (1857). *Adversus Haereses.* Ed. W.W. Harvey, 1965. 2 vols. Cambridge: Cambridge University Press; reprint Ridgewood, New Jersey.

James, William (1902). *The Varieties of Religious Experience.* New York: Modern Library.

Jonas, Hans (1958). *The Gnostic Religion*, 2nd Ed. Boston: Beacon Press.

Jung, C.G. (1916). The Transcendent Function. *Collected Works*, Vol. 8. Princeton: Princeton University Press, pp. 67–91.

Jung, C.G. (1947). *On the Nature of the Psyche. Collected Works*, Vol. 8. Princeton: Princeton University Press, pp. 159–234.

Jung, C.G. (1952). *Psychology and Religion.* Answer to Job. *Collected Works*, Vol. 11. Princeton: Princeton University Press, pp. 355–470.

Jung, C, G. (1954). The Development of Personality. *Collected Works of C.G. Jung*, Vol. 17. Ed. and Trans. Gerhard Adler and R.F.C. Hull. Princeton, NJ: Princeton University Press.

Jung, C.G. (1961). *Memories, Dreams, Reflections.* Revised Ed. Ed. A. Jaffe. Trans. R. and C. Winston. New York: Vintage.

Kandinsky, Wassily (1911). *Concerning the Spiritual in Art.* Trans. Michael T.H. Sadler, 2006. Boston: MFA Publications.

Kant, Immanuel (1781/1787). *Critique of Pure Reason.* Trans. Norman Kemp Smith, 1929. New York: St. Martin's Press.

Kant, Immanuel (1790). *Critique of Judgment.* Trans. Werner S. Pluhar. Forward Mary J. Gregor, 1987. Indianapolis: Hackett.

Kirkpatrick, Lee (1999). Attachment and Religious Representations and Behavior. In J. Cassidy and P.R. Shaver (Eds.), *Handbook of Attachment: Theory, Research, and Clinical Applications.* New York: Guilford, pp. 803–822.

Klein, Melanie (1946). Notes on Some Schizoid Mechanisms. *International Journal of Psycho-Analysis* 27: 99–110, reprinted in Klein (1988), *Envy and Gratitude and Other Works, 1946–1963.* London: Virago Press, pp. 1–24.

Kohut, Heinz (1971). *The Analysis of the Self.* Madison, CN: International Universities Press.

Krauss, Lawrence (2013). *A Universe from Nothing: Why There is Something Rather than Nothing.* New York: Atria.

Lacan, Jacques (1953). The Function and Field of Speech and Language in Psychoanalysis. In *Écrits: A Selection.* Trans. Alan Sheridan, 1977. New York: Norton, pp. 30–113.

Lacan, Jacques (1957–1958). *Le Séminaire 1957–1958, Livre V: Les Formations de l'Inconscient.* Paris: Seuil, 1998.

Lacan, Jacques (1973). *The Four Fundamental Concepts of Psycho-Analysis.* Ed. J.A. Miller and Trans. A. Sheridan, 1977. New York: Norton.

Laërtius, Diogenes (1925). *Lives of Eminent Philosophers*. Trans. Robert Drew Hicks. Loeb Classical Library.

Landau, Elizabeth (2013). Scientists More Certain that Particle is Higgs boson. CNN, updated 10:45 AM EDT, March 15. www.cnn.com/2013/03/14/tech/innovation/higgs-boson-god-particle.

Le Poidevin, Robin (1996). *Arguing for Atheism*. London: Routledge.

Lin, Paul J. (1977). *A Translation of Lao Tzu's Tao Te Ching and Wang Pi's Commentary*. Ann Arbor: Center for Chinese Studies, University of Michigan.

Locke, John (1690). *An Essay Concerning Human Understanding*. Ed. John W. Yolton. London: Everyman, 1993.

Luther, Martin (1546). The Last Sermon in Wittenberg, 1546. *Luther's Works*, 54 vols. Philadelphia: Muhlenberg Press, pp. 374–375.

Maimonides, Moses (1995). *Guide of the Perplexed*. Trans. Chaim Rabin. Indianapolis: Hackett.

Maimonides, Moses (1937). *Mishneh Torah: The Book of Knowledge*. Trans. Moses Hyamson, 1971. New York: Bloch; reprinted Jerusalem: Feldheim.

Maimonides, Moses (2000). *Treatise on the Resurrection*. Trans. Hillel G. Fradkin. In Ralph Lerner, *Maimonides' Empire of Light*. Chicago: University of Chicago Press, pp. 154–177.

Maitzen, Stephen (2006). Divine Hiddenness and the Demographics of Theism. *Religious Studies*, 42, pp. 177–191.

Martin, Michael and Monnier, Ricki (Eds.) (2003). *The Impossibility of God*. Amherst, NY: Prometheus Books.

Matt, Daniel (1995). *The Essential Kabbalah*. San Francisco: Harper Collins.

Merkur, Dan (1996). The Numinous as a Category of Values. *The Sacred and its Scholars*. Leiden: E.J. Brill, pp. 104–123.

Merkur, Dan (1999). *Mystical Moments and Unitive Thinking*. Albany: SUNY Press.

Merkur, Dan (2014*). Relating to God: Clinical Psychoanalysis, Spirituality, and Theism*. Lanham, MD: Aronson/Rowman & Littlefield.

Miller, Jonathan (2004). *The Atheist Tapes*. BBC documentary series.

Mills, Jon (2002a). *The Unconscious Abyss: Hegel's Anticipation of Psychoanalysis*. Albany: SUNY Press.

Mills, Jon (2002b). Whitehead Idealized: A Naturalized Process Metaphysics. *Process Studies*, 31 (1): pp. 32–48.

Mills, Jon (2005). *Treating Attachment Pathology*. Lantham, MD: Aronson/Rowman & Littlefield.

Mills, Jon (2010). *Origins: On the Genesis of Psychic Reality*. Montreal: McGill-Queens University Press.

Mills, Jon (2013). Jung's Metaphysics. *International Journal of Jungian Studies*, 5 (1), pp. 19–43.

Mills, Jon (2014a). *Underworlds: Philosophies of the Unconscious from Psychoanalysis to Metaphysics*. London: Routledge.

Mills, Jon (2014b). Jung as Philosopher: Archetypes, the Psychoid Factor, and the Question of the Supernatural. *International Journal of Jungian Studies*, 6 (3), pp. 227–242.

Nagel, Thomas (2012). Reply. *The New York Review of Books*, Nov. 8, LIX (17), p. 74.

Newberg, Andrew and D'Aquili, Eugene (2001). *Why God Won't Go Away: Brain Science and the Biology of Belief*. New York: Ballantine Books.

Nietzsche, F. (1892). *Thus Spoke Zarathustra*. Trans. Walter Kaufmann, 1954. New York: Penguin.

Norris, Pippa and Inglehart, Ronald (2004). *Sacred and Secular: Religion and Politics Worldwide*. New York: Cambridge University Press.

O'Dea, Thomas and Janet O'Dea Aviad (1983). *The Sociology of Religion*. Englewood Cliffs, NJ: Prentice Hall.

Oppenheimer, Mark (2010). Atheists Debate How Pushy to Be. *The New York Times*. October 15. www.nytimes.com/2010/10/16/us/16beliefs.html?_r=2.

Otto, Rudolf (1917/1950). *The Idea of the Holy*, 2nd. Ed. London: Oxford University Press.

Otto, Rudolf (1932). The Sensus Numinis as the Historical Basis of Religion. *Hibbert Journal*, 30, pp. 283–297; 415–430.

Pagels, Elaine (1979). *The Gnostic Gospels*. New York: Vintage.

Parsons, Keith M. (2007). Some Contemporary Theistic Arguments. In Michael Martin (Ed.), *The Cambridge Companion to Atheism*. Cambridge: Cambridge University Press, pp. 102–117.

Parsons, Keith M. (2013). Problems with Theistic Arguments. In C. Meister and P. Copan (Eds.), *The Routledge Companion to Philosophy of Religion*, 2nd Ed. New York: Routledge, pp. 490–499.

Pew Research Center (2012). The Global Religious Landscape: Religiously Unaffiliated. www.pewforum.org/2012/12/18/global-religious-landscape-unaffiliated/.

Pfaller, Robert (2014). *On the Pleasure Principle in Culture: Illusions Without Owners*. London: Verso.

Plantinga, Alvin (1983). Reason and Belief in God. In A. Plantinga and N. Wolterstorff (Eds.), *Faith and Rationality: Reason and Belief in God*. Notre Dame: University of Notre Dame Press, pp. 16–93.

Plantinga, Alvin (2000). *Warranted Christian Belief*. Oxford: Oxford University Press.

Plantinga, Alvin (2011). *Where the Conflict Really Lies: Science, Religion, and Naturalism*. Oxford: Oxford University Press.

Plato. *Republic*. In E. Hamilton and H. Cairns (Eds.), *The Collected Dialogues of Plato*. Princeton: Princeton University Press, 1961, pp. 575–844.

Plato. *Sophist*. In E. Hamilton and H. Cairns (Eds.), *The Collected Dialogues of Plato*. Princeton: Princeton University Press, 1961, pp. 957–1017.

Plato. *Timaeus*. In E. Hamilton and H. Cairns (Eds.), *The Collected Dialogues of Plato*. Princeton: Princeton University Press, 1961, pp. 1151–1211.

Plotinus. *The Enneads*. Trans. Stephen MacKenna, 1992. Burdett, NY: Larson Publications.

Popper, Karl (1959). *The Logic of Scientific Discovery*. London: Routledge.

Rey, Georges (2012). Can Religious Belief be Tested? *The New York Review of Books*, Nov 8, (LIX) 17, pp. 73–74.

Rizzuto, Ana-Maria (1979). *The Birth of the Living God: A Psychoanalytic Study*. Chicago: University of Chicago Press.

Roberts, K. (1990). *Religion in Sociological Perspective*. Belmont, CA: Wadsworth.

Rudolph, Kurt (1977). *Gnosis: The Nature and History of Gnosticism*. San Francisco: Harper & Row.

Ruse, Michael (2013). The Sociobiological Account of Religious Belief. In C. Meister and P. Copan (Eds.), *The Routledge Companion to Philosophy of Religion*, 2nd Ed. New York: Routledge, pp. 511–521.

Russell, Bertrand (1927/1957). *Why I Am Not a Christian and Other Essays on Religion and Related Subjects*. New York: Touchstone.

Russell, Bertrand (1975/2009). *Autobiography*. London: Routledge.

Sartre, Jean-Paul (1946). *Existentialism is a Humanism*. In Stephen Priest (Ed.), *Jean-Paul Sartre: Basic Writings*. London: Routledge, 2001.

Schneider, Nathan (2013). *God in Proof*. Berkeley, CA: University of California Press.

SCImago: Journal & Country Rank (2013). *Religious Studies*. www.scimagojr.com/journalrank.php?category=1212&area=0&year=2012&country=&order=sjr&min=0&min_type=cd

Segal, Robert A. (2011). Mysticism and Psychoanalysis. *Religious Studies Review*, 37 (1), pp. 1–19.

Sennett, James F. (Ed.) (1998). *The Analytic Theist: An Alvin Plantinga Reader*. Cambridge: William B. Eerdmans Publishing Co.

Shelley, Percy Bysshe (1880). *The Necessity of Atheism*. In H. Buxton Forman (Ed.), *The Works of Percy Bysshe Shelley in Verse and Prose*, 1880. http://terpconnect.umd.edu/~djb/shelley/necessity1880.html.

Spilka, B., Hood, R. and Gorsuch, R. (1985). *The Psychology of Religion*. Upper Saddle River, NJ: Prentice Hall.

Spinoza, Baruch (1992). *The Ethics, Treatise on the Emendation of the Intellect, and Selected Letters*. Trans. Samuel Shirley and Ed. Seymour Feldman. Indianapolis: Hackett.

Stein, Howard F. (1981). Review of *The Birth of the Living God. A Psychoanalytic Study*. *Psychoanalytic Quarterly*, 50: pp. 125–130.

Stenger, Victor J. (2006). *The Comprehensible Cosmos*. Amherst, NY: Prometheus Books.

Stenger, Victor J. (2007). *God: The Failed Hypothesis*. Amherst, NY: Prometheus Books.

Swinburne, Richard (1979/2004). *The Existence of God*, Rev. 2nd Ed. Oxford: Clarendon Press.

Tillich, Paul (1952). *The Courage to Be*. Glasgow: Collins.

Tougas, Cecile T. (2013). *The Phenomena of Awareness: Husserl, Cantor, Jung*. London: Routledge.

Vaihinger, Hans (1925). *The Philosophy of 'As-If:' A System of the Theoretical, Practical and Religious Fictions of Mankind*. New York: Hartcourt, Brace & Co.

Vilenkin, Alexander (1983). Birth of Inflationary Universes. *Physical Review*, D27, pp. 2848–2855.

Virgil. *The Aeneid*. Trans. Robert Fitzgerald, 1990. New York: Vintage Books.

von der Luft, Eric (1994). Comment. In Robert L. Perkins (Ed.), *History and System: Hegel's Philosophy of History*. Albany, NY: SUNY Press.

Walsh, David (1994). The Historical Dialectic of Spirit: Jocob Boehme's Influence on Hegel. In Robert L. Perkins (Ed.), *History and System: Hegel's Philosophy of History*. Albany, NY: SUNY Press.

Walton, Kendall (1978a). Fearing Fictions. *Journal of Philosophy*, 65, pp. 5–27.

Walton, Kendall (1978b). How Close are Fictional Worlds to the Real World? *Journal of Aesthetics and Art Criticism*, 37, pp. 11–23.

Weeks, Andrew (1991). *Boehme: An Intellectual Biography of the Seventeenth-Century Philosopher and Mystic*. Albany, NY: SUNY Press.

Whitehead, Alfred North (1926). *Religion in the Making*. New York: Macmillan.

Whitehead, Alfred North (1929a). *Process and Reality*. Corrected Edition. New York: Free Press.

Whitman, Walt (1855). Leaves of Grass, Song of Myself, Part 24. http://iwp.uiowa.edu/whitmanweb/en/writings/song-of-myself/section-24

Wicks, Robert. (1993). Hegel's Aesthetics: An Overview. In F.C. Beiser (Ed.), *The Cambridge Companion to Hegel*. Cambridge: Cambridge University Press.

Wilson, Edward O. (1978). *On Human Nature*. Cambridge, MA: Harvard University Press.

Wilson, Edward O. (2012). *The Social Conquest of Earth*. New York: Liveright/Norton.

Winnicott, D.W. (1971). *Playing and Reality*. London: Routledge.

Yinger, J.M. (1967). Pluralism, Religion, and Secularism. *Journal for the Scientific Study of Religion*, 6, p. 18.

Žižek, Slavoj (1989). *The Sublime Object of Ideology*. London: Verso.

Žižek, Slavoj (1997/2007). How to Read Lacan. 7. "God is Dead, but He Doesn't Know It": Lacan Plays with Bobok. www.lacan.com/zizbobok.html.

Zuckerman, Phil (2007). Atheism: Contemporary Numbers and Patterns. In Michael Martin (Ed.), *The Cambridge Companion to Atheism*. Cambridge: Cambridge University Press, pp. 47–65.

Index